Trail from Denver to Durango

A Colorado High
The Official Guide to the Colorado Trail

by
Randy Jacobs

**With contri-
butions by:**   Hugo Ferchau
David L. Gaskill
John R. Dyni
Peter D. Rowland

Drawings by: Jerry Albright

International Standard Book Number 0-944639-02X
Library of Congress Catalogue Card Number 89-80772

Second Edition Copyright © 1989 by Randy Jacobs

Published by The FreeSolo Press for The Colorado Trail Foundation

The Colorado Trail Foundation would like to acknowledge
Martin Marietta Corporation, Kady Cone and the CTF Board
of Directors for their support and assistance with this guide.

Contents

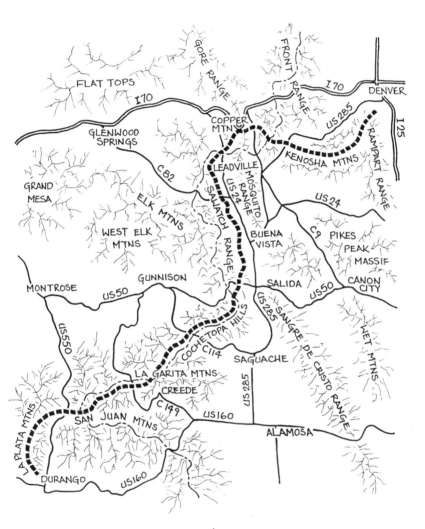

FLAT TOPS
GORE RANGE
FRONT RANGE
I 70
DENVER
I 25
GLENWOOD SPRINGS
COPPER MTN.
US 285
RAMPART RANGE
C 82
LEADVILLE
MOSQUITO RANGE
KENOSHA MTNS
GRAND MESA
SAWATCH RANGE
US 24
ELK MTNS
US 24
WEST ELK MTNS
BUENA VISTA
C 9
PIKES PEAK MASSIF
MONTROSE
GUNNISON
US 50
SALIDA
US 550
CANON CITY
US 550
COCHETOPA HILLS
US 285
SANGRE DE CRISTO RANGE
WET MTNS
C 114
SAGUACHE
LA GARITA MTNS
US 285
LA PLATA MTNS
CREEDE
C 149
US 160
ALAMOSA
SAN JUAN MTNS
DURANGO
US 160

COLORADO TRAIL

N

The Colorado Trail

The Colorado Trail is a continuous, non-motorized recreational trail that crosses Colorado for 469 miles from Denver to Durango. The trail passes through seven national forests and six wilderness areas, traverses five major river systems and penetrates eight of the state's mountain ranges. What makes the trail even more impressive is that it was created through a massive volunteer effort involving literally thousands of dedicated people.

The CT is administered through an unusual joint venture involving the private sector, represented by the Colorado Trail Foundation, and the public sector, in the form of the United States Forest Service. Because of this special relationship, the trail has been built and maintained largely through donated funds for just a small fraction of the cost that would otherwise have come out of taxpayers' pockets.

As of the publication of this guide, the trail had been fully linked from Denver to Durango, but much work still needs to be done to fully realize the goals of the CT's planners. You can help by lending your support to the Colorado Trail Foundation in any of three ways: by volunteering to serve on a trail crew, helping to improve and maintain the CT; by contributing a tax-deductible donation to the Foundation and thereby becoming a "Friend of the Colorado Trail"; or by "adopting" a section of the CT to maintain as your very own.

The Colorado Trail Foundation is a nonprofit Colorado corporation administered by volunteers. All money raised by the Foundation is used to supply and equip base camps and purchase food for the trail crews. There are no salaries or overhead costs. For more information, write to the Colorado Trail Foundation, 548 Pine Song Trail, Golden, CO 80401. Profits from the sale of this guide go exclusively to support future work on the CT.

Background of the Colorado Trail

It is possible that the original leaders of the Colorado Mountain Trails Foundation took lightly the concept of a Colorado Trail. That was back in 1975, when talk of a trail corridor across the state was being discussed as a mere linking together of existing trails.

Two years earlier, Merrill Hastings had proposed in the July issue of *Colorado Magazine* a Colorado Trail connecting Denver and Durango. But if anyone is to be given credit for the idea of today's Colorado Trail it would have to be Bill Lucas, who was at that time regional forester for the Rocky Mountain region of the United States Forest Service. Basing his concerns on an alarming increase of visitation to the national forests and hoping to reduce the pressure on existing trails, Lucas organized a day-long session of interested forest user groups to discuss the possibility of a recreation corridor complete with side trails, access points and, eventually, even a hut system. Additional considerations were the realities of shrinking budgets, which made the Forest Service's contributions doubtful, and the energy crisis, which heightened concern for trail access at places served by public transportation. The November, 1973 meeting produced more questions than answers, but it did result in the establishment of the Colorado Mountain Trails Foundation, a nonprofit organization that was to make the CT a reality, using primarily volunteer labor.

Initially funded with a $100,000 grant from the Gates Foundation as well as numerous smaller grants, the CMTF planned on making the trail a Colorado Centennial-United States Bicentennial project. Gates promised additional funding, assuming progress on the trail continued, and completion was tentatively set for 1978.

In its first years, the CMTF organized groups to inventory existing trails and to propose a definite route for the main trail corridor as well as the side trail system. Dr. Hugo Ferchau, a biology professor at Western State College in Gunnison, spent his summers fielding groups of students and documenting trail inventories from Lake Pass to Molas Pass. In the meantime, Gudy Gaskill had been named executive trail director by the CMTF to recruit volunteers for the inventory elsewhere on the proposed route and to begin trail construction.

When the Environmental Assessment Report for the CT was printed by the Forest Service, it was estimated that three quarters of the route followed existing trails. Based on this report, an official decision on the location of the Colorado Trail was made and various alternate routes proposed. The report also made vague reference to a proposed alternate route around a highly controversial and heavily used portion of the Weminuche Wilderness which, if adopted by the CT, would only compound an already serious overuse of the area.

At the same time, questions were being raised about the ability of the CMTF to continue coordinating the trail effort. The Foundation had exhausted nearly all of its original seed money on overhead costs and, although not officially disbanded, had become severely polarized and seemed to many to be unable to establish a unified course for the project.

Here the story of the CT might have come to a dismal end were it not for Gudy Gaskill. Gaskill had been recruiting volunteers for the CMTF from its infancy and also chaired the Colorado Mountain Club's Trail and Huts Committee, which was established solely for the purpose of organizing volunteer trail crews to preserve the state's network of hiking trails. When the Foundation collapsed, she continued to organize volunteers through the Trail and Huts Committee. Slowly, year by year and mile by mile, progress continued on the trail.

The first section of the CT to be completed by Gaskill and her volunteers was on the South Platte district, the section closest to Denver. Next, the crews moved to the Leadville and Salida districts where, in 1984, they were visited by journalist Ed Quillen. The resulting "Trail To Nowhere" cover story in *Denver Empire* (December 9, 1984) was decidedly pessimistic in describing the jubilant beginnings and unfortunate downfall of the Foundation, and raised serious doubts whether the trail could ever be finished. The disturbing article did, however, raise the eyebrows of one influential Coloradan — Governor Richard Lamm.

Soon after "Trail To Nowhere" appeared, Lamm and Gaskill devised an ambitious schedule for completing the original links and thus finally joining Denver to Durango via the CT. The resulting two-year plan, which had the support of the Forest Service, called for completing nearly 60 miles of trail on six Forest Service districts during the 1986 and 1987 seasons, using only volunteer labor. Almost half the total mileage would be constructed in the Animas District of the San Juan National Forest, where the proposed Hermosa Highline detour would lead trekkers around the originally proposed route down Vallecito Creek in the Weminuche Wilderness. Other areas needing attention were a 20-mile stretch between Copper Mountain and Tennessee Pass and neglected sections around Twin Lakes Reservoir and Mount Princeton.

Concurrent with this renewed focus on the CT, a new Colorado Trail Foundation was formed to organize the volunteers, provide leaders and supply trail crew base camps. Unlike the businessmen who dominated the original Foundation board, the new board of directors consisted of individuals who had been affiliated with the volunteer activities of the CMC Trail and Huts Committee or similar organizations, and was headed by the energetic Gaskill.

The effort put forth during those two years by the volunteers can only be described as unprecedented in the state's history. In 1986, some 400 volunteers labored in 20 trail crews building new tread for the CT. The following year, nearly a thousand volunteers happily took up their tools in 46 trail crews. The complicated logistics taxed the Foundation's volunteer organizers, who used their own vehicles to supply and relocate the trail-crew base camps that moved along with the progression of trail work. The effort was helped immensely, however, by the Forest Service, especially in the Animas District, where the bulk of the work on the Hermosa Highline detour took place.

The CT's volunteers enjoyed one of the greatest feelings of accomplishment imaginable when, on September 4, 1987, "golden spike" ceremonies were held on Molas Pass, Camp Hale and Mount Princeton to commemorate the linking of the CT from Denver to Durango. But that ceremony did not by any means mark the true completion of work on the trail. Much remains to be done, improving the sometimes obscure routes of existing trail adopted into the main corridor and rerouting portions of the trail which presently follow roads. A system of connector and loop trails is still planned, as well as official trailhead access points, which now are not well identified. Eventually, a shelter system along the trail may eliminate the need for long-distance trekkers to shoulder the extra weight of tents.

Please join us for a walk on the trail that was built by the people for the people. And, more importantly, be part of the continuing effort to maintain a regional landmark that highlights a unique aspect of the history of Colorado.

Proposed Improvements and Future Plans

Trail construction and rerouting along the entire length of the CT will be ongoing for the foreseeable future, until the trail system as originally conceptualized is completed. Obviously, any such construction or rerouting will make this guide partially obsolete almost as soon as it rolls off the press. A synopsis of proposed changes and future plans for the trail system is included here to give an idea of major differences which may be encountered due to new trail construction. Anyone planning a hike on the CT should contact the Colorado Trail Foundation or the Forest Service district(s) through which they will be passing for detailed information concerning any changes in the route.

Animas District: Work will commence in 1989 and continue through 1990 to remove the CT route from logging roads and improve neglected sections of existing trail in the vicinity of Orphan Butte. See Segment 27.

Cebolla District: Work will conclude in 1989 on a short section of trail contouring around the north side of Point 11,862 just east of Windy Peak, eliminating approximately 250 feet of elevation gain and loss. See Segment 16.

Creede District: Rerouting of the CT at the head of Miners Creek is scheduled for 1989. See Segment 21. Also scheduled for 1989 is a rerouting of approximately 1.2 miles starting from the 4WD road near the site of Beartown. See Segment 24.

Dillon District: At present the CT follows a road from the top of Georgia Pass down the Swan River from Colorado 9 for a distance of 11 miles. Work began in 1988 on a trail that parallels the road and will separate hikers from the noxious fumes and noise of cars on this section. See Segment 6. Trail crews are also expected to more clearly mark the route over the Tenmile Range in 1989. See Segment 7.

Holy Cross District: Trail crews are tentatively scheduled to reroute the CT away from FS 726 for approximately one mile in 1990. See Segment 8.

Leadville District: Depending on the acquisition of necessary rights-of-way through private property, the CT route may change dramatically in the vicinity of Twin Lakes Reservoir. The timetable for the changes depends on clearance of the proposed easement. See Segment 11.

Salida District: Trail construction which would avoid use of five miles of county roads north of Chalk Creek is still awaiting clearance of proposed rights-of-way. See Segment 13. Scheduled for 1989 is the elimination of 1,000 feet of elevation gain between Chalk Creek and Raspberry Gulch. See Segment 14.

South Park District: Trail construction in 1989 will change the route of the CT on the east side of Georgia Pass to avoid a snowbank. See Segment 6. A new section of trail planned for 1989 just west of the stream crossing at Johnson Gulch will avoid the boggy areas of the valley bottom. See Segment 5.

Gunnison Loop: In 1988 work began on the Gunnison Loop of the Colorado Trail. This 150-mile loop trail, originally envisioned as a possible route for the main CT corridor, will peel off the CT near Halfmoon Creek, top the Continental Divide at Lake Pass, continue south to Matchless Mountain, cross BLM property and enter Gunnison on the campus of Western State College. From there the loop will continue south via Sawtooth Mountain and Agency Peak, rejoining the CT at Cochetopa Creek. As of 1988, the first section of the loop was marked and open from Gunnison to the vicinity of Doctor Park. Work scheduled for 1989 will complete tread north to Matchless Mountain. Work on the Gunnison Loop will continue into the foreseeable future until it is complete. For more detailed information, contact the Foundation, the Cebolla and Taylor River

Ranger Districts of Gunnison National Forest and the Leadville Ranger District of San Isabel National Forest.

Mancos Spur: Trail crews scheduled for 1989 will begin work on this spur, which will connect the CT near Kennebec Pass with the town of Mancos via the Sharkstooth Trail. Mancos Ranger District, San Juan National Forest.

Colorado Trail Heritage

The unique heritage of the Colorado Trail parallels that of the mountain West. In fact, the CT's story goes back much further than just the mid-1970s, when the first trails crews were taking to the hills. Some of the trails we still use today were created by the Plains Indians, who had traveled the fertile mountain parks of Colorado for generations to hunt and to fight amongst themselves for those hunting grounds. In the process they created many trails, some of which we still pass over, totally unaware of their long-departed originators.

The Utes, the mountain people, are probably the best known of the Indian tribes in Colorado because of the skirmishes between them and white settlers, battles which eventually saw the Utes exiled to a small corner of the southwestern part of the state. Prior to the 1863 Treaty made with the Utah Tabeguache Band, the Utes had laid claim for centuries to most of the mountainous area of the state. The 1863 treaty, however, limited them to a reservation whose boundaries followed the Continental Divide on the east and south, the Colorado and Roaring Fork rivers on the north, and the Uncompahgre River on the west. Soon they would be restricted even further, as pressure from an ever-increasing flood of migrating Easterners and mining entrepreneurs persuaded the government to move the Utes farther west in 1868, to a reservation in western Colorado bounded by the 107th meridian. Two agencies were set up to distribute goods and food to the Indians, one to the north on the White River and one to the east on Los Pinos Creek at the foot of the Utes' ancestral Continental Divide passage over Cochetopa Pass.

The promise of profitable mining in the San Juan Mountains resulted in a council at the Los Pinos agency in 1872, at which the government attempted to persuade the Utes to turn over even more of their reservation. They were not successful, however, on this particular try. Chief Ouray, official representative of all the Ute bands, "with rare eloquence, demolished every detail of their carefully arranged program," as one observer put it, adding that the great chief put "them to shame by exposing the violation of their pledges, the injustice and wrong of their attempt to nullify a contract, which had been agreed to and ratified by the Senate of the United States, and the commissioners, worsted, fell back to Washington in anything but good order." The government commissions remained persistent, however, and the following year Felix Brunot, with the help of Otto Mears, persuaded the Utes to turn over nearly four million acres in what was to become the rich San Juan mining district around present-day Silverton. This infamous agreement came to be known as the Brunot Treaty.

By 1879, tensions were high because of the white man's continuing relocations and attempts to convert the nomadic Indians into farmers. When White River agent Nathanial Meeker plowed up the Utes' horse track for planting, the Indians responded by killing Meeker and nine other agency employees and by attacking a cavalry unit sent to subdue them. The Utes thus assured that their future lay on tiny, comparatively less hospitable reservations. The White River Utes, who were responsible for the killings, and the Uncompahgre Utes were driven out of Colorado to a reservation in Utah; the Southern Ute bands were removed to two small reservations bordering New Mexico.

Chief Ouray, who had attempted to save his Indian nation by cooperating with the government, witnessed the tragic decline of the Ute people, whose important contributions and culture are unknown to most people today. Several towering mountain peaks in the southern Sawatch Range immortalize some of the names of these mountain people.

Early Explorers and Expeditions

The Spanish for centuries had been well entrenched in the regions south of present-day Colorado, but they had little if any knowledge of the region traversed by the CT until Fathers Escalante and Dominguez, during their expedition of 1776, viewed the western San

Juan country. Their unarmed party hoped to discover a more pleasant trail than the well known, but rather perilous, southern route. The friars' ramblings took them on a roundabout tour of western Colorado and eastern Utah, and they described the La Plata and San Miguel Mountains northwest of Durango as well as many future tourist destinations. Escalante and Dominguez never made it to California, as they had hoped, but their adventure helped New Mexico Governor Juan Bautista de Anza when he visited the eastern San Juan Mountains, the Cochetopa Hills and the San Luis Valley three years later.

De Anza led an army north from Santa Fe in pursuit of a Comanche band that was terrorizing Spanish colonists, and thereby became the first European to enter the central portion of the Southern Rockies. Along the way, de Anza noticed that the Rio Grande had its beginnings on the eastern flank of the San Juans, not far to the north as previously had been assumed. He was also the first white man to lay eyes on the ancient Continental Divide crossing known to the Utes as "Pass of the Buffalo," or Cochetopa. He correctly deduced that further west, beyond the ridges seen from the San Luis Valley, flowed the headwaters of the western San Juan rivers described by Father Escalante. De Anza continued north to Poncha Pass, descended into the Arkansas Valley near today's Salida, and viewed the skyscraping Sawatch Range before disposing of Comanche Chief Greenhorn's war party near the Wet Mountains.

In the adventurous half century between 1813 and 1863, expeditions in the American West were sponsored by the War Department's newly formed Corps of Topographical Engineers. Major Stephen Long's 1820 expedition, which skirted the east slope of the Rampart Range, was organized under the auspices of the Corps. Long's group was timid about penetrating the Rockies, but it did struggle a few miles up Platte Canyon, which was destined to become the eastern trailhead of the CT. The group then headed south, where the party's botanist, Edwin James, ascended Pikes Peak and discovered the blue columbine, Colorado's state flower. There is an ironic end to this otherwise rather uneventful expedition. James, while admiring and cataloguing the delicate alpine flowers on the slopes of Pikes Peak, noticed that his unattended campfire far below was raging out of control, consuming an entire forest.

Later expeditions, led by Captain John Charles Frémont, probed the La Garita Mountains, South Park and the upper Arkansas River. Frémont, the son-in-law of influential Senator Thomas Hart Benton, conducted several expeditions into the Rockies for the Corps. He is probably best known in Colorado for the disaster which struck his expedition during the winter of 1848-49 in the rugged La Garita Mountains.

In 1853, Congress authorized the Corps to conduct preliminary transcontinental railroad surveys through the Rockies. Captain John W. Gunnison explored what seemed to be the only logical route in Colorado, that is, over Sangre de Cristo Pass, across the San Luis Valley and over Cochetopa Pass. Unfortunately, the river drainage west of Cochetopa Pass cut down into the impregnable gorge of the Black Canyon. Even more unfortunately, Gunnison and seven others in the party were killed later that summer in Utah, by a band of Piutes out to avenge the murder of their chief's father by a group of uprooted settlers. The railroad was eventually built through Wyoming, and as a further reminder of the tragic end of the Gunnison expedition, Cochetopa Pass has remained a rather minor Continental Divide passage.

The Great Surveys

After the Civil War, the most significant of the Colorado surveys were led by Ferdinand Hayden and Lieutenant George Wheeler. The Plains Indians were used to seeing the peculiar figure of Hayden digging in worthless soil and, thinking him a harmless eccentric, gave him a name which translates as "man who picks up stones running." By 1869, Hayden had lobbied Congress sufficiently to fund his civilian United States Geological Surveys of the Territories. During the three summers between 1873 and 1875, the Hayden Survey covered most of Colorado's high country, climbing and naming many of its major summits, which were used as triangulation points. Hayden skillfully staffed his teams with competent topographers, geologists and experts in fields ranging from anthropology to paleontology. Pioneer photographer William Henry Jackson gained fame with the Hayden Survey in Wyoming and Colorado. After a decade of exploring and preparing invaluable maps and reports, the Hayden Survey came to an end in 1879 with the creation of the

United States Geological Survey.

The Wheeler Survey, unlike Hayden's civilian expeditions, was sponsored by the War Department and concentrated mainly on topographic features. Its premature demise in 1878, before the completion of its work, was at least in part the result of intense competition among the surveys. As a result, Wheeler never gained the prominence that Hayden did. Both of these great surveys, however, provided maps and valuable information which guided railroad builders and prospectors and led to further taming of the mountains.

Early Entrepreneurs

The CT meanders through a wide band of territory, known popularly as the Mineral Belt, which begins west of Boulder and trends southwesterly to Silverton. The riches of this region supported some of Colorado's most rip-roaring boom towns of old, towns that were eventually to be connected by a web of stage roads, trails and railroad tracks.

An early route for prospectors was pointed out by Frémont in 1844. Prior to the Civil War, a group of Southerners used the route, which became known as Georgia Pass, and panned their way to prosperity at Parkville near the headwaters of the Swan River. The rival town of Breckenridge gained prominence in the valley by 1862 and has been the center of a busy mining area ever since.

At the same time the Fiftyniners were digging their first placers at Parkville, prospectors were filtering into California Gulch near the headwaters of the Arkansas. A rich placer boom in the 1860s was responsible for the brief appearances of the towns of Oro, Granite and Dayton. But the real boom had to wait until 1878, when miners uncovered silver deposits concealed in lead carbonate, which gave the rejuvenated camp its new name of Leadville. For a short time the satellite communities of Kokomo and Robinson, in the Tenmile Mining District, competed with Leadville for prominence in the area.

It was in Oro, Granite and later Leadville that an eccentric entrepreneur, Horace Austin Warner Tabor, got his start as a prospector and merchant. Tabor's better half, Augusta – the first white woman in the valley – was the classic pioneer woman: thrifty, self-reliant and concerned for the welfare of the young miners in camp. These were also attributes that would sustain her in the inevitable crash that follows all booms.

Lieutenant Charles Baker, tired of the Yankee company in California Gulch, followed the Continental Divide south into the San Juans, where his party panned unsuccessfully for gold around Bakers Park. Even though it meant trespassing on the Ute reservation, Baker pushed south to test the soil at a new location, on the shores of the Animas River just north of present-day Durango, which he christened Animas City. Being a true confederate, the Lieutenant took a brief leave from prospecting to fight in the Civil War. He then returned to southwestern Colorado, where he was promptly killed by Indians. The area was still technically closed to whites, but other encroaching prospectors uncovered rich mineral deposits there, and when the Brunot Treaty removed the Utes in 1873, the area boomed with the production of silver, gaining a new name, Silverton.

Toll Roads and Railroads

Clever little Otto Mears built roads out of the San Luis Valley along routes that had been pioneered by earlier explorers. Mears' objective, in which he was quite successful, was to maintain toll booths and freighting companies to supply the boom towns with goods he produced in the valley. His first enterprise was to build a road north over Poncha Pass to the placers on the upper Arkansas. Mears teamed up with Enos Hotchkiss to build the Saguache-San Juan toll road via Cochetopa Pass and Los Pinos agency in 1874. Originally intended to go up the Lake Fork over Cinnamon Pass and down into Silverton, that stretch of road was delayed when Hotchkiss discovered the Golden Fleece mine while building a road near Lake City.

Mears did more than build roads. As the San Juans produced more minerals, he developed an interconnecting network of railroads to serve them. The most prominent was the Rio Grande Southern, whose 168 twisting miles of track between Durango and Ridgway passed some of the Rocky Mountains' most stunning scenery.

Perhaps most persistent of the mountain railroads was the Denver and Rio Grande. In 1870, General William Jackson Palmer incorporated the D&RG and planned to build his railroad from Denver to Mexico City. But plans changed and Palmer's railroad, using narrow gauge track and equipment that could climb steeper grades and turn tighter corners, became Colorado's premier railroad. The small cars and locomotives were soon puffing over passes and into mining communities to the cheers of the citizenry.

Spurring the D&RG on were competing mountain railroads such as Governor John Evans' Denver South Park and Pacific and the Colorado Midland. The DSP&P was constructed in the 1870s from Denver up Platte Canyon to Kenosha Pass. From there, one branch continued across South Park to Leadville and Gunnison via the legendary Alpine Tunnel. The other branch ascended the Continental Divide at Boreas Pass to serve Breckenridge and the Tenmile Mining District. The entire line survived until the 1930s.

The more ambitious, standard gauge Colorado Midland was built by a feisty easterner named John J. Hagerman, who came to Colorado to die of tuberculosis but instead lived to build a railroad. The Midland was a well respected, although short lived, railroad that linked the silver mines at Aspen to the eastern slope via Leadville and

the breathtaking 11,528-foot Hagerman Tunnel on the craggy north shoulder of Mt. Massive.

The prosperity of the late 1800s in Colorado was based largely on the mining of silver, and by 1893 the value of silver production exceeded that of gold by nearly four to one. Thus the silver camps of the San Juans, Leadville, Aspen and the Tenmile District were in a precarious state when the Sherman Silver Purchase Act was repealed that same year and the nation moved toward a monetary system based on the gold standard. The battle over the monetary standard caused wrenching agony and displacements nationwide, and was at least partly to blame for the Panic of 1893. Silver mining districts across Colorado went into a collapse from which they never fully recovered. H.A.W. Tabor, the silver king of Leadville, lost everything and died a pauper. Other fortunes were likewise wiped out.

Fortunately for the overall economy of the state, some of the mining districts also had rich veins of gold. About the same time that Congress repealed the Silver Purchase Act, a drunken cowboy named Bob Womack stumbled across a peculiar-looking rock outcrop while herding cattle, and laid first claim to Colorado's glorious gold field on the banks of Cripple Creek. Displaced miners from the silver camps poured into the gold district in the shadow of Pikes Peak with restored hope. But life would never be quite the same with the passing of Colorado's silver era.

Modern Development

A perplexing ore penetrating the slopes of 13,555-foot Bartlett Mountain at the head of Tenmile Creek on the Continental Divide baffled early-day prospectors until specialists at the Colorado School of Mines identified the mineral as molybdenum. The claim, named Climax because of the loftiness of its location, was not developed until 1911, when its value in steel alloy was realized. It has been a mainstay of the upper Arkansas Valley economy ever since. The Climax Molybdenum Mine is widely known as the state's most notorious strip mine. It is in fact no longer possible to find the summit of Bartlett Mountain, which has been mined away over the years. Today the mountain's digested remains clog the headwaters of Tenmile Creek, under the ignominious tailings ponds which have completely buried the historic sites of Robinson and Kokomo.

Other Colorado valleys have likewise disappeared, not buried under mine tailings but drowned under thousands of acre-feet of water. Denver began damming waterways as early as 1890, building the Castlewood Dam on Cherry Creek in that year and Cheesman Dam on the South Platte in 1905. In addition, East Slope water districts cast longing eyes west of the Continental Divide. They laid ambitious plans to siphon off significant flows from the Colorado River watershed and transport the runoff to thirsty cities using an intricate system of diversion points, tunnels and reservoirs.

The most prominent water project along the CT today is the Fryingpan-Arkansas diversion system, known locally as the Pan-Ark. This complex system diverts 69,200 acre-feet of water per year from the West Slope's Fryingpan River, a tributary of the Colorado, to the Arkansas River using a network of six reservoirs, 16 diversion structures and ten tunnels. The Pan-Ark project was begun in the 1960s to shore up East Slope municipalities and agricultural water users.

Summit County's Dillon Reservoir, named for the little community it flooded, and 23-mile-long Roberts Tunnel comprise a system that funnels excess flow from the Blue River eastward into the headwaters of the South Platte, eventually to reemerge at faucets all over Denver. The reservoir, besides providing water for Denver, provides summer water sports in one of the state's most highly developed mountain recreation areas. Once an active mining region, Summit County typifies the metamorphosis which has taken place in Colorado's mountain communities. The county's economy now revolves around its appeal as a glamorous vacation destination, focusing on the many posh ski resorts in the surrounding area.

The seeds of the state's ski industry had been unknowingly sown by local enthusiasts well before World War II, but the Army installation at Camp Hale from 1942 to 1945 dramatically emphasized Colorado's potential as a winter recreation area. The training that the troops received at the Rocky Mountain outpost was not lost upon the men of the 10th Mountain Division. Many of them returned to Colorado after the war to fulfill their dreams of elegant ski resorts and to help the state develop its reputation as the nation's premier winter wonderland. The ruins of Camp Hale now rank as one of the state's most recent and unusual ghost towns.

The latest development proposed along the CT is Two Forks Dam and Reservoir, which would inundate scenic Platte Canyon 25 miles southwest of Denver. If built, Two Forks would be larger than Dillon Reservoir and would drown several miles of the trail in the craggy canyon, which is popular with hikers, anglers and kayakers.

Balancing the demands of a growing state with an unparalleled natural setting and a dynamic tourism industry is no small task. And if the past is indeed prologue to the future, then development is destined to build on development. However, this trend will not continue without a price. That price includes visual deterioration, loss of wildlife habitat and, through the construction of highways and transit systems, bringing the noise and congestion of the cities into once-peaceful mountain settings. Still, despite all the development, many isolated niches remain seemingly untouched by the imposing hand of our species. The 469 miles of the CT highlight the continuing history of a remarkable state, and if travelers can keep it all in perspective, it can be quite a trip.

The Buffalo Peaks

Hiking the CT

The Colorado Trail assumes varying characteristics as it meanders through eight mountain ranges with dissimilar topographic and geologic features. For its entire 469 miles, the trail imposes diverse demands on its users, and their ability to adjust to those changing demands helps determine how much they will enjoy their trek. Whether it is the repetitious gain and loss of elevation in the Sawatch Range, or the obscurity of the route in the La Garitas, there is always something along the way to challenge some and to intimidate others.

As with other trails in the state, the CT is not developed to the point that it can be followed blindly. Nor should it be, especially in the many wilderness areas through which it passes. This guide assumes that all users of the CT are familiar with basic backcountry techniques, precautions and orienteering skills. For those who are not, organizations such as the Colorado Mountain Club hold regular sessions to acquaint neophytes with these virtues before they venture out on the trail.

Planning a Hike

Probably only a very few of the total number of those hiking the Colorado Trail will do so straight through, from one end to the other. A more realistic and certainly less taxing plan would be to travel the route segment by segment, in either dayhike or backpack fashion, and take advantage of the various side trips available along the main corridor.

When planning a hike, keep in mind that portions of the trail below 9500 feet generally are accessible from May to November, depending on weather extremes and the orientation of the trail. Above 9500 feet, the hiking season can be dramatically shorter, again depending on the trail location and the amount of snowfall.

One of the main considerations in planning a hike for early summer is lingering snow. If you intend to sample different segments of the trail as you feel inspired, then you can visit a given area whenever conditions are best. Long-distance trekkers, however, cannot be choosy about avoiding a snowed-in segment if it happens to lie in their path. Many high crests and ridges are likely to be laden with snow until early July, especially on their north sides. If you have to cross a lot of snow, plan to do so at a time of day when the snow is neither too hard nor too soft. An otherwise perfect day can be ruined by having to "posthole" through deep, soft snow with a full pack or suffering a terrifying, uncontrolled glissade down a slippery, icy slope.

Those planning a 469-mile trek should consider that, if they start at the eastern end, it is more than 70 miles before they top out at timberline on Georgia Pass. If they begin at the western end, however, timberline comes in less than 20 miles, at Kennebec Pass. Thus a trek starting at Denver and progressing to Durango could be started earlier. In any event, setting out from Denver before the third week of June, or from Durango before the first week of July, would generally be impractical because of the hazards of lingering snowfields.

The logistics of returning to your starting point can be troublesome and should not be overlooked until the last minute. Several towns along the way have regular bus service. Denver and Durango are connected by regular airline service. Those wishing to take advantage of railroad passenger service may do so by planning a hike around the Durango and Silverton narrow gauge line, which runs daily during the summer between the two towns. For information on fares and schedules, write the Durango and Silverton Railroad, 479 Main Avenue, Durango, CO 81301.

Day-hikers have less complicated options from which to choose. They can either walk as far as they wish and then retrace their steps to their starting point, arrange a car shuttle between trail access points, or swap car keys with a party hiking in the opposite direction. In future years it is hoped that additional loop trails and trailhead points will make such backtracking and detailed logistics unnecessary for the day-hiker.

Whether you are day-hiking or backpacking, the isolation of the trail in the Cochetopa Hills and the La Garita and San Juan Mountains can be mind-boggling. It would be worthwhile to prepare one's psyche for this stretch and have a compatible companion along, someone with whom all outstanding differences have already been resolved. Because this part of the CT is rarely visited, it is more of a challenge to follow. In addition, the high route through the La Garitas and San Juans, which parallels the crest of the Continental Divide, may very likely be blanketed with snowfields until mid-July. This compounds the area's isolation from civilization, and heightens the need for hikers to keep a steady head and possess good mountaineering and orienteering skills.

Contrary to some overblown stories, wild animals are not likely to molest you during your trip. A clean camp is your best insurance against midnight visitors. Wild animals are generally not crazed and are after food, not you. The most important factor is to keep food secured and out of your tent. Mosquitoes are the wilderness occupants you are most likely to encounter, and they, too, are looking for a meal, so bring repellent. An occasional flock of domestic sheep likely will be seen also, especially in the San Juans. If you find yourself part of a flock, the shepherd's advice is to leash your pets to prevent a chaotic stampede and to avoid eye contact with the animals — lest they interpret your stares as a prelude to an attack, which could also precipitate a stampede.

Supplying Your Trek

Based on their own experiences and preferences, different travelers will come up with slightly varying lists of supplies to have along on a backpacking trip. The essentials aside, some comments are included here to help plan a trek on the CT.

If you are planning a long trek, it would be impractical to carry all your food from the beginning. Unfortunately, with the exception of Copper Mountain, supply points along the way lie well off the trail, and most likely would not cater to your specific tastes. But they do offer possibilities for resupplying an empty pack and, more importantly, provide restaurants for satisfying the ravenous cravings one inevitably develops after an extended period in the wilds. It is also possible to pack your nonperishable meals into boxes before leaving and then mail them to yourself, in care of "General Delivery," to post offices in towns where you plan to stop. Your local post office can give you tips on how to do this. Another alternative is to rely on friends or relatives to meet you with fresh supplies at access points along the trail.

Clothing, the traveler's first line of defense against the elements, deserves careful consideration. The CT experiences extremes of mountain weather conditions, with the dry warmth of the less lofty elevations in the Rampart Range and lower Arkansas Valley contrasting sharply with the exposed, alpine ridges of the La Garita and San Juan Mountains. An appropriate combination of cotton and wool garments, including hat and gloves, plus rain gear, is essential, even though any number of these layers of clothing will probably be taking up space in your pack most of the time. It is conceivable that some garments, especially socks, will wear out in 469 miles. Special measures should be taken to replace certain items you feel might succumb to that fate.

Your boots and feet will take a beating on the trail. And even though there are some sections that might lend themselves well to the use of light-weight boots and tennis shoes, only heavier footgear will see you through the high-altitude march along the Continental Divide, where snowfields and talus will be encountered. If your boots are well broken in, but not nearing the end of their life, they will likely see you through the entire trek.

Sometime in the future, a system of shelters may exist along the trail. At present, however, there is only one official shelter along the entire length of the CT, and some kind of portable protection from the elements is necessary to see you through the series of rainy days you will inevitably experience.

Drinking water is generally readily available along the CT, although there are a few sections where adequate supplies are as far as 13 miles apart. These stretches require some planning and foresight if you do not want to be caught at a dry camp. Unfortunately, grazing is common along most of the trail, and all water, with the exception of domestic supplies at camprounds, should be treated or filtered to screen out protozoa that might otherwise bring your trek to an untimely halt.

Maps and a compass, as well as a knowledge of their use, should be part of every hiker's basic provisions. The maps in this guide are intended only to describe the area of each trail segment, and should be supplemented by either detailed USGS topographical maps or the Colorado Trail Foundation's series of topographical maps. Forest Service maps provide additional information, such as campground locations and 4WD and Forest Service roads. (Mountain cyclists traveling any of the mountain bicycle detours described at the end of this guide will find Forest Service maps particularly useful.)

In addition to the above-mentioned essentials, it is prudent to take a first-aid kit along. Even better is to have as many members of the group as possible schooled in first-aid techniques — they can be lifesavers in emergencies. Organizations such as the Red Cross give basic instruction in first-aid practices.

Safety

An experienced mountaineer will be prepared and take no unnecessary chances. Along the more isolated portions of the CT, assistance will be many hours – even days – away, so travelers should keep the following points in mind:

Be aware of the conditions. The varied terrain of the CT puts you at risk for both hypothermia and dehydration. Plan for the possibility of each, as well as for the lightning hazard of exposed ridges. Snowfields, as mentioned earlier, will likely be encountered early in the season. If you plan an early start through the San Juans and La Garitas, consider carrying an ice axe, glacier glasses and possibly crampons — assuming, of course, that you know how to use these items properly.

Start hiking early. You will encounter storms of varying intensity, whether they are midsummer thunderstorms or late-summer snow showers. Generally, mornings are more likely to be clear, and leaving early gives you a better chance to get to your destination and set up camp in comfort.

Travel with a companion. Backpacking or hiking alone is not recommended, even for the experienced. If you do so, make sure your itinerary is known by others and check in as often as possible.

Be in shape.   Your best insurance against accidents is to be in top physical condition. Acclimatize yourself before beginning your trek, and guard against fatigue. Pushing yourself too hard in rugged terrain can be an invitation to disaster.

Using this Guide

The 28 CT segments described in this guide begin and end at points accessible by car. Some have additional trail access points within the segment. The average length of a segment is 17 miles, although actual distances vary from nine to 29 miles. Each individual segment could be completed by day-hikers with light loads, although some might make for a very long day. Backpackers with heavy packs could conceivably take two to three days to cover some of the longer segments. Those going from end to end might need two months to complete the entire distance, assuming they will hike about nine miles per day, with one day off per week for side trips or relaxation.

The trail descriptions are laid out progressing from Denver to Durango. We apologize to those who wish to travel in the opposite direction; perhaps a later edition of this guide will include a Durango-to-Denver description. The descriptions indicate the distance of recognizable landmarks from the beginning of the trail segment. Accompanying the mileage count, in parentheses, is the elevation of that landmark. These mileages were obtained over a two-year period using a "rolotape" device in the field, and are as accurate as humanly possible.

A vicinity map accompanies each description for general orientation purposes. Topographic maps covering the trail segment are listed as well. Also included are altitude profiles which give a graphic summary of the elevation gain and loss along each segment. A short paragraph describes supply points along the way and what can be expected at each.

Instructions for reaching trailheads and trail access points are given at the beginning of each segment. Generally, "trailhead" refers to an access point with a parking area, which can sometimes be primitive and skimpy. "Trail access" refers to a point where the trail crosses a vehicular artery but where no parking is provided. One of the priorities in the next few years is to increase the number of trailheads on the CT. In the meantime, be careful where you park your car.

Trail Markings

It is surprising how quickly the extreme environment of the Rockies can alter a trail's appearance. Overgrowing vegetation, downed trees and avalanches can render the trail difficult to follow regardless of how well it was marked originally. Portions of the CT as described here may be altered over time by these natural forces or because of ongoing trail construction and maintenance. This guide generally does not refer to trail markers and signs because they are often vandalized or stolen.

Over the years, CT markers have varied considerably. Their one common, eye-catching characteristic has been the incorporation of the CT's unique logo. Trail markers can be either triangular or diamond-shaped, and may be fashioned from wood, metal or plastic. Reflective metal markers were once used extensively on the trail, but have been discontinued because of their expense and appeal to souvenir hunters. Esthetic redwood markers have survived on isolated sections in the Cebolla District. Less expensive, triangular plastic markers are now being used and may solve the theft problem, since they will self-destruct when removed by those wanting a memento of their hike.

In more remote stretches and wilderness areas, the CT is marked

Continental Divide above Lake San Cristobal

by wooden posts, rock cairns and blazes on tree trunks. Some older blazes are almost completely healed over and difficult to see. Some districts use unimpressive but practical carsonite posts to identify the route. These are long, slender slats, dark brown in color and made of a material resembling fiberglass. They tend to nod conspicuously back and forth in any but the lightest breeze.

You may run across pieces of gaudily colored forester's tape (flags) that have been tied to tree branches to mark obscure portions of the trail. Since many other individuals and agencies also use this material for countless other designations, these flags should not be followed mindlessly. You might also encounter routes marked with blue diamonds; these identify winter cross-country ski routes and are not necessarily intended to mark the CT.

Miscellaneous Notes

The abbreviation "FS" refers to Forest Service roads. FS-543, for example, means Forest Service Road 543. These roads can generally be traveled by conventional automobiles. If not, the designation "4WD" identifies the road as suitable for four wheel drive vehicles only.

The CT is generally a footpath, but in places it follows roads of varying quality. The trail descriptions refer to several types of roads. A "jeep track" is the lowest quality of road, and typically appears as a parallel double track or trail separated by a hump of grass. Jeep tracks usually run through meadows or tundra and can be either closed to vehicular traffic or still actively used. A "jeep road" can likewise be closed or opened to vehicles and is usually narrow, rough and sometimes steep. The guide also refers occasionally to "old roads," which are long-abandoned supply routes that now more closely resemble rough, widened trails.

"Route" is a term sometimes used to describe the CT in general. However, for stretches where the trail is so obscure that no tread is visible, "route" is used to indicate the lack of an obvious trail. A "posted route" or "cairned route" has been marked with either wooden posts or rock cairns, respectively.

Directional indicators such as right, left, north and south are used occasionally within parentheses. When taking compass readings, be sure to compensate for magnetic declination. Finally, there are two

Stony Passes and two Windy Peaks referred to in this guide — be careful not to confuse them.

Cycling the Colorado Trail

Mountain bicycles are becoming more popular year by year and will be encountered increasingly on the CT. They are not, however, allowed in wilderness areas. This guide explains adequate detours for mountain bicycles around the six wilderness areas through which the official route passes. These detours generally use county roads, 4WD roads, Forest Service roads and highways. Cyclists can also custom-design their own detours, using Forest Service maps and a state highway map.

Regulations and Backcountry Ethics

The CT lies almost entirely on National Forest lands. In some areas, the route uses rights-of-way and easements across or adjacent to private property. Negotiations for certain easements are still underway. Keep in mind that rights-of-way can be withdrawn by owners if problems associated with their use arise.

All users have a responsibility to maintain the pristine condition of the backcountry as they find it. Refrain from cutting switchbacks and other practices which lead to trail erosion. Use existing campsites where possible, and resist the temptation to develop new ones by rearranging rocks for fire rings or digging drainage channels. Use a backpacker's gas stove for all your kitchen chores and limit your consumption of firewood, which is becoming increasingly scarce in many areas of the Colorado high country. Before starting your trek, check with the Forest Service for the current forest fire danger, which can sometimes be extreme. Walking and talking softly is in tune with the backcountry code and increases your overall awareness of the wilderness.

Forest Service occupancy regulations are primarily designed to limit wear and tear in fragile wilderness areas, although some heavily used, non-wilderness areas also have campsite restrictions. Within wilderness areas groups cannot exceed 25 members, camps and tethered pack animals are not permitted within a hundred feet of lakes and streams, and pets must be kept on a leash. These are good rules to follow even outside of wilderness areas.

Addresses for Additional Information

The CT crosses ten Forest Service districts, each of which usually maintains information concerning the portion of the trail within its jurisdiction. Addresses for the districts are:

South Platte District: Pike National Forest, P.O. Box 25127, 11177 West 8th Avenue, Lakewood, CO 80225

South Park District: Pike National Forest, P.O. Box 219, Fairplay, CO 80440

Dillon District: Arapaho National Forest, P.O. Box 620, 135 Highway 9, Silverthorne, CO 80498

Holy Cross District: White River National Forest, P.O. Box 190, 401 Main, Minturn, CO 81645

Leadville District: San Isabel National Forest, 2015 North Poplar, Leadville, CO 80461

Salida District: San Isabel National Forest, 230 West 16th Street, Salida, CO 81201

Saguache District: Rio Grande National Forest, P.O. Box 67, 626 Gunnison Avenue, Saguache, CO 81149

Creede District: Rio Grande National Forest, P.O. Box 270, 220 Creede Avenue, Creede, CO 81130

Cebolla District: Gunnison National Forest, 216 North Colorado, Gunnison, CO 81230

Animas District: San Juan National Forest, 10 West 11th, Durango, CO 81301

Natural History of the Colorado Trail

by Hugo A. Ferchau
Thornton Professor of Botany, Western State College

This brief look at Rocky Mountain ecology is intended for those who wish to enjoy the Colorado Trail country but have previously had no contact with it, as well as for locals who have only rarely ventured into its vastness. Veterans of these wilds could probably write an equally good account of the inhabitants of the open spaces. Regardless, there is no question that the natural history of this region is the prize, the reward for the effort made in hiking the CT. This opportunity to observe the Rocky Mountain ecosystem also underscores the need to *walk,* not run, while making one's daily tour on the trail. In ten years of leading groups of students through the Rockies, it has been my experience that hikers who reach camp two hours before the rest can rarely relate any interesting observations. They might as well have worked out in a gym. To get the most out of your sojourn on the CT, take the time to look, to sit, to let nature present itself to you, and to soak up all that it has to offer — you may pass this way but once.

Observing Wildlife

For some reason, we commonly use the term "wildlife" to refer only to animals. Plants, evidently, are considered to be somewhat trapped or tamed, or at least subdued. There is less drama associated with plants because we can prepare for our encounters with them, whereas animals tend to take us by surprise — they are there all of a sudden and gone all of a sudden. As a botanist, I must recognize that most people would rather talk about a bear than about the bearberry.

The native fauna of the Rockies may readily be viewed from the CT. At this point, perhaps, I should make a digression concerning the domestic dog. Some hikers feel the hiking experience is not complete without their dog. To be sure, when a backpacker is on the trail alone, companionship is pleasant. When hiking in a group, however, a dog can be a distinct nuisance. If you are interested in being a part of the surrounding ecosystem, your dog (which is *not* a part of that ecosystem) should be left at home.

But back to the question of those birds, bees, and the larger and more impressive animals you may encounter. Having been over most of the CT, I cannot think of a single day's hike which did not reveal much of the Rocky Mountain fauna. By the same token, I have seen students hike for days without seeing a single animal. This apparent contradiction can be explained by the fact that native animals are not in a zoo. They have learned behavior and instincts which assure them of avoiding threatening outsiders, such as hikers. You must meet the animals on their own terms. Several general rules may be followed. Dawn and dusk are when animals tend to be most active. Animals require water regularly. Many animals will learn to ignore you if you are part of the scenery, which means being relatively quiet and still. Do not try to see all of the fauna in a single sitting. Obtain some of the local fauna texts and become familiar with the behavior of the animal or group of animals you wish to observe, and make a conscious effort to make the observations. You will probably have the most success with birds. Also, do not discount what might be considered the less dramatic animals, such as the small nocturnal rodents. A log to sit on at night and a flashlight will often allow you some captivating moments. Rising early in the morning and getting on the trail ahead of the group can also increase your chances of seeing wildlife.

Early-season hikers should note that fawning of deer and calving of elk occur in June. Try to avoid being disruptive if traveling during this time of year.

Some hikers may be fearful of encountering wildlife, but there is little need for them to worry. After taking students into the Rockies for more than ten years, we have never been attacked by anything. I have seen mountain lion and bear at reasonable distances, and I am sure they have observed me from distances which, were they known, would have excited me. I have seen bear droppings on the trail on a cold morning that were so fresh the steam was still rising off them. My wife woke up from a nap one afternoon, and there were fresh bear-claw marks on a tree over her head. Good judgment will discourage your being molested. An animal seeks food, not your company. If you have no food in your presence, you will generally not be bothered. If you choose to keep food, even nuts or a candy bar, in your tent, you may wake up at night to find a hole cut in the floor and confront the steely eyes of a mouse or pack rat. After arriving in camp, place your food away from the sleeping area — 75-100 yards is a good distance.

Plant Communities

The highly variable topography of the central Rocky Mountains provides for a kaleidoscopic variety of vegetation. The accompanying diagrams give some indication of the vegetation types encountered on the CT, as well as their relationships to each other. Note that the zones are not defined by elevation alone, but depend also on local climatic factors. In the field, of course, matters can be even more complicated. In areas that have been disturbed, for example, as by fire or logging, different types of vegetation will exist in different relationships. Diagram 1 (page 36) shows the relationships between various plant communities in a "climax" situation, that is, in an ecologically stable, undisturbed environment. Where the land has been disturbed, the plants proceed through a "succession" phase before eventually evolving back into a climax state. Diagram 2 (page 37) shows the relationships between various types of vegetation during succession. Because of the severe climate and short growing season in the Rockies, successional vegetation patterns may persist for more than a hundred years. In addition, a single hillside may be covered with successional vegetation in one place and climax vegetation in another.

Riparian Vegetation

This is the vegetation found along streambanks, and it plays a variety of important roles, such as controlling erosion and providing cover and feed for wildlife. On the Western Slope, lower-elevation streambanks are dominated by assorted cottonwood trees, alder, maple and red-osier dogwood. With increasing elevation the cottonwoods become less evident, while the shrubs persist, eventually being

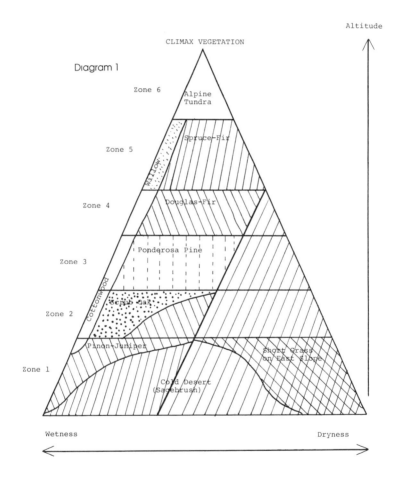

Diagram 1

Ferchau, 1970

dominated by willows. On the Eastern Slope the cottonwoods are not as evident but, as on the Western Slope, a mixture of shrubs prevails, becoming increasingly dominated by willows at higher elevations.

Despite what appears to be very aggressive growth by riparian species, they are among the most sensitive to human activity. And, because of their proximity to water, they are typically among the most threatened and endangered.

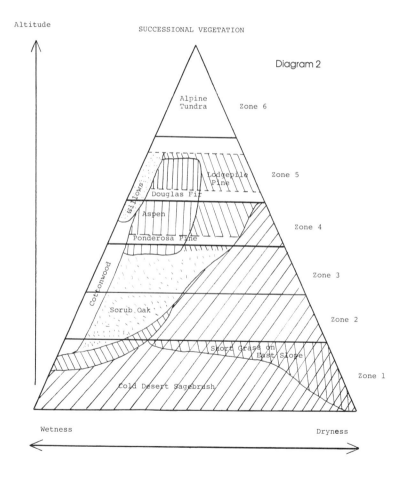

Altitude

SUCCESSIONAL VEGETATION

Diagram 2

Alpine Tundra — Zone 6

Willows
Lodgepole Pine — Zone 5
Douglas Fir
Aspen
Ponderosa Pine — Zone 4

Cottonwood

Scrub Oak — Zone 3

Zone 2

Short Grass on East Slope

Cold Desert Sagebrush — Zone 1

Wetness

Dryness

Ferchau 1970

Sagebrush

The sagebrush, the cold-desert scrubland of the Rockies, can be found from low to surprisingly high elevations. It is interspersed with grasses, and is the primary grazing land of central and western Colorado. It is also quite dry, with little water available for hikers; ranchers typically maintain water supplies in stock tanks for their cattle, but those supplies are definitely not recommended for humans. During the day, this environment can become quite hot, while at night even summertime temperatures can drop to near freezing. During June, watch out for ticks.

Scrub Oak and Piñon-Juniper Woodland

This dryland plant community is most evident along the CT where it climbs through the foothills above Denver. It will also be seen occasionally at higher elevations, on the driest and most stressed sites, until near Kenosha Pass. Junipers tend to be widely spaced, with grasses interspersed in between, while the scrub oak tends to be clumped together so closely as to be almost impenetrable. This sort of vegetation makes for good game habitat, and hikers should be prepared for deer to pop up most anywhere, particularly in early June. In late summer, the scrub oak/piñon-juniper woodland is prone to wildfire, which can move rapidly through the dry terrain. Such fires are often started by lightning strikes, and occasionally by hikers, who are reminded to pay attention to their campfires.

Ponderosa Pine

This is the lowest-elevation timber tree. Because of its good lumber quality and proximity to civilization, it has been the most extensively cut. Thus you may see large, old ponderosa stumps among woodland vegetation, indicating a logged ponderosa forest where the tall pines have not yet returned. These long-needled pines tend to grow well spaced, with grasses flourishing between trees. As a result, ranchers like to graze their stock among the ponderosa, particularly in early spring. On the Eastern Slope, ponderosa pine is found on less stressed south-facing hillsides. On the Western Slope, it is the tree one encounters above the open, arid countryside of the sagebrush community.

Douglas-fir

This predominant tree is not to be confused with the giant firs of the Pacific Northwest, though it is related to them. Here in the Rockies, we have the runts of the litter. The Douglas-fir occupies moist, cool sites. On the Eastern Slope it is found on the slopes opposite the ponderosa pine, and on the Western Slope it grows above the level of the ponderosa. In either case, as a result of the moister environment and shorter growing season, Douglas-fir trees tend to grow closer together, with little ground cover underneath. Much of both the Eastern and Western slopes is Douglas-fir habitat, but because it is also the type most likely to be burned, much of that habitat is occupied by successional vegetation. Hikers, again, should remember to be careful with fire.

Spruce-Fir Forest

This, the highest-elevation forest, is composed of Engelmann spruce and subalpine fir. Because of the late snowmelt, moist summertime conditions and early snowfall, this vegetation type has been least altered by fire. Many of the spruce-fir forests in the Rockies are as much as 400 years old. These dense forests tend to contain many fallen logs, which can be a real deterrent to hiking. The logs are typically moist, and hikers walking over them may be surprised when the bark slips off and they lose their footing. Ground cover may be lacking, and a thick humus layer may be present.

As one approaches timberline, the spruce-fir stands tend to be more open. The trees are clustered, with grasses and beautiful wildflowers interspersed between them. These tree clusters provide refuges for elk during the night. At the timberline itself, the trees are bushlike, weatherbeaten and windshorn. They often grow in very dense clumps which can provide an ideal refuge for hikers. Winds of 50 mph can whistle by virtually unnoticed while you sit in a clump of timberline trees. Animals are aware of this, too, and thus, while waiting out a storm, you may have the pleasure of observing a great deal of small mammal activity.

Lodgepole Pine and Aspen

These are ordinarily successional species which can occupy a given site for up to 200 years. The lodgepole pine often succeeds disturbed Douglas-fir and spruce-fir communities and grows on the driest sites. Its seed-cones are opened by fire, and a wildfire will cause the deposition of thousands of seeds — and, a few years later, the appearance of many dense stands of seedlings and saplings. These pine stands are often referred to as "horsehair." There is virtually no groundcover in the deep shade beneath the saplings, and competition is fierce between the closely spaced trees. The dryness of the site encourages repeated fires.

The aspen occupies moister sites. A clump of aspen among lodgepole pines suggests a potential source of water. Aspen reproduce from root suckers, and any ground disturbance, such as a fire, causes a multitude of saplings to appear. On drier sites, aspen is typically interspersed with Thurber fescue, a large bunchgrass. In moderately moist sites the ground cover will consist of a multitude of grasses, forbs and shrubs. Wet-site aspen often has a ground cover dominated by bracken fern. Aspen groves can be attractive for camping, but during June and July may be infested with troublesome insects.

Alpine Tundra

Though it strikes many people as odd, the tundra can be likened to a desert because it enjoys only minimal precipitation. During the winter, fierce winds prevent snow from accumulating anywhere except in depressions. During the summer, the snowmelt drains quickly off the steeper slopes, leaving the vegetation there to depend for survival on regular afternoon showers. Despite the harsh conditions, the alpine tundra is quite diverse, and includes such different environments as meadows, boulder fields, fell fields, talus and both temporary and permanent ponds. The cushion-like meadows are a favorite site for elk herds. The boulder fields provide homes for pikas, marmots and other animals, and the protected spaces between the boulders can produce some of the most beautiful wildflowers. The fell fields are windswept sites from which virtually all mineral soil has been blown away, leaving behind a "pavement" which, despite its austerity, may have some interesting plants. The talus fields consist of loose rock; they also host some interesting plants and animals. The ponds often teem with invertebrates and can provide good sites for observing the fascinating bird known as the ptarmigan.

Geological Tales

by David L. Gaskill
and John R. Dyni

What forces have determined the magnificent landscapes of Colorado? What do the rocks tell of the past? Why are fossil seashells found far from any sea? How do rocks form, differ and change? What is the special environment of gem stone, metalliferous ores, or coal? What relation do topographical features have to earthquakes, volcanoes, drifting continents or extraterrestrial events?

Mountain-building, deposition of sediments along ancient streams and in vanished seas, and the restless process of weathering by physical and chemical disintegration, water, wind and ice have shaped the landscapes of past and present. The mountains exhibit complex structures at extraordinary scales, requiring enormous forces to build and support. Some are carved from relatively hard, unfractured rock, others from soft, easily eroded rock. Many are huge blocks, the result of vertical uplift along faults. Some are broad crustal upwarps or great piles of eroded extrusive rock. Some are folded and imbricated, or broken by thrust plates that stack older rocks over younger. Many are associated with igneous intrusions. Some may owe their origins to the collisions of continents. Some stand on the foundations of older mountains with deep structural roots; others rest on weak, easily deformed substrata.

The rock formations seen along the CT vary widely in composition and architecture. Minerals found in some of these rocks are responsible for much of Colorado's colorful history. During the frontier days of the late 1800s, gold and silver mining was Colorado's major industry. The discovery of placer gold in the stream beds of the Front Range led to the discovery of metalliferous veins and lodes in the mining districts of Central City, Leadville, Aspen, Telluride, Cripple Creek and other areas. Other mineral commodities important to the state's economy are limestone for making cement and steel; sand, gravel and building stone; molybdenum, lead and zinc, coal, oil and natural gas; and vast reserves of oil shale. The mountains capture and conserve the vital water of this semi-arid region, in forest soils and snowbanks, valley alluvium and porous fractured bedrock. The rocks and geologic structures reveal a succession of visual clues to events in the earth's history dating back 1.8 billion years in Colorado.

Briefly, the plains of eastern Colorado are underlain by relatively flat-lying, interlayered beds of shale, sandstone, conglomerate, limestone, coal and volcanic ash ranging in age from very new to about 570 million years old. This sedimentary rock sequence is 13,000 feet thick in the Denver Basin (see map below) and rests on a much

Figure 1—Geological structures underlying the CT

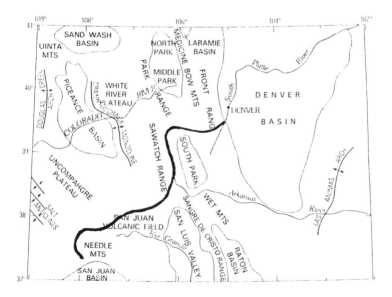

older Precambrian basement complex of crystalline granitic and metamorphic rocks. At the CT's eastern terminus, where plains and mountains meet, these sedimentary and crystalline basement rocks are folded, faulted and bowed up. Some of the rock layers form flatirons (the Fountain Sandstone at the Garden of the Gods, Red Rocks and elsewhere) and hogbacks (the Dakota and Morrison Formations seen from I-70). The basement rocks form the core of the Front Range, having been uplifted some 20,000 feet relative to their position underlying the plains. Westward, the CT crosses the 170-mile-long by 45-mile-wide Front Range, an area that has been repeatedly uplifted during the past 330 million years. The Pikes Peak batholith and other granitic bodies intrude older schists and gneisses, quartzites, marbles and metamorphosed volcanic rock along this portion of the trail.

On the west flank of the Front Range, sedimentary units of the eastern plains are preserved in synclinal basins (such as South Park) and fault blocks. These sedimentary rocks are intruded by mineralized granodiorite porphyry stocks, 40-70 million years old, of the mountain-building Laramide Orogeny.

North of Georgia Pass, the trail passes through part of the Breckenridge mining district, an area of old gold-dredge tailings and the site of the largest gold nugget found in Colorado (now at the Denver Museum of Natural History). The trail climbs over the Tenmile Range, a narrow, upfaulted block of Precambrian gneiss and migmitite. Then it traverses a mosaic of faults on the divide southwest of Copper Mountain, where ancient reefs of dolomite and limestone are interbedded with arkosic grits, conglomerates and sandstones of the Maroon and Minturn formations. These layered rocks are intruded by thick sills and laccoliths of quartz monzonite-latite and granodiorite porphyry.

Two miles east of Camp Hale, the CT crosses a 29-million-year-old rhyolite formation and swings south through the Tennessee Pass mining area, passing over mineralized Cambrian, Devonian, Mississippian and Pennsylvanian strata that host gold deposits.

South of Tennessee Pass, the trail crosses 1.7-billion-year-old gneisses and schists cut by pyritic, quartz-sulfide (silver) veins of the St. Kevin-Sugar Loaf mining district. Some of the turquoise deposits in this area were worked by early Indians. The trail circles Turquoise

Lake on a 1.4-billion-year-old granite batholith, meanders southwest over Precambrian and younger intrusive rocks, and crosses lateral and terminal moraines deposited by extinct glaciers of the Sawatch Range. Turquoise, Twin and Clear lakes, now augmented by dams, formed behind terminal moraines. Both the Clear Creek and Pine Creek glaciers extended across the Arkansas Valley, damming the Arkansas River and forcing it to cut a new channel in bedrock on the east side of the valley.

The upper Arkansas Valley (above Salida) is a rift valley (a down-dropped block, or graben), bounded by the Sawatch fault zone on the west and a series of faults on the east. Well preserved fault scarps of several ages, and numerous hot springs, including the hottest spring in Colorado (the Hortense) and the Mt. Princeton hot spring, are located along the Sawatch fault zone. The fault scarps offset unconsolidated valley fill and glacial deposits more than ten feet in places. Estimated displacement on the Sawatch fault is 3,000 feet or more. Roughly parallel faults on the eastern side of the Arkansas Valley are progressively down-dropped to the west about 1,000 feet on each fault, and seismic studies indicate that the valley in the Buena Vista area is filled with unconsolidated material to a depth of 1,200 to 1,400 feet.

The trail edges the Mt. Princeton-Antero quartz monzonite batholith (about 30 million years old) and the hydrothermally-altered quartz monzonite of the Chalk Cliffs at the Mt. Princeton hot springs. Aquamarine beryl, topaz, garnet and other rare minerals occur near the summit of Mt. Antero, and topaz, garnets and sanadine crystals are found near the town of Nathrop.

Southwest of Marshall Pass, the trail crosses an area known to geologists as the San Juan Volcanic Field (Fig. 1), an immense pile of layered volcanic rock thousands of feet thick. Many cubic miles of welded (and non-welded) ash flow tuff (erupted as incandescent ash) were ejected during violent eruptions from a dozen huge craters, the largest being 20 miles in diameter! The rich silver and gold mining camps of Creede, Silverton, Platoro, Lake City and Bonanza are located either on the edge of or within such calderas. The varied products of other, more passive, eruptions blanket thousands of square miles within the area. Rocks from these volcanic sites range from 3.5 to 35 million years old. The great caldera eruptions occurred intermittently between 22 and 30 million years ago.

Near the Rio Grande headwaters and north flank of the Needle Mountain uplift, the trail crosses Precambrian terrain that includes spectacular upthrust beds of quartzite, slate and phyllite in the Grenadier Range. On the west rim of the Animas River Canyon, a layer of quartzite overlies 1.4-billion-year-old Precambrian rocks. The erosional unconformity between the two represents some 800 million years of unrecorded time here.

From Molas Lake, the trail climbs up through progressively younger sedimentary strata (the Elbert, Ouray, Leadville, Rico, Hermosa, Molas, Cutler, Dolores, Wanakah, Entrada and Morrison formations). Many of these rock units have different sediment source areas than rocks in eastern Colorado, but some, like the Dakota, Morrison, Entrada and Leadville, are lithologic and time-equivalents to like-named rocks in central and eastern Colorado. Other formations, like the 2,000-foot-thick Mancos Shale in this area, interfinger with, and are in part equivalent to, formations in other areas. Mancos strata were deposited in the same sea as the Pierre Shale of eastern Colorado, but as the seashore migrated eastward so did the deposition of younger sediments in the Pierre-Mancos seaway.

On the ridge south of Grizzly Peak, indurated clays, marlstones of the Morrison Formation (famous for dinosaur bones) and the Dakota Sandstone (ancient beach and lagoon deposits) are intruded by igneous dikes, sills and laccolithic bodies. Here the trail follows a high divide, providing grand views of the San Miguel, San Juan, La Plata and Needle Mountains. The nearby Grizzly Peak, Sultan Mountain, Ophir, Mt. Wilson and Rico intrusive centers probably represent roots or local vents for some of the extrusive rocks of the San Juan volcanic field. Continuing south to the La Plata Mountains, the trail crosses mostly continental red shales, siltstones, mudstones, grits and conglomerates of the Cutler Formation. The La Platas are a dissected dome of sedimentary rocks intruded by sills and laccoliths of diorite-monzonite porphyry and granitoid stocks of Laramide age. Gold-silver telluride, ruby silver, copper and lead deposits have been mined from this district since 1873.

The trail descends into the canyon of Junction Creek through progressively younger strata, including the "type section" of the Junction Creek Sandstone member of the Wanaka Formation, to the southern terminus of the CT.

The Geologic Map of Colorado (U.S. Geological Survey, 1979 edition) shows the state's major geologic features, relative ages of the rock units, and references. Many other published maps and reports cover areas along the CT in greater detail. Many of these references are available by mail or over the counter from the U.S. Geological Survey Public Inquiries Office, 15426 Federal Building, Denver, CO; from U.S. Geological Survey Map Sales, Denver Federal Center, Denver, CO; and the U.S. Geological Survey Map Information Office, Washington, DC. Free, non-technical pamphlets, also available from these agencies, include: *Geological Maps, Portraits of the Earth; Mountain and Plains, Denver's Geologic Setting; Volcanoes of the United States; Landforms of the United States; Earthquakes; Geologic Time; Prospecting; Collecting Rocks* and many other titles.

Heaven Underfoot: A Backcountry Essay

"Sensitivity to fine scenery is indeed an index of the plane on which men and women are living" — Prof. G.M. Trevelyan.

It has often been said that the great masses of humanity live lives of quiet desperation, with little time to be anything but machines, spending the best part of their lives making it possible to experience the questionable liberty of enjoying the least valuable part of their existence. Undoubtedly there are many men so occupied with the artificial cares of life that its finer fruits are never plucked by them. Their time is frittered away by details and they often live mean and servile lives, making themselves sick that they might save something against a sick day. Yet these same men from every walk of life are discovering the tonic of the wilderness. They come to the wild places worried and sick at heart, and change under the stimulus of wilderness living into happier, more joyous and carefree individuals. Who can say exactly what they have found — but it is something as definite as life itself, perhaps a heaven underfoot. To many the wilderness has become a way of life as important as their love of home and family, a vital part of their living which brings happiness and lasting content. There can be little melancholy in those who live in the midst of nature and still retain their senses. Thoreau once said that "while I can enjoy the friendship of the seasons nothing can make life a burden to me."

I have no wish to trouble the peace of those who are satisfied with life as they find it — though it often seems that many of our luxuries and so-called comforts are often quite dispensable and even a positive hindrance, and it has been said that with respect to luxuries and comforts, the wisest have ever lived a simple life. Some of the wisdom of life, in part, may consist in the elimination of nonessentials and of finding contentment in those things closest to us. Lin Yutang, the Chinese philosopher, remarked, "There seems to be a great deal of wistfulness . . . to be on a plot of grass under tall trees and just do nothing," and it is at such moments that our soul utters, "Life is beautiful."

But it is he who strays from the shelter of the broad, cool verandas, the beaten path and man-made trails, who may reach the most sublime heights of emotional and spiritual climax, and enjoy experiences treasured and remembered throughout one's years. It is well known that a knowledge of art or music adds greatly to the capacity to enjoy. The musically ignorant may be much moved emotionally by a great piece of music, but the educated listener will be more discriminating and understanding. And so it is with the work of nature. An eye sensitive to beauty may see only the contours and colors, which exert in themselves an emotional influence on the beholder. But the scientists are making it more and more possible for even casual travelers to learn something of the age-old forces, the fingerprints of geology, that have created the scene. The informed may become discriminatingly appreciative. Atmosphere, too, is conducive to one's greatest enjoyment. Acoustically near-perfect music halls and beautiful art galleries help the admirer to lose himself in contemplation of that which stirs his senses. But only faintly can the finer music of the wilderness be heard from the highways, graveled paths and country clubs.

But for those who yearn for the wilderness as a way of escape from the problems of everyday living, and who long for freedom from machines and pressing responsibilities, who are not afraid of physical discomfort and elemental factors of muscle and self reliance, there may be reward in peace of mind. And with it may come the perspective that men recognize in the back country, the ability to become conscious of a unity with primary forces in life, a unity that destroys feelings of futility, frustration and unreality. Maybe we are too serious and hence our world is too full of troubles. The mountains remind of God, who is too easily forgotten in our living complicated by life's fears, talk of economic boom and slump, unemployment, survival of the fittest — here on the heights these things seem relatively unimportant. The mountains teach us a creed of beauty and simplicity — to live decently in sight of heaven and one's fellow man, realizing that life as we know it is but a fragment of Eternity.

Mountains are big things, and they suggest to those who love them even more than they are and hint at more than they say. Perhaps there is more than we realize in the familiar saying of the prospector, who also was searching for something — "There's Gold in them thar hills!"

— From "Philosophy of Mountaineering," by Dave Gaskill, originally published in *Trail & Timberline*, September 1949, Colorado Mountain Club, Denver

Little Molas Lake

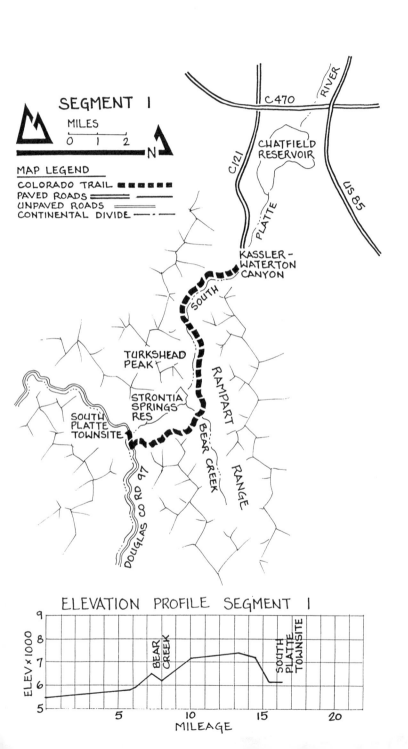

Segment 1
Kassler to South Platte Townsite

Introduction

The Colorado Trail officially begins at an obscure trailhead deep within Pike National Forest, 6.2 miles beyond the Waterton Canyon parking area. Access to this point is provided via an old railroad grade, which is now an asphalted road restricted to foot and bicycle traffic or vehicles of the Forest Service and the Denver Water Board. If Two Forks Dam is constructed, this road access might be closed to the public and another approach would have to be provided to the trailhead. Therefore, it would be prudent to inquire about the situation with the South Platte Ranger District if planning a departure from the Waterton Canyon parking area. The Denver Water Board allows no dogs or camping along this first 6.2-mile section.

On your way to Waterton Canyon from the east, notice the hogbacks leaning against the ancient core of the Rampart Range. With a little imagination it is possible to visualize these leftover sedimentary rocks crumpling and eroding away through the eons as the Rampart Range forced its way up from below. Beyond the initial sedimentary layers at the outlet of the canyon, the gorge narrows and reveals its 1.6-billion-year-old metamorphic walls.

Although this canyon was no doubt visited by many Indians and was briefly explored by the Long Expedition of 1820, it was not permanently disrupted until 1877, when territorial governor John Evans built his Denver South Park and Pacific Railroad up the Platte on its way to exploit Colorado's mineral belt. The canyon has known little peace since, and received a major trauma in the early 1980s, when work began on Strontia Springs Dam. Plans for the massive Two Forks project just upstream will continue the cycle, as well as inundate a significant portion of the CT.

Trailheads/Access Points

Kassler (Waterton Canyon Trailhead): There are several routes to the trailhead at Waterton Canyon. Least confusing is to take I-25 south from Denver through the suburbs to Colorado 470. Travel west on C-470 (which is a freeway) 12.5 miles to Colorado 121 (Wadsworth Blvd). Go left (south) on C-121 for 4.5 miles, after which the road officially ends, just before the entrance to a Martin Marietta plant. Turn left, off of C-121 and onto a side road. Continue 0.3 mile, following the signs to Waterton Canyon parking area.

South Platte Townsite: See Segment 2.

Supplies, Services and Accommodations

Denver and its southern suburbs have the full array of services expected in a megalopolis. The trailhead at the mouth of Waterton Canyon has limited interurban bus service.

Maps

USGS Quadrangles: Kassler, Platte Canyon. USFS Maps: Pike National Forest. CT Series: Maps 1 and 2.

Trail Description

From the parking area at the Kassler water treatment plant, begin your journey up Waterton Canyon on the old railroad grade. Cottonwoods along the banks of the Platte provide shade on warm summer days. At 5520 feet above sea level, this point is the lowest anywhere along the route of the CT, and serves as a gateway from the eastern plains grasslands to the foothills life zone. Immediately above the shadows of the cottonwoods, the dry, rocky slopes of the canyon support little more than yucca, gambel oak and juniper. High up on the cooler, moister mountain slopes, dark patches of ponderosa and Douglas-fir are visible.

Pass Strontia Springs Dam at mile 5.8 (5800) and continue straight ahead (south) on the dirt road, which steadily steepens. The public must exit the road at a switchback to the right, 0.2 mile beyond the dam. Here, a spur to the left (south) leads through an impressive portal of multicolored metamorphic boulders at mile 6.2 (5920) to the official beginning of the CT. A sign here reads "Colorado Trail #1776, Bear Creek—1.6, South Platte Townsite —10.0." Perhaps another entry should be added to the sign, stating, "Junction Creek Trailhead, Western Terminus—462.5." The wide trail switchbacks up through a shaded Douglas-fir forest, offering intermittent glimpses of the rocky summit called Turkshead. From the saddle at mile 7.3 (6560), descend and cross Bear Creek at mile 8.0 (6200). Bear Creek is the last reliable point for water until you reach South Platte townsite 8.0 miles beyond.

A barely visible path can be seen descending alongside the creek here. This was an old logging road built by C.A. Deane, who had a sawmill at the confluence of Bear Creek and the South Platte River. Besides providing ties to the DSP&PRR during its construction, Deane later expanded his profitable operation by adding a hotel and the whistle stop which became known as Deansbury.

Continue 0.1 mile on the CT to the crossing of West Bear Creek. At mile 9.0 (6640) the CT shares its route with Motorcycle Trail 692 for a half mile, until just after the second crossing of West Bear Creek. Here the trail diverges from the motorcycle trail and proceeds uphill and to the right. Ascend another 0.6 mile to the ridge at mile 10.1 (7200), where the motorcycle trail crosses the CT a final time. Begin a traverse along the north slope of Platte Canyon. Rock outcrops provide convenient perches for rest stops, from which the reservoir below and the foothills to the north and west can be viewed.

At mile 13.0 (7280) the trail rounds an elevated valley and passes along a ridge, then begins a switchbacking descent into the valley. Pass below the shoreline of the proposed Two Forks Reservoir, then join up with Douglas County Road 97 at mile 15.4 (6120). A widened roadway here provides plentiful parking for this unmarked trailhead. Long-distance trekkers will have to share the route north for the next 0.7 mile with sometimes inconsiderate motorists on the road, which was originally graded for the DSP&PRR Nighthawk Branch. Cross the South Platte River on a beefy bridge, designed to support heavy locomotives, and enter the historic railroad junction where the boarded-up South Platte Hotel recalls memories of another era. The first CT segment ends here at mile 16.1 (6100).

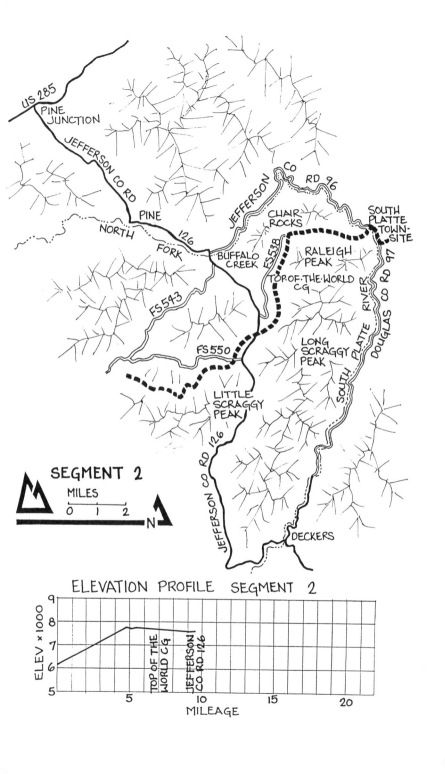

US 285

PINE
JUNCTION

JEFFERSON CO RD

PINE

NORTH   FORK   126

BUFFALO
CREEK

JEFFERSON   CO   RD 96

CHAIR
ROCKS

FS 538

RALEIGH
PEAK

TOP OF THE WORLD
CG

SOUTH
PLATTE
TOWN-
SITE

FS 543

FS 550

LITTLE
SCRAGGY
PEAK

LONG
SCRAGGY
PEAK

SOUTH PLATTE RIVER

DOUGLAS CO RD 97

JEFFERSON CO RD 126

DECKERS

SEGMENT 2

MILES

0   1   2

N

ELEVATION PROFILE SEGMENT 2

9

8

7

6

5

ELEV × 1000

TOP OF THE
WORLD CG

JEFFERSON
CO RD 126

5   10   15   20

MILEAGE

Segment 2

South Platte Townsite to Jefferson County Road 126

Introduction

During its heyday, South Platte saw many trains pass the confluence of the South Platte River and its North Fork. Today the shuttered South Platte Hotel serves as a lone reminder of that age. If completed, Two Forks Reservoir will submerge this historic junction as well as significant portions of the canyon itself, which is popular with anglers, kayakers, hikers and rock climbers.

The CT route in this segment, except along the South Platte River at the outset, is completely without water. Even Top of the World Campground is waterless, so pack plenty if you wish to make use of the many potential campsites along the way.

This trail segment makes a transition from the Rampart Range to the Kenosha Mountains, and all along are splendid examples of the rounded outcrops of the Pikes Peak batholith, outcrops which take on dramatic, fortress-like appearances. The pink coloration of this billion-year-old granite is disguised by the green and black lichens which grow profusely on it.

This segment ends at Jefferson County Road 126 approximately 3.2 miles south of Buffalo Creek town. The Forest Service has provided a parking area 0.3 mile south of this point, on the west side of the highway.

Trailheads/Access Points

South Platte Townsite Trailhead: Travel approximately 32 miles west from Denver on US 285 to Pine Junction. Go left (south) on Pine Valley Road (Jefferson County Road 126), following the signs to Pine and Buffalo Creek. Continue on Jefferson County Road 126 for 9.4 miles to the outskirts of Buffalo Creek. Turn left onto Jefferson County Road 96, which parallels the North Fork 10.6 miles to the trailhead, at the boarded-up South Platte Hotel. Ample parking is available here.

This trailhead is also accessible from US 24 at Woodland Park by traveling north on Colorado 67 to Deckers. Continue down the Platte River on Douglas County Roads 67 and 97 approximately 14 miles to the trailhead. This trailhead is subject to closure if work commences on Two Forks Dam.

Top of the World Campground: At Buffalo Creek, continue on Jefferson County Road 126 approximately 2.5 miles and go left onto FS-538, which is marked "Top of the World CG." It is approximately 1.5 miles to the campground, on a spur which takes off to the right as FS-538 continues ahead. Drive to the cul-de-sac at the end of the campground and park at the small area provided. Follow a short side trail down to the CT, which runs to the east and just below the long ridge where the campground is situated.

Jefferson County Road 126: See Segment 3.

Supplies, Services and Accommodations

There is a Forest Service work center in Buffalo Creek. Services here are quite limited.

Maps

USGS Quadrangles: Platte Canyon, Deckers. USFS Maps: Pike National Forest. CT Series: Map 2.

Trail Description

From the confluence of the South Platte River and the North Fork, the CT temporarily follows a Forest Service road around the old hotel's right side and then south across the North Fork on a rickety, one-lane bridge. This crossing provides the last reliable water for almost 13 miles. A few hundred feet beyond the bridge, the trail leads right at a well marked junction and switchbacks uphill through a forest of ponderosa pine and Douglas-fir. Several miles up the trail a large outcrop of pink Pikes Peak granite, which could make a lazy afternoon's destination, affords views of Pikes Peak, Devil's Head and Platte Canyon.

Immediately beyond a jeep road crossing at mile 3.8 (7360) the trail makes a sharp right which may not be obvious to westbounders. If you miss this turn, however, a well trampled unofficial route rejoins the official pathway in 0.2 mile.

The next stretch of trail is a bit confusing. At mile 4.3 (7600), the CT follows an old road, but only for about 150 feet. Westbounders will make a sharp left onto this short piece of adopted route, then a right off of it and back onto the trail at a more obvious junction. The route is more confusing for eastbounders. The right turn for you off of this old road is unmarked and hidden by a bushy pine.

Continue your ascent north of Raleigh Peak through a Douglas-fir forest to a ridge at mile 4.7 (7760), where Chair Rocks are visible to the west. Descend from the ridge to a dry gully, then ascend to mile 5.4 (7760) and FS-538 at a three-corner intersection. Follow FS-538 west 0.1 mile to where the road turns south. The trail resumes here and heads off the road to the left (south) through a forest that consists of ponderosa with an occasional juniper. The trail continues to bear south, paralleling FS-538 and crossing several old, abandoned roads. Take care not to wander off the main trail where dirt bikes have illegally created spur trails.

Through this section, the striking vistas to the east justify a pace slow enough to allow you to fully appreciate Raleigh Peak, Long Scraggy and Pikes Peak's rarely seen northwest profile. Pass the short side trail up to Top of the World Campground at mile 7.1 (7680). Although this location would make a good trailhead for the CT, no markers have been posted to lead those interested from the campground's cul-de-sac down to the trail. If you have a few minutes to spare, ascend the short distance to appropriately designated Top of the World, whose 360-degree panorama reveals the Pikes Peak massif, the entire Rampart Range and the southern end of the Front Range. Also visible to the west is the CT route along the Kenosha Mountains and Windy Peak.

South of Top of the World Campground, the trail continues in and out of several shallow gullies planted alternately with ponderosa and Douglas-fir forests. At mile 9.0 (7520), a new section of trail splits off to the right from an older section that is being revegetated, then crosses a dirt road 400 feet beyond. Continue on the trail to Jefferson County Road 126 at mile 9.4 (7600), which is the end of this segment. This is a potentially dangerous highway crossing at a blind corner. The town of Buffalo Creek is approximately 3.2 miles north from this point, and the Forest Service trailhead parking area is 0.3 mile south on the west side of the highway.

Long Scraggy Peak

Segment 3
Jefferson County Road 126
to FS-543 (Second Crossing)

Introduction

Squeezing between two parcels of private property, the CT begins this segment at Jefferson County Road 126 approximately 3.2 miles south of Buffalo Creek town. The Forest Service has conveniently provided a parking area 0.3 mile south of the trail crossing on Road 126. This segment crosses several streams in its middle section and provides many potential campsites, including the Forest Service's Buffalo Campground, for those wanting a taste of civilization. (Meadows Campground is available through reservation only). You will pass through the heavily-used Buffalo Creek Recreation Area in this segment. The original trail just west of Tramway Creek was obliterated by logging activity and has since been rebuilt. The new tread winds above the logged area, at times just skirting it, and ends up on the logging road for a short section.

The CT crosses FS-543 twice in this segment. Mountain bicyclists should note that they need to exit this described route at the first crossing of FS-543 to detour around Lost Creek Wilderness (refer to the Mountain Bicycle Route). The trail crosses FS-543 a second time at the end of this segment, where a parking area is provided.

Trailheads/Access Points

Jefferson County Road 126 Trailhead: Travel approximately 32 miles west from Denver on US 285 to Pine Junction. Go

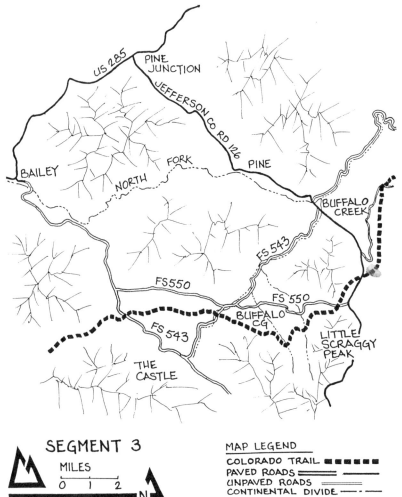

SEGMENT 3

MILES

0   1   2

N

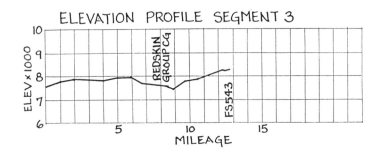

ELEVATION PROFILE SEGMENT 3

left (south) on Pine Valley Road (Jefferson County Road 126) and follow the signs to Pine and Buffalo Creek. Continue approximately 3.2 miles south of Buffalo Creek on Road 126 to where the CT crosses the highway. This is the start of this segment, but you can't park on the road shoulder, so continue 0.3 mile south to the trailhead parking area on the right (west) side of the road. The CT is about 0.2 mile to the west, beyond the gate, on a Forest Service road that has been closed to motorized traffic.

FS-550 Trail Access: From Buffalo Creek, continue south on Jefferson County Road 126 approximately 4.0 miles and go right (west) on FS-550. Drive approximately 0.5 mile to where the CT crosses the road. No parking is provided here.

FS-543 Trail Access (First Crossing): At Buffalo Creek, leave Jefferson County Road 126 and follow FS-543 toward Wellington Lake. Drive approximately 6.5 miles to a fork and go left, continuing on FS-543 barely another 0.1 mile. Look for the obscure trail crossing. No parking is provided here.

FS-543 Trailhead (Second Crossing): See Segment 4.

Supplies, Services and Accommodations
Available at Buffalo Creek. See Segment 2.

Maps
USGS Quadrangles: Deckers, Green Mountain, Windy Peak. USFS Maps: Pike National Forest. CT Series: Maps 2 and 3.

Trail Description
Hurry across Jefferson County Road 126 at a blind curve and continue through the ponderosa forest to mile 0.3 (7720), where you join an abandoned road which leads south, paralleling Road 126. A spur to the left here heads east about 0.2 mile to the trailhead parking area on the highway. The trail leaves the road to the right (west) at mile 1.3 (7800) and continues a half mile, where the CT briefly follows an old jeep road. Follow the jeep road for just a hundred feet and resume on the trail at left (south), which curves around the west side of an impressive and massive granite outcrop.

Cross FS-550 at mile 1.9 (7840). The trail traverses through ponderosa and Douglas-fir forests to mile 2.8 (7800), where it joins an old road and descends slightly on a rounded ridge sprinkled with fragments of quartz. The trail reemerges to the left 0.2 mile beyond and assumes a more southerly bearing into Morrison Creek Canyon. Pass under a huge mass of granite blocks on the steeply descending north ridge of Little Scraggy Peak and continue to mile 4.1 (7760), where the trail seems to end at a jeep road. Bear to the right on the road and notice how, a few steps beyond the creek crossing, the trail resumes at left and ascends 0.2 mile to the crest of the ridge. Descend and cross a small tributary of Morrison Creek on a corduroy bridge. Head up the west side of this tributary to mile 5.0 (7960), where a sharp right will take you across several gullies. The CT joins and descends an old road beginning at mile 5.8 (8000) and crosses Tramway Creek a half mile further on.

On the north side of a clearing at mile 6.7 (7680), the trail picks up again at a sharp left and continues a traverse to mile 7.2 (7600), where it crosses a logging road which descends to the right. The trail continues to wind in and out of small gullies forested with ponderosa pine and Douglas fir. The logged area is visible from time to time below. Bear left (west) at mile 8.8 (7560) where the trail briefly joins the logging road. Continue 0.2 mile on the logging road and look for the obscure trail to resume at right (north). If the trail marker here were vandalized this junction would be virtually impossible to spot.

Pass through Meadows Group Campground 0.1 mile further on; Buffalo Campground is a half mile east on FS-550. At mile 9.5 (7400) the CT, Buffalo Creek and FS-543 (first crossing) converge. The trail ascends steeply 0.7 mile west of FS-543 to a flat-topped ridge. The Castle's granite bulwark is visible to the south through a ponderosa forest. Be careful not to prick yourself on the nearby yuccas, plants whose leaves were once woven into moccasins by the Indians and whose roots were pounded into soap.

The CT crosses an old road, then assumes another as its route at mile 11.0 (7920). This road begins a slow transition back into a trail a half mile beyond. Descend into a small gully at mile 13.1 (8160), where the CT crosses a faint road. Then ascend a bit and drop down to the second crossing of FS-543. A parking area is provided here at the end of this segment at mile 13.4 (8280).

Segment 4
FS-543 (Second Crossing) to FS-817

Introduction

If traveling westbound, you will gain a lot of elevation in this segment as you climb to the rounded ridges of the Kenosha Mountains. The exposed Precambrian crest of this range is largely hidden from view by thick lodgepole and aspen forests until you travel further west. Backpackers will find several reliable sources of water, but heavy grazing in upper Lost Park may taint the supply.

Mountain cyclists are once again reminded that they must detour around the Lost Creek Wilderness, through which this segment passes (see the Mountain Bicycle Route).

Most of this segment of the CT follows an old logging road that was built between 1885 and 1887 by W.H. Hooper for $1,700. The cost was higher than expected because of several marshy stretches that needed corduroy treatment. Hooper also ran a sawmill operation in Lost Park that was eventually shut down by the Department of the Interior for persistent illegalities.

Misfortune also befell the Hayden Survey's Gustavus Bechler in 1875, when he was on a nearby mountain top making observations and noticed his camp burning below. Typical of the dedication of his lot, Bechler remained on the summit to finish his calculations before descending to contend with the disaster.

Trailheads/Access Points

FS-543 Trailhead (Second Crossing): Travel west from Denver on US 285 about 39 miles to Bailey.   Go left on Park

County Road 68, which becomes FS-543. Continue approximately eight miles from Bailey to where the CT crosses the road. A small parking area is provided here.

Lost Park Campground: Travel west from Denver on US 285 approximately 58 miles to Kenosha Pass. Continue on the highway another 3.2 miles to the turnoff marked Lost Park Road (FS-127). Turn left (east) onto the dirt road and drive 19.4 miles to the end of the road at Lost Park Campground. A somewhat indistinct and unmarked trail goes north from the campground 1.7 miles and joins the CT.

FS-817 Trail Access: See Segment 5.

Supplies, Services and Accommodations

Limited supplies are available in the town of Bailey, eight miles west from the trailhead on FS-543.

Maps

USGS Quadrangles: Windy Peak, Topaz Mountain. USFS Maps: Pike National Forest. CT Series. Maps 3 and 4.

Trail Description

From the trailhead parking area on FS-543, the CT ascends a logging road to mile 0.3 (8360), where a gate closes the road to public vehicles. At this point, Rolling Creek Trail bends to the left and the CT leaves the road and continues to the right. Observe the wilderness regulation sign here. At mile 0.9 (8560) the CT joins up with the old road built by Hooper and begins a serious ascent, bearing generally southwest. Pass through a gate a half mile further on and enter Lost Creek Wilderness at mile 1.8 (9100). The wilderness boundary is marked by an inconspicuous little metal sign. Because of the thick stand of lodgepole pines blanketing the area, the only vista along here is of nearby Windy Peak when it aligns itself with the swath cut for the old Hooper Road. Go left where the trail forks at mile 2.3. Continue straight ahead on the CT at mile 3.1 (9320), where the Craig Creek Trail descends to the right. The CT continues its ascent southwest on the old Hooper Road, alternately passing through lodgepole and aspen forests. Cross a small stream at mile 4.5 (9360), where the carcass of a long-forgotten truck recalls the

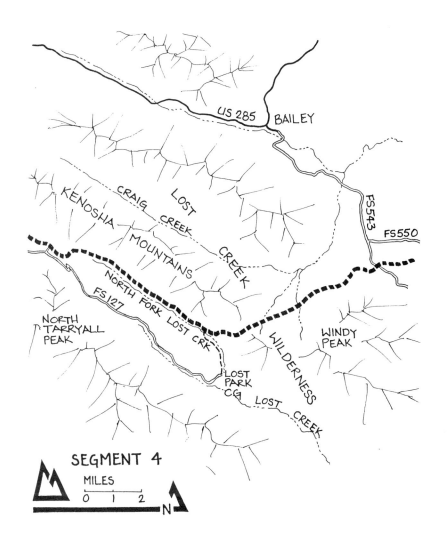

US 285 BAILEY

FS543

FS550

KENOSHA

CRAIG CREEK

LOST CREEK

MOUNTAINS

NORTH FORK LOST CRK

FS 127

NORTH
TARRYALL
PEAK

LOST
PARK
CG

WINDY
PEAK

WILDERNESS

LOST CREEK

SEGMENT 4

MILES

0　1　2

N

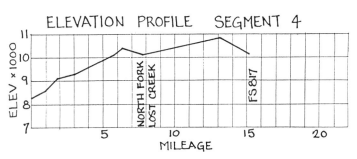

ELEVATION PROFILE   SEGMENT 4

ELEV × 1000

11

10

9

8

7

NORTH FORK
LOST CREEK

FS 817

5   10   15   20

MILEAGE

enterprising prewilderness days of this road.

The CT detours to the left off of the old road at mile 5.7 (10,160) to avoid the marshy areas that caused Hooper to exceed his budget. The CT rejoins the Hooper Road half a mile further on, above the soggy stretch. Pass over a low, forested ridge of the Kenosha Mountains at mile 6.3 (10,480) and descend to the elongated alpine meadow of the North Fork of Lost Creek 1.1 miles beyond. Pass the cutoff to Lost Park Campground at mile 7.8 (10,200) and notice the ruins of an old sawmill to the south across the creek. Could this be the remains of Hooper's busted operation?

Begin a slow ascent northwest, paralleling the creek on the north side of this broad alpine valley. A contingent of curious cattle will mostly likely be observing your progess. Avoid the spur which leads uphill to the right into the forest at mile 8.0 (10,240) and continue on the CT straight ahead up the valley. Cross a small tributary stream 0.1 mile beyond and pass through a gate. Continue the easy ascent northwest along the north edge of the linear meadow. In a few places, the nearby craggy metamorphic ridge of the Kenosha Mountains comes into view.

Top the saddle at the head of the North Fork at mile 13.2 (10,880). A newly built section of the CT bends to the left here, off the old Hooper Road, and contours beyond the saddle through a spruce forest. At a point 0.2 mile beyond the saddle, the trail abruptly curves around to a westerly exposure offering the first glimpse of the Continental Divide, through a mixed forest of lodgepole, spruce, limber pine, bristlecone pine and aspen. The trail loses elevation quickly as it switchbacks down to a stream crossing in an area of washed-out beaver ponds at mile 15.2 (10,160). The CT crosses an obscure, eroded spur 0.1 mile beyond the beaver ponds; this spur leads down to an unofficial but popular parking area and trail access point at the end of FS-817 on the Lost Park Road.

Segment 5
FS-817 to Kenosha Pass

Introduction

Grazing cattle will accompany you on this segment, especially during those few times when water is available at both Rock Creek and the tiny seasonal trickle of Johnson Gulch. Water can be pumped during the summer from a well located in Kenosha Campground at the end of this segment.

Travelers have complained about the obscurity of the route between FS-817 and Kenosha Pass, especially in the grassy meadows through which the trail often passes. Be alert for remnants of trail in these meadows and for posts and cairns, often vandalized, which mark the route.

Trailheads/Access Points

FS-817 Trail Access: Travel west from Denver on US 285 approximately 58 miles to Kenosha Pass. Continue on US 285 another 3.2 miles to the turnoff marked "Lost Park Road" (FS-127). Turn left (east) onto the dirt road and travel 11.0 miles to FS-817, an inconspicuous side road which branches left and is only about 0.2 mile long. Park your car at the end of this short road and hike up the eroded jeep road, which has been barricaded with a large hump of earth. Continue a short distance up the steep, abandoned road and watch for the trail which crosses it at right angles.

FS-133 (Ben Tyler Trail) Trail Access: This trail access is on a rough, but not necessarily 4WD, road. Travel approximately

7.5 miles on Lost Park Road (FS-127) east from US 285 and go left onto FS-133, which is marked "Ben Tyler Trail." Continue up the rough road 1.3 miles to the point where the CT crosses it. No parking area is provided.

Kenosha Pass Trailhead: See Segment 6.

Supplies, Services and Accommodations

The town of Jefferson is 4.5 miles from Kenosha Pass on US 285. Here you will find a small general store with basic provisions.

Maps

USGS Quadrangles: Topaz Mountain, Observatory Rock, Mount Logan, Jefferson. USFS Maps: Pike National Forest. CT Series: Maps 4 and 5.

Trail Description

The CT continues west above FS-817 through aspen forest, then curves to the north, descending slightly into upper Black Canyon. Cross over to the north side of the canyon and continue a slow descent to Rock Creek at mile 7.1 (9520), just downstream from the old cabin of Rock Creek Cow Camp. Here the trail vanishes momentarily in thick, shrubby cinquefoil which conceals the wooden-timber creek crossing.

On the west side of Rock Creek, follow the old road 0.1 mile downstream (southeast) and be alert for the trail, which veers to the right off the road and immediately enters a spruce forest. Ascend 0.1 mile and pass through a red gate, then make a sharp right onto another old road. Continue an ascent 0.3 mile west-northwest on the abandoned road and look for the trail to resume at left as the road begins to level out. Cross Ben Tyler Trail (actually a road) at mile 7.7 (9720), then descend through a grassy clearing to Johnson Gulch and cross the tiny seasonal flow on a wooden timber at mile 8.2 (9520).

Immediately west of the stream, follow a faint route west-southwest for about 300 feet, crossing a jeep road and angling over a grassy rise. From here on, the route is marked by a series of posts which lead northwest up the grassy, shallow valley. The posts that mark the route are about 75 feet to the right of an old road that

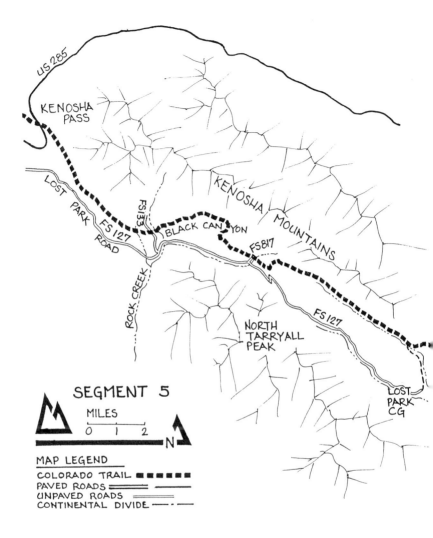

SEGMENT 5

MILES

0   1   2

N

MAP LEGEND

COLORADO TRAIL ■ ■ ■ ■ ■
PAVED ROADS ═══════
UNPAVED ROADS ═══════
CONTINENTAL DIVIDE ─ · ─

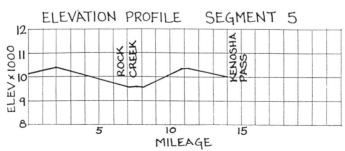

ELEVATION PROFILE   SEGMENT 5

ELEV × 1000

MILEAGE

parallels them for slightly more than a mile. The trail through here is intermittent at best, so you will need to blaze through the grass from post to post or follow the old road which parallels the CT route.

Enter a mostly-aspen forest at the head of the valley at mile 9.5 (9840), where the posted route joins the jeep road. The jeep road slowly changes into a trail and climbs to an open area, where the CT route over the Continental Divide at Georgia Pass is visible to the west. Look back over your shoulder before reentering the trees for one of the nicest views you will ever have of the Black Canyon and the Kenosha Mountains.

After descending through a forest of aspen, bristlecone and spruce, the trail abruptly leads into another grassy expanse at mile 10.5 (9960). There is no hint of a trail through here; proceed 0.2 mile north-northwest, following a cairned route that is frequently vandalized. Cross several faint roads until you end up at the base of a bald hill that is scarred with jeep tracks. The CT resumes to the left here, ascending the southwest side of the hill and passing through stands of aspen and stately bristlecone. Openings in the trees reveal the dramatic scenery of South Park and the Mosquito Range. The trail makes a left turn onto a jeep road at mile 11.1 (10,200). Continue bearing generally north to mount a broad forested ridge, then take the right fork where the jeep road splits at mile 11.3 and begin a traverse at the 10,400-foot level. Notice the old stock driveway signs along here, which recall an era when animals were   transported largely on the hoof.

Descend to a junction with another old road at mile 12.4 (10,240), and go right (north). Continue for just 300 feet on this old road before rejoining the trail to the left. Resume your descent in an aspen forest that shimmers with a golden glow in autumn. Go left where the trail adopts a jeep road at mile 13.5 (10,080) and left again where the jeep road forks 0.2 mile further on. With a few more steps you will enter the large, open saddle at Kenosha Pass. Proceed to the trailhead on the east side of US 285 at mile 14.0 (10,000).

Segment 6
Kenosha Pass to Goldhill Trailhead

Introduction

The CT west of Kenosha Pass is poorly marked and difficult to follow when compared with the trail up to this point. Beyond Jefferson Lake Road the route becomes easier to follow, but still care must be taken to look for the rather obscure cairns that mark the way.

Water and facilities are available during the summer at the campgrounds on Kenosha Pass and Jefferson Lake Road. Beyond Jefferson Creek, there is no reliable water supply until the trail drops down into the headwaters of the Swan River, on the west side of Georgia Pass. Camping within Jefferson Creek Recreation Area is restricted to established campgrounds only. The Swan River is also the site of past and present private enterprises. Many of the mining operations here are still active, so please behave accordingly.

The first official loop on the CT occurs within this segment. It is a 10.6-mile round trip with 1,520 feet of elevation gain and is designed as a long day hike or as an overnight backpack. Trailhead parking is provided at either Beaver Ponds Picnic Ground for day-hikers or at the backpacker parking area just outside of Jefferson Creek Campground for overnighters. Both of these trailhead points are on Jefferson Creek Road. The trail description for this loop appears at the end of this segment.

From the site of Parkville, west of Georgia Pass, the route of the CT splits. The official route follows the Swan River to Colorado 9 and continues as Segment 7 up Miners Creek to Wheeler Flats Trailhead at Copper Mountain. The advantage of this route is that it

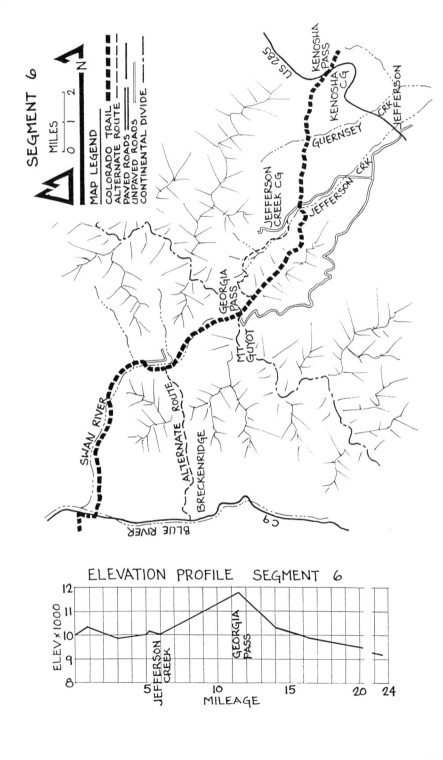

SEGMENT 6

N

MILES
0 1 2

MAP LEGEND
COLORADO TRAIL
ALTERNATE ROUTE
PAVED ROADS
UNPAVED ROADS
CONTINENTAL DIVIDE

US 285

KENOSHA PASS

KENOSHA CG

GUERNSEY

JEFFERSON CRK

JEFFERSON

JEFFERSON CREEK CG

JEFFERSON CRK

GEORGIA PASS

MT GUYOT

SWAN RIVER

ALTERNATE ROUTE

BRECKENRIDGE

BLUE RIVER

C9

ELEVATION PROFILE   SEGMENT 6

ELEV × 1000

12
11
10
9
8

JEFFEERSON CREEK

GEORGIA PASS

5   10   15   20   24

MILEAGE

avoids the bustling town of Breckenridge. However, some long-distance trekkers may want to pass through the old mine-town turned ski-resort. The alternate route that will lead them there will be described as Segment 7-Alternate.

Kenosha Pass had long served as an Indian trail into the fertile hunting grounds of South Park and was crossed by Anglo parties as early as 1830. In the mid 1840s, Col. John C. Frémont crossed the pass, and when miners began streaming into the Blue River drainage, they paralleled the old Indian trail and then veered west over Georgia Pass, approximating the route of today's CT.

In 1860, a 25-year charter was given by the Kansas Territorial Legislature to John McIntyre, Major Bradford and Judge Steke to build and maintain a toll road from Denver to California Gulch (the future Leadville) using, in part, the Kenosha Pass route. The following year, a stage line began operating over the road. It was Clark Herbert, a driver for the line, who named the pass after his hometown of Kenosha, Wisconsin. Twenty years later, Governor Evans built his DSP&P Railroad over the pass. The DSP&P chugged to Breckenridge and, eventually, Gunnison.

At the same time the California Gulch stage road was being built, a group of southern miners were working Georgia Gulch west of the divide and defending their claims as others poured over Georgia Pass. The energetic town of Parkville developed at the mouth of the gulch, but mining activity was so great that by the 1880s the town had been inundated by the tailings of its own prosperity.

A more drastic means of recovering the gold was introduced in the early 1900s by Ben Stanley Revett. His efficient but destructive dredge boats did recover well-hidden gold deep within the valley bottoms, but at the same time they created enormous piles of rock which still run parallel with the Swan and Blue rivers and French Creek.

Mount Guyot (13,370 feet) is a prominent landmark in this segment and was named in honor of Princeton geography professor Arnold Guyot, who was grateful for having his name attached to a peak just a few miles south and on the same ridge as the two fourteeners named for his well-known colleagues, John Torrey and Asa Gray. Professor Guyot also has a less dramatic mountain in the Appalachians named for him, and yet another in the Sierra Nevada.

Interestingly, a "guyot" is also a geologic term denoting an underwater volcano. Colorado's Mt. Guyot is neither submerged nor a volcano, but an igneous intrusion somewhere in the neighborhood of 40 to 72 million years of age, much younger than the granite knobs and metamorphic rocks of the Rampart Range and the Kenosha Mountains.

Trailheads/Access Points

Kenosha Pass Trailhead: Travel on US 285 approximately 58 miles west from Denver to the summit of Kenosha Pass. The trail crosses the highway at Kenosha Campground. Parking is available at the trailhead point several hundred feet east on the Forest Service access road. Parking spaces are also provided within Kenosha Campground, though you may have to pay for the privilege.

Jefferson Lake Road Trail Access: From Kenosha Pass, continue on US 285 4.5 miles to Jefferson. Go right on the side road marked "Jefferson Lake Road." Drive 2.1 miles, then go right again at the sign which marks the way to Jefferson Lake. Continue 3.1 miles to where the CT crosses the road. A tenth of a mile further there is temporary parking at Beaver Ponds Picnic Ground. More permanent backpacker parking is available 0.6 mile up the road, near the entrance to Jefferson Creek Campground.

Goldhill Trailhead: See Segment 7.

Supplies, Services and Accommodations

Available in Jefferson (see Segment 5).

Maps

USGS Quadrangles: Jefferson, Boreas Pass, Keystone, Frisco. USFS Maps: Pike National Forest, Arapaho National Forest. CT Series: Maps 5 and 6.

Trail Description

West of US 285, the CT passes through the southern portion of Kenosha Campground. Once inside the campground, bear to the left twice, until the road passes through a gate. Notice that the trail resumes to the right, just beyond the fence, and climbs northwest through a forest of aspen and lodgepole. In July the understory is

thick with golden banner, paintbrush and columbine. At mile 0.7 (10,400) the noise of US 285 disappears as the trail passes over a ridge and begins a descent through inclined meadows and aspen groves. The hay piles visible far below in the expansive fields of South Park are reminiscent of freshly baked loaves of bread. As you walk through the aspen forests, notice where ravenous wildlife has stripped patches of bark off the tree trunks.

Cross an old road at mile 1.4 (10,280) and continue west. The trail is inobvious for the next hundred feet. The CT follows a minor ridge, with more views of South Park, then descends through the trees to an open area full of shrubby cinquefoil at mile 2.3 (10,120). The trail vanishes here, but the route continues west, marked by cairns that have been partially demolished by cattle. Pick up the trail again in 0.1 mile and resume a descent in the open. Cross FS-807 at mile 2.9 (9880) and continue ahead on a faint trail hidden by shrubby cinquefoil. Enter an aspen grove 150 feet beyond the road and then pass over Guernsey Creek, which is spanned by a huge timber.

The CT exits the aspens a hundred feet beyond the creek and crosses an indistinct old road just north of a primitive but popular car camping spot. The faint trail bears west-southwest, then west. Avoid trail forks that might lead you to FS-807, which is several hundred feet to the south. The CT continues west and just grazes the north edge of a small group of aspens, then fades out completely in the meadow grasses. Follow a line of cairns west across the meadow to mile 3.4 (9880), where the trail again becomes visible and leads through alternating pockets of aspen and meadow. At mile 0.2, the faint trail enters a small meadow and crosses a jeep road. Continue west to west-northwest and quickly reenter the aspens, where the trail becomes obvious as it rises slightly and then briefly parallels an old irrigation ditch. Bear to the right off of the ditch route at mile 4.0 (10,040) as the trail continues in the aspen forest and rises slowly. Follow the trail 0.3 mile, until it appears to end at the edge of a small, esthetic grouping of bristlecone pines. Just 200 feet west-northwest through the bristlecones you will cross FS-427. Continue west 0.1 mile on the obscure trail, then go right onto an old, abandoned road just before the ford on Deadman's Creek. If you want to keep your feet dry, there is a timber over the creek a few steps downstream from the ford. Return to the road after crossing the creek and continue a slight ascent north to north-northwest. Bear to the left (west) on the trail 400 feet past the creek as the old road continues ahead. Go right (north-northwest) onto a jeep road at mile 4.7 (10,160). Continue on this road for just 0.2 mile. As the road assumes a more westerly bearing and crosses a small stream, look carefully for the obscure trail which reemerges at left (south-southeast). The faint trail passes through a rather dismal, burned-out section of forest that is slowly reseeding itself. Reenter the unharmed lodgepole forest beyond, and ascend to a saddle which extends north from Jefferson Hill at mile 5.2 (10,200). Pass through a gate here, then descend a half mile and cross another old road. Continue 0.1 mile on the trail to mile 5.8 (10,000), where you will cross Jefferson Lake Road. Beaver Pond Picnic Ground is only a few hundred feet north on the road.

Continue on the trail 0.1 mile, then cross Jefferson Creek and begin a gradual ascent. Exchange the trail for an old road at mile 6.1 (10,000) and proceed 300 feet north-northwest to where the trail resumes at left and continues up switchbacks that ease the ascent. The CT adopts an abandoned road near the head of the elevated gully at mile 6.5 (10,320). Continue 0.4 mile west on the old road, until a timber barricade deflects you to the left, back onto the trail. Proceed on the trail to yet another road at mile 7.2 (10,400). Follow the road north 300 feet to where it curves left. Continue straight ahead here on the resurrected trail. At mile 7.3, cross the road for a final time and continue on the trail past several gentle switchbacks on the southeast side of this broad, forested ridge, an extension of the Continental Divide. The CT heads northwest through a lodgepole forest along an old road for about 300 feet at mile 9.0 (10,880). Admire the little niche of bristlecone pines at the head of Ohler Gulch and notice that, as the trail approaches timberline, the dominant tree becomes the spruce.

At mile 10.5 (11,400) the trail enters the krummholz zone, the interesting transition between forest and tundra. The prevailing wind pattern is immortalized in the postures of these stunted flag-trees. The trail becomes obscure in thick tundra grasses at mile 11.1 (11,520). It is here that the Jefferson Creek loop trail takes off to the right to return to the valley.

Pick up a somewhat unreliably posted route and continue, bearing generally northwest. Mount Guyot (13,370 feet) is prominent here, as is the entire ridge of the Continental Divide just ahead. At mile 11.6 (11,880) you should be standing on a small, rounded knob of the Continental Divide, east of and slightly above Georgia Pass, which is visible below. If your journey across the divide here had been made prior to February 28, 1861, when Colorado Territory was created, you would have been passing from Kansas Territory into Utah Territory.

Descend west, without the aid of a trail or markings, to Georgia Pass at mile 11.9 (11,600). One of Colorado's earliest trans-continental water projects was the Mt. Guyot flume, which channeled water from upper Michigan Creek on the east slope to serve placers to the west on the Swan River. This is curious, because today the precious resource is diverted in the opposite direction.

Once on the jeep road at the top of the pass, avoid the left-hand spur to Mt. Guyot and the right-hand spur to Glacier Peak. Descend the steep jeep road northward into the Swan River drainage. The road is marked with esthetic 4-inch by 4-inch posts emblazoned with the distinctive CT insignia. The jeep road grazes the edge of a meadow at mile 12.8 (10,920), then curves left and up. If you want to save yourself a few paces and some elevation gain, continue straight ahead on the cleared and marked route, which links up again with the road in 400 feet.

The jeep road bears northwest, paralleling the Swan River as it continues its descent. The route levels off somewhat near Moe's Cabin, at mile 14.0 (10,280). After crossing the Swan River on a bridge you will come to an intersection at mile 15.4 (10,000), just south of the site of Parkville. A jeep road branches off to the left here and is identified by a sign as American Gulch, although actually the road ascends the ridge between American and Georgia gulches and continues to Humbug Hill and, eventually, Breckenridge. If you wish to follow this alternate route for some R&R in Breckenridge, consult the Segment 7-Alternate trail description.

If you wish to proceed on the official route, continue northward down the road. Pass by the path to historic Parkville Cemetery 0.2 mile beyond the cutoff to Breckenridge and proceed to an intersection with another dirt road at mile 16.3 (9840). Turn left (north) here and continue on the county road, which parallels the Swan River and the unsightly tailings left by the gold dredges in the valley. The county road slowly assumes a westerly bearing and eventually joins **up with** Colorado 9 at mile 22.7 (9240). Carefully cross this busy highway to the paved bicycle path which parallels it. Bear right (north) onto the bike path and continue to mile 23.4 (9200), where you will find Goldhill Trailhead parking area at the intersection of Summit County Road 950 and Colorado 9.

Jefferson Creek Loop Trail

Start the loop trip at mile 5.8 (10,000), where the trail crosses Jefferson Lake Road just south of Beaver Ponds Picnic Ground. Continue on the official CT to timberline at approximately mile 11.1 (11,520). The Jefferson Creek Loop Trail inconspicuously takes off to the right (northeast) as the official trail is engulfed by the thick tundra grasses ahead. The loop trail slowly descends north and then east through a large bowl just below the Continental Divide. Snow accumulations here might linger into mid-summer, obscuring the trail and making the crossing hazardous.

The loop trail enters the protection of a spruce forest 0.6 mile after leaving the official CT. Negotiate at least 14 switchbacks as the trail drops into the headwaters of Jefferson Creek, then continue several miles, bearing generally southeast just above the level of the marshy creek bottom. Cross over to the south side of Jefferson Creek and proceed another mile along a rocky, old road through a lodgepole forest to a locked green gate within Jefferson Creek Campground. Turn left onto the campground road, cross to the north side of Jefferson Creek and finally follow Jefferson Creek Road 0.6 mile southeast to your starting point at Beaver Ponds Picnic Ground.

Segment 7
Goldhill Trailhead to Copper Mountain

Introduction

Hikers choosing this official CT route, as opposed to the alternate route through Breckenridge, probably won't have too much company, at least once they progress a mile or two beyond Goldhill Trailhead. The logging roads which intercept the trail in several places along the first two miles make the going a little confusing, and the blue-diamond markers on tree trunks in the initial portion of this segment identify cross country ski trails, not necessarily the CT.

The CT route over the Tenmile Range has no trail and is not well marked. The steep, alpine mountainsides here will challenge even the seasoned hiker, and inclined snowfields may linger well into July. Mountain cyclists should not attempt this section, but should instead use the detour around the Tenmile Range described as part of the Mountain Bicycle Route. Less experienced hikers may also want to consider this detour, which follows the Tenmile Bike Path to Frisco and up Tenmile Canyon to Wheeler Flats Trailhead at Copper Mountain.

A trail access point on Miners Creek, reached via Frisco and Rainbow Lake, is mentioned here only in passing because it is extremely rough, even for 4WD vehicles.

This segment rejoins Segment 7-Alternate on the west side of the Tenmile Range, then drops down to Wheeler Flats Trailhead, which is conveniently located near Copper Mountain Resort.

Trailheads/Access Points

Goldhill Trailhead: Travel west from Denver approximately 73 miles on I-70 and take the Frisco/Breckenridge/Colorado 9 exit.

Proceed approximately five miles south of Frisco on Colorado 9 toward Breckenridge. Goldhill Trailhead will be on your right (west) at the intersection with Summit County Road 950.

If you are coming in from the south on Colorado 9 over Hoosier Pass, continue north approximately four miles beyond Breckenridge. Goldhill Trailhead will be on your left (west).

Wheeler Flats Trailhead (Copper Mountain): See Segment 8.

Supplies, Services and Accommodations

Breckenridge is four miles south of the Goldhill Trailhead on Colorado 9. The town has a variety of overnight accommodations and a large grocery store. There are also sporting goods and hardware stores. If you need to resupply or recuperate in Breckenridge, you should consider following the Segment 7-Alternate route, which splits off the official route at the site of Parkville, goes through the town and rejoins the CT on the west side of the Tenmile Range.

Bus service is not available in Breckenridge or Copper Mountain, but buses do serve Frisco, five miles north of Goldhill Trailhead on Colorado 9.

Maps

USGS Quadrangles: Frisco, Breckenridge, Copper Mountain, Vail Pass. USFS Maps: Arapaho National Forest. CT Series: Maps 6, 7.

Trail Description

Begin at the convenient trailhead point just off of Colorado 9. The trail starts just opposite the small, informal parking area and continues through an alternating landscape of sagebrush meadows and lodgepole forest with an understory of lupine. The trail appears to end at a confusing, three-way logging road intersection at mile 1.0 (9680), but actually it bears to the left (southwest) from this intersection, on the south side of the road which continues straight ahead. The CT steadily gains elevation in a lodgepole forest, bearing generally south to south-southwest, then takes a more westerly direction before it crosses a logging road at mile 1.6 (9960). Continue 700 feet uphill, then bear right (north) as the trail joins an old road. Go right at the intersection with another road at mile

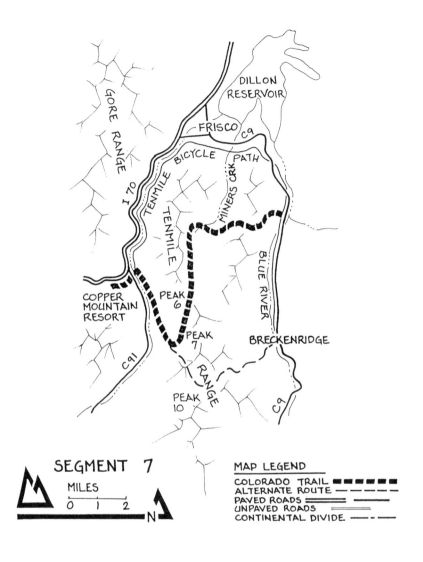

DILLON RESERVOIR

GORE RANGE

I 70

FRISCO

C9

TENMILE BICYCLE PATH

TENMILE

MINERS CRK

BLUE RIVER

COPPER MOUNTAIN RESORT

C 91

PEAK 6

PEAK 7

RANGE

BRECKENRIDGE

PEAK 10

C9

SEGMENT 7

MILES

0 1 2

N

MAP LEGEND

COLORADO TRAIL ▬▬▬▬▬

ALTERNATE ROUTE — — — —

PAVED ROADS ═══════

UNPAVED ROADS ═══════

CONTINENTAL DIVIDE —·—·—

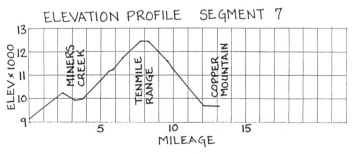

ELEVATION PROFILE SEGMENT 7

ELEV × 1000

13

12

11

10

9

MINERS CREEK

TENMILE RANGE

COPPER MOUNTAIN

5   10   15

MILEAGE

1.9 (10,120). Continue 200 feet further and take the right fork onto an old road, then go left as the old road forks again in another 600 feet. The road leads generally west and slowly takes on a more trail-like character as it ascends to a somewhat rounded, rocky summit at mile 2.3 (10,240). A sparse lodgepole forest allows glimpses of the crest of Tenmile Peak to the west.

Descend 0.4 mile from the rocky summit and cross the last logging road. At mile 3.2 (9920), join up with the Peaks Trail, which connects Breckenridge with Frisco. Go left (south) and uphill on this short section of the Peaks Trail for 0.3 mile, then bear right (west) onto the Miners Creek Trail. The wide, rocky trail ascends to the southwest, paralleling a tributary stream of Miners Creek for 0.6 mile, then abruptly leaves the drainage and climbs to a ridge. Traverse a steep side-cut as the trail makes its way to the 4WD trail access point on Miners Creek at mile 4.8 (10,560). Sign in at the register, then continue west from the small, primitive trailhead parking area. Proceed 200 feet to a point where you will encounter a barricade on the original trail ahead. Go right (west-northwest) here, onto a newly constructed trail, and, after a few steps, cross over Miners Creek using a bumpy corduroy bridge. The trail then ascends, steeply at times, through a spruce forest. The CT next veers southward near timberline at mile 5.5 (11,120) and breaks out momentarily into a finger of alpine tundra which reaches down from a glacial cirque on Tenmile Peak.

Ascend steeply beyond the timberline to a small saddle at mile 6.6 (11,840), where the trail disappears. The CT for the next three adventurous miles leads without a trail through the scenic tundra; hikers must rely entirely on cairns to stay on the route. Follow the cairns southward, ascending toward the crest of the Tenmile Range on the steeply sloping mountainside. About 0.5 mile beyond the saddle, the route becomes difficult to follow because of the rough, inclined terrain. Climb steeply as you approach the crest to avoid a precipitous rocky area ahead. Mount the Tenmile Range at mile 7.8 (12,440), on a long saddle that connects Peaks 5 and 6. Follow the broad saddle south toward Peak 6 and enjoy the abundant views on either hand. Can you distinguish Mount of the Holy Cross far away to the west?

After a half-mile walk along the saddle, the cairned route bears slightly to the right (south-southwest) as it approaches Peak 6 and begins a steady descent on the west side of the mountain range. Pick up a very faint trail in spots as the route continues its descent of the steep mountainside. The route bears more westerly as it approaches timberline, picking up a definite trail just inside the trees at mile 9.6 (11,640). Continue descending for 0.4 mile to the intersection with Wheeler Trail at mile 10.0 (11,240), where Segment 7-Alternate rejoins the official CT. Descend on the Wheeler Trail and cross several small streams along the way. The steep terrain in this area would be a definite impediment to camping.

Intersect an old jeep road which parallels the east side of Tenmile Creek at mile 12.1 (9760). Then bear to the right (north) and follow the jeep road to the paved Tenmile Bike Path at mile 13.1 (9720), near the confluence of Tenmile and West Tenmile creeks. Turning left onto the bike path will bring you in a few steps to the Wheeler Flats Trailhead parking area.

Peak 8-9 Pass, Tenmile Range

Segment 7-Alternate
Parkville to Copper Mountain

Introduction

This alternate route gets you to the same destination (Copper Mountain) as Segment 7, but passes through scenery dominated by our own species' handiwork. This segment diverges from the official route just south of the long-abandoned site of Parkville, and for the first 12 miles follows roads largely adjacent to private property. Please respect "No Trespassing" signs observed along the way. West of Breckenridge, this alternate route follows the Wheeler Trail over the Tenmile Range, and rejoins the official CT on its descent to Wheeler Flats Trailhead.

The alpine zone traversed along the Wheeler Trail is exquisitely carpeted with tundra foliage in late July and early August and provides a scenic foreground for the ancient metamorphic rocks of the Tenmile Range. This linear mountain range connects the southern end of the Gore Range with the northern end of the Mosquito Range. It is named for the creek on its western boundary and is known for its sequentially numbered peaks.

When a southern miner named Highfield discovered gold in Georgia Gulch, the usual rush was on and soon the little town of Parkville was the most active in the area. Its prominence was short-lived, however. In 1862 the county records were taken to Breckenridge, and by the 1880s hydraulic mining had removed any sign of the enterprising little community on the Swan River. Other placers in French Gulch were worked in part by Harry Farncomb, who discovered delicate wire-gold specimens here. This valley is the site of the greed-induced Ten Years War, a lengthy legal battle for the

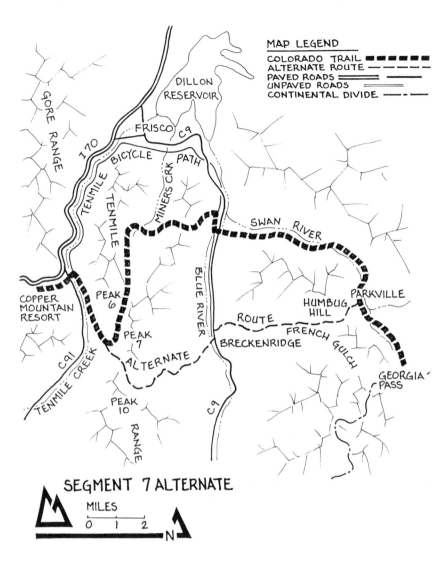

SEGMENT 7 ALTERNATE

MILES
0 1 2

N

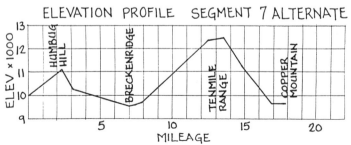

ELEVATION PROFILE   SEGMENT 7 ALTERNATE

riches of the gulch. The "war" ended in a dramatic shootout, which resulted in three deaths, and the insolvency of a bank.

Beyond the site of Lincoln City in French Gulch, you will pass an enormous, elongated pile of worked-over boulders, the tailings of the destructive dredges. These huge, mechanized gold boats slowly worked their way upstream in dirty ponds of their own making. Their duty was to scavenge the valley bottoms and recover gold left by earlier placers. These inglorious tailings are the legacy of the dredge era in the Blue River and its tributaries.

At the end of this segment you enter the reborn 1860s town of Breckenridge. It was originally named Breckinridge (note the spelling), after James Buchanan's vice president. But when the citizens discovered that the town's namesake had confederate leanings, the irate miners distinguished their town from the rebel by changing the spelling of its name.

Trailheads/Access Points

Wheeler Flats Trailhead (Copper Mountain): See Segment 8.

Supplies, Services and Accommodations

The purpose of this alternate route is to provide hikers a detour through Breckenridge, which has a variety of overnight accommodations, a large grocery store, and sporting goods and hardware stores. Bus service is available in Frisco, nine miles north on Colorado 9.

Maps

USGS Quadrangles: Boreas Pass, Breckenridge, Copper Mtn., Vail Pass. USFS Maps: Arapaho National Forest. CT Series: Map 6.

Trail Description

Begin this alternate route just south of the unrecognizable Parkville townsite, at the intersection of the South Fork Swan River Road and the jeep road ascending Humbug Hill, which is signed as American Gulch. Continue on the American Gulch Road, which actually switchbacks up the ridge between American and Georgia gulches. As the main road switchbacks to the right at mile 2.0 (10,840), don't be tempted to continue straight ahead on the road which traverses into the American Gulch tailings. An inspection of dramatic Georgia Gulch is possible at mile 2.2 (10,960), where the road crosses the tailings slope.

End your ascent at mile 2.3 (11,080) on a low point along Humbug Hill's summit ridge, where the route joins another jeep road coming up from French Gulch. Turn left (south) onto this intersecting road and in a few steps bend to the right (west) and descend into French Gulch. Be sure to savor the panorama of the ski area and the Tenmile Range before dropping into the dense aspen forest below.

Join French Gulch Road at mile 3.1 (10,280) and then continue downstream (west) past the remains of Lincoln City and mountainous piles of gold-dredge tailings. Go left where the road forks at mile 5.8 (9680) and continue on the county road, which becomes Wellington Road within the city limits of Breckenridge. Intersect Main Street, which is also Colorado 9, at mile 6.9 (9560), then turn left (south) and proceed two blocks to Washington Street. Notice that Washington doesn't continue west beyond Main, but that a footbridge over the Blue River is situated where the street would go if it continued that far. Cross this footbridge and proceed west to South Park Street. Then cross the street and pick up what would appear to be Washington Street but has been renamed Four O'clock Road. Continue west 0.2 mile along the concrete sidewalk of Four O'clock Road to Kingscrown Street at mile 7.4 (9680). Turn left (south) onto Kingscrown and notice a brown Summit County maintenance shop on the southwest corner of this intersection. Immediately south of this building, follow Summit County Road 751 as it ascends into a lodgepole forest. Cross a ski run at mile 7.8 (9840). Follow the road back into the trees, where it switchbacks to the right and enters Arapaho National Forest. Notice the private property warnings here.

Switchback up the road through the middle of Breckenridge's Peak 9 ski area, avoiding the spurs which lead to ski lift terminals and maintenance shops. Pass the last and the highest of the ski area's buildings at mile 11.0 (11,480) and continue on the rough road above timberline to mile 12.5 (12,360), where you intersect the Wheeler Trail. Although wet in spots and a terrible place to be caught in an electrical storm, the alpine meadow here in the shadow of Peak 10 is the first decent campsite since the upper Swan River. Traverse northwest on the Wheeler Trail toward the Peak 8-9 saddle visible ahead. The trail crosses glorious, rolling fields of alpine flowers and talus slopes where the mountain's banded metamorphic rocks have been exposed. If you arrive early in the season, you will see marsh marigold peeking out of the slowly unfolding blanket of snow. Visible to the northeast is the alpine ridge of the Continental Divide as well as the two "fourteeners" named for botanists John Torrey and Asa Gray.

Top the saddle at mile 13.5 (12,400), where the Gore Range comes into view. This saddle has been unofficially designated as Lucas Pass, after the parents of Bill Lucas, who conceived the idea of the CT. Descend half a mile northwest from Lucas Pass and enter an area featuring the characteristic flag-trees of the krummholz zone. From here, the immense tailings ponds of the Climax Molybdenum Mine are visible up the Tenmile Creek valley. These ignominious tailings, which have buried the valley and inundated the old mining camps of Kokomo and Robinson, are the remains of Bartlett Mountain.

Join up with the official route of the CT at mile 14.8 (11,240) at an intersection where huge bouquets of columbine bloom in July. Continue downhill, crossing several small streams along the way. The steep angle of the mountain slope would impede camping along here. Intersect the jeep road which parallels the east side of Tenmile Creek at mile 16.9 (9760). Proceed to the right (north) on the jeep road to mile 17.9 (9720) and intersect the paved Tenmile Bike Path near the confluence of Temile and West Tenmile creeks. Turning left onto the bike path will lead you in a few steps to the Wheeler Flats Trailhead near Copper Mountain.

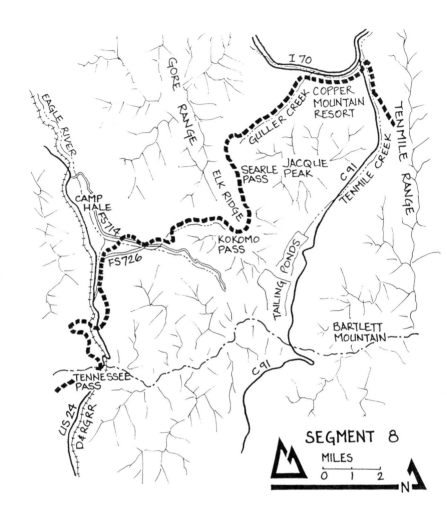

GORE RANGE

EAGLE RIVER

I 70

GULLER CREEK

COPPER MOUNTAIN RESORT

SEARLE PASS

JACQUE PEAK

TENMILE RANGE

ELK RIDGE

C 91

TENMILE CREEK

CAMP HALE

FS 714

KOKOMO PASS

FS 726

TAILING PONDS

BARTLETT MOUNTAIN

C 91

TENNESSEE PASS

US 24

D & RGRR

SEGMENT 8

MILES

0   1   2

N

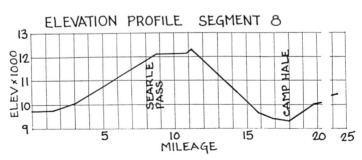

ELEVATION PROFILE   SEGMENT 8

ELEV × 1000

13

12

11

10

9

SEARLE PASS

CAMP HALE

5   10   15   20   25

MILEAGE

Segment 8
Copper Mountain to Tennessee Pass

Introduction

The DSP&PRR once had a whistle stop known as Solitude on its Tenmile Canyon line near present-day Copper Mountain Resort. Unfortunately, with the activity of the ski area and busy I-70, the isolation of the valley is a thing of the past. As recently as 1970, before the ski area was built and the highway widened, this valley was still known as Wheeler Flats, a throwback to the days when Judge John S. Wheeler would drive his stock over the Tenmile Range to graze in the valley's lush, boggy meadows. A little settlement developed here and served the Tenmile Mining District.

A case study in the transformation from mining community to ski area is available to CT hikers as the route makes its way through the resort. Some hikers might be persuaded to linger awhile in the embrace of civilization, while others might pass through quickly, attempting to ignore what they consider a "ruined" area. Whatever their inclination, the resort does provide weary backpackers the opportunity to recharge their batteries before submerging themselves again in the wilderness.

Hikers in this segment have a tremendous perch on Elk Ridge from which to view the Climax Molybdenum Mine and the immense tailings ponds which have completely inundated the historic Tenmile Mining District towns of Robinson and Kokomo. This mining district got its start when Leadville businessman George B. Robinson grubstaked two miners who subsequently discovered ten mines in the headwaters of Tenmile Creek. Robinson's namesake town had the distinction of being Colorado's highest incorporated town, and for a time threatened Leadville for dominance in the area. The little community of Kokomo, named by Indiana miners for their hometown, developed just downstream from Robinson.

Both the D&RG and the DSP&P felt confident enough about the upstart mining district to lay tracks into the valley. Merchant Robinson gained enough influence to emerge as Colorado's lieutenant governor in 1880, but unfortunately he enjoyed only one month of his term before being cut down in a shoot-out involving a controversy over the ownership of the Smuggler Mine. Captain J.W. Jacque, for whom Jacque Ridge, Jacque Creek and Jacque Mountain apparently were named, was also involved in the fatal dispute.

As hikers descend into the headwaters of the Eagle River, they will pass through Camp Hale, one of Colorado's most fascinating ghost town sites. Construction of this Rocky Mountain outpost, named for Brigadier General Irving Hale, began in 1942 and was the war-time training base of the 10th Mountain Division. The troops were eventually attached to the 5th Army and sent to fight in Italy's Apennine Mountains. At its height in 1944, the camp held 15,000 men who trained during the summer and winter in the surrounding mountains. Cooper Hill Ski Area on Tennessee Pass was originally constructed as part of the camp. Here troops attached slats to their feet and learned techniques on the ski run that at the time had the world's longest T-bar. Camp Hale was largely abandoned after WWII, although sporadic use continued until 1963, after which the camp was completely dismantled. Trail crews working here in 1987 unearthed hundreds of spent ammo rounds while building trail in the vicinity of the shooting range.

Portions of the CT above Camp Hale follow the narrow gauge railroad grade that the D&RG abandoned in 1890, when the line was realigned and widened to standard gauge. The segment ends on Tennessee Pass, which was discovered in 1845 by Col. John Frémont.

Except along the first two miles of this segment through Copper Mountain Resort, backpackers will have an abundant selection of campsites from which to choose. The exposed, high-altitude section from Searle Pass to Kokomo Pass, along which you are likely to find domestic sheep, has only skimpy water supplies. Snowfields here may linger well into July. This same area has several abandoned vertical mine shafts, some of which are disturbingly close to the CT and partially camouflaged by low, bushy willows. Backpackers wandering on a somewhat independent course through here near dusk would be putting themselves at an obvious risk.

The Forest Service requests that horses and pack animals refrain from using the Tenmile Bike Path between Copper Mountain and Guller Creek. Those traveling with stock should use a short bypass through the lower end of the Union Creek Base area. This bypass, outlined at the end of the trail description, is provided in order to avoid a direct confrontation between skittish animals and bicyclists flying down from the top of Vail Pass.

Trailheads/Access Points

Wheeler Flats Trailhead (Copper Mountain): Go west from Denver approximately 79 miles on I-70 to the Copper Mountain/Leadville/Colorado 91 exit. Take the exit and cross over the freeway on an overpass, then drive just a few hundred feet and turn left onto the side road, identified by an Amoco station just opposite the entrance to Copper Mountain Resort. Continue down the side road 0.4 mile to where it dead-ends at the Wheeler Flats Trailhead parking area.

Camp Hale (Eagle Park) Trail Access: From the top of Tennessee Pass, descend north on US 24 for 2.5 miles to the point where the CT crosses the highway. Then continue another half mile and go right on FS-726. Gradually descend on FS-726 for three miles, to where it joins up with FS-714. The CT is directly ahead of you at this junction and continues up the meadow to your right toward Cataract Creek. In the opposite direction, the CT adopts a short section of FS-714 to the left before it ducks back into the meadow. No official parking area exists here.

Tennessee Pass: See Segment 9.

Supplies, Services and Accommodations

The CT passes through Copper Mountain Resort. Accommodations are available here, but it might be wise to make reservations if you know your schedule in advance. A small grocery store carries a variety of food, but no dehydrated or freeze-dried packaged meals. Bus service is available in Frisco.

Maps

USGS Quadrangles: Vail Pass, Copper Mountain, Pando, Leadville North. USFS Maps: Arapaho National Forest, White River National Forest. CT Series: Maps 7 and 8.

Trail Description

The CT follows the paved road 0.4 mile from Wheeler Flats Trailhead parking area past the Amoco station to the stop sign at Colorado 91. Carefully cross the highway to the main entrance of Copper Mountain Resort and continue on the busy street, which is named Copper Road. Stay on Copper Road as it slowly bends around the north end of the resort to mile 1.5 (9760), where the road crosses West Tenmile Creek on a wide bridge. Embark here on the paved bike path, which continues west, paralleling the creek.

In 0.3 mile you will pass the cutoff to Union Creek Base building, where horses and pack animals should detour off the bike path. Pedestrians can continue west on the path, which runs close by I-70, to mile 2.6 (9960). A convenient bridge crossing here takes you across West Tenmile Creek. After crossing the bridge, bear to the left (southeast) on an obscure trail for a hundred feet and cross Guller Creek on a wide bridge. Next, angle to the right (south) and climb to the level of a low bench above the brushy bank of the creek. There is no recognizable trail as you progress southwest, paralleling Guller Creek on its east bank. Cross under the eastbound I-70 bridge, whose cover might be appreciated on a stormy day. Continue another 800 feet and ford to the west bank of Guller Creek. (If the flow here is particularly fast and deep, you may want to bushwhack to this point by paralleling Guller Creek on its west bank from the West Tenmile Creek bridge at mile 2.6.)

From the ford on Guller Creek, proceed 600 feet beyond to mile 3.0 (10,040), where the horse and pack animal bypass descends from the east and joins the official route on the west bank. The trail slowly ascends, through occasional wet spots and willow patches, following Guller Creek as it trends generally southwest. Cross over to the east bank at mile 3.9 (10,400) on a log bridge. Stride across Jacque Creek, a tributary of Guller, 150 feet beyond on a similar log bridge. The grassy, rolling meadow here in the shadow of Jacque Ridge is ideal for camping.

The CT bears to the right as the trail forks 300 feet beyond Jacque Creek. Then, in just a few more steps, it crosses back over to the west side of Guller Creek. At mile 4.7 (10,600), enter a linear meadow which extends along Guller Creek almost to timberline. The CT stays near the edge of the spruce forest, though at times it breaks into the elongated meadow, where there are ideal campsites. Guller Creek, always nearby, is usually hidden in a mass of thick willows. The trail makes several switchbacks as it nears timberline and exits the trees at mile 7.4 (11,600).

Above timberline the route is delineated mainly by posts and cairns, although several short sections of excellent trail do exist between here and Searle Pass. Cross the small upper headwaters of Guller Creek and continue past two switchbacks marked with cairns. The final approach to the pass is rocky and rough but again well marked with numerous cairns. Searle Pass, at mile 8.6 (12,040), can

be uncomfortably windy, but try to take time to admire the fine vistas it affords of the Tenmile and Gore ranges. From Searle Pass, the marked route makes a traverse, bearing generally south at approximately 12,000 feet and wandering in and out of many little side drainages. Exposed campsites abound in the soft alpine grasses.

Approximately 2.4 miles beyond Searle Pass, pick up a faint trail which becomes more obvious as the CT ascends through several switchbacks to the rocky southern end of Elk Ridge. At mile 11.2 (12,280) the trail levels out on the ridge, which offers instructive views of the unsightly remains of Bartlett Mountain, once 13,555 feet high but now reduced to the huge piles of tailings below.

Descend a half mile along the trail, which is cut deeply into the hillside in places, to 12,000-foot Kokomo Pass. Follow a short but steep ravine north-northwest from the pass down into a rolling alpine meadow on the headwaters of Cataract Creek. Cross a small tributary stream as the trail nears the timber and then descend to the left 0.1 mile beyond as an obscure animal trail continues ahead. The trail enters the trees and descends through three long switchbacks, then assumes a westerly heading parallel to and slightly above the level of Cataract Creek. Continue descending in a spruce forest to an abandoned sawmill site in a meadow near the creek at mile 13.5 (11,000). For the next 2.4 miles, the CT follows an old logging road as it descends the steepening gorge of Cataract Creek.

Follow the road through a switchback to the left at mile 15.1 (10,200), ignoring the faint continuation of another road which climbs ahead here. There is a challenging ford of Cataract Creek 400 feet beyond, and unless it is late summer you will probably get your feet wet. Ignore the ascending fork which branches left 600 feet beyond the ford on Cataract Creek, and continue straight ahead on the logging road. The final pitch of the road descends steeply to the upper end of a long meadow on the East Fork Eagle River. From this point, continue on the CT a few hundred feet to mile 15.9 (9680), where an esthetic arched bridge spans Cataract Creek just a few feet downstream from the falls.

Continue along the trail in a meadow of fragrant sage and cinquefoil, gaining views west toward the upper end of the park, which not so long ago bustled with the wartime activities of Camp Hale. The trail joins up temporarily with FS-714 at mile 16.7

(9400); FS-726 peels off to the south here and continues on to US 24. Continue 800 feet west on FS-714 and look for the obscure route which veers off into the meadow north of the road. The CT heads west here, paralleling FS-714 for 0.6 mile, after which it again joins the road. Continue approximately 600 feet west on FS-714 and then go left (south) on an intersecting road which takes you past a series of earthen mounds that were part of the old Camp Hale shooting range.

Cross the East Fork Eagle River on a bridge at mile 17.9 (9320), just beyond the shooting range and near a line of dilapidated concrete bunkers. For the next 400 feet, the trail disappears into thick, marshy meadow grasses, but it is visible on the hillside ahead. The route bears southwest through here and is marked by a cairn of crumbling concrete piers taken from some long-forgotten military building. Regain the trail as it enters a lodgepole forest and begins an ascent. Turn through two short switchbacks and continue west to southwest a half mile, then exit briefly onto the upper end of the old "B" slope ski run, which is slowly being reclaimed by the forest. This vantage point gives one of the nicest views possible of the site of Camp Hale.

The CT now reenters the lodgepole forest, heading in a more southerly direction and joining up with FS-726 at mile 18.8 (9680). Continue south on asphalted FS-726 for one mile, at which point the CT takes off to the left (east) as a somewhat obscure jeep road. This obscure point of departure is only 0.2 mile before FS-726 joins US 24. Continue for just 250 feet on the jeep road, then follow the trail which takes off to the right (southeast) and ascends into a lodgepole forest. Follow the trail to US 24 at mile 20.7 (10,000) and carefully cross to the west side of the busy highway. Pass through a gate and proceed 200 feet on a railroad maintenance driveway, which drops slightly to the railroad tracks. Cross the tracks and continue ahead (west) 400 feet on the faint, elevated grade of an abandoned railroad siding to a small stream, which is crossed on a dirt-fill bridge. Continue along the grade, which fades away as it bears to the right (northwest). When the route becomes unrecognizable, continue on the level (north-northwest, then northwest) between a small finger of high ground protruding downward to your left and an eroded, shallow gully to your right. Cross Mitchell Creek at mile 21.1 (9820) and then head southwest on the abandoned narrow-gauge railroad grade up a broad, marshy valley. Continue 0.8 mile on the old railroad grade, after which the trail peels off to the left (southeast), toward the opposite side of the meadow. Take time to observe the water fowl nesting in the abundant ponds along here.

The trail ascends slowly and enters a lodgepole forest after about 800 feet. At mile 22.4 (10,200), the trail joins a jeep road, which is again the abandoned narrow gauge route of the D&RG. Head east-northeast on the road a short distance, then assume a more southerly bearing for 1.0 mile. The route slowly bends to the east and passes the remains of several large coking ovens. The ski runs of Cooper Hill are visible in places along here to the southeast. Continue on the jeep road to Tennessee Pass at mile 24.3 (10,424), where this segment ends on the west side of US 24 at the trailhead parking area.

Horse and Pack Animal Bypass

Follow the regular trail description through Copper Mountain Resort on Copper Road to a point just before the intersection with the bike path at mile 1.5. Turn right on Beeler Place, which leads to the stables. Proceed on the road to a parking area cul-de-sac and continue ahead toward the Union Creek Base building on the ski area maintenance road. Bend around the base building and cross under the "H" and "K" ski lifts, then proceed 200 feet further to a switchback. Follow the ascending side road which takes off to the right at this switchback and continue for a half mile to the base of "L" lift. An obscure trail forks to the right (west) here off the ski maintenance road. Continue on this meandering trail through alternating meadows and lodgepole forests for a half mile, until an abrupt descent is made to the east bank of Guller Creek. Ford the creek and pick up the official CT at mile 3.0 (10,040).

Segment 9
Tennessee Pass to Old Hagerman Road

Introduction

At Tennessee Pass, the CT enters the skyscraping Sawatch Range and begins a trek southward along the eastern flank of these mountains. The Sawatch includes some of the highest elevations in Colorado, including the highest, Mt. Elbert. There are many grand, glacier-scoured valleys leading into the range, and lovely, lake-filled basins as well. Much of the route follows the old Main Range Trail, which began as a Civilian Conservation Corps project in the 1930s.

This segment passes through a corner of Holy Cross Wilderness, where backpackers will find many campsites with backdrops of the Continental Divide's glaciated walls. Mountain cyclists must detour around the wilderness areas in Segments 9 and 10 (see the Mountain Bicycle Route). A series of blue-diamond markers, beginning at Tennessee Pass, identifies a cross-country ski route and not necessarily the CT.

The trail rounds the west edge of Turquoise Reservoir, a water storage basin for the immense Fryingpan-Arkansas Project. The original Turquoise Lake, which received its name from the precious stone mined in the area by early Indians and later collectors, was greatly enlarged by Sugarloaf Dam. This reservoir is one of six in the system, whose purpose is to divert water from the west slope's Fryingpan River and pipe it under the Continental Divide to east slope users via the Arkansas River. The trail parallels the project and visits Clear Creek and Twin Lakes reservoirs further south, as well as the Mt. Elbert powerplant, all links in the long chain of the Pan-Ark Project.

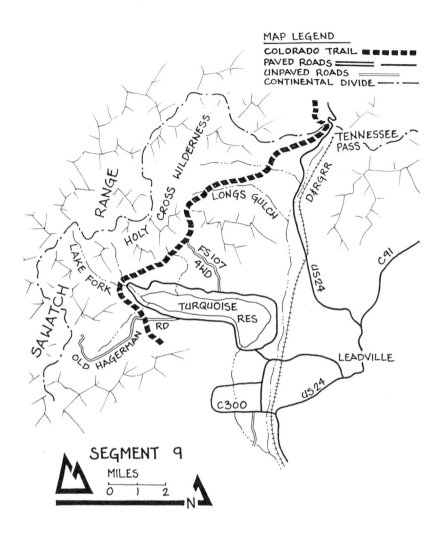

MAP LEGEND
COLORADO TRAIL
PAVED ROADS
UNPAVED ROADS
CONTINENTAL DIVIDE

TENNESSEE PASS

HOLY CROSS WILDERNESS

LONGS GULCH

RANGE

LAKE FORK

FS 107
4WD

SAWATCH

TURQUOISE RES

OLD HAGERMAN RD

D&RGRR

US 24

C 91

LEADVILLE

C 300

US 24

SEGMENT 9

MILES
0   1   2

N

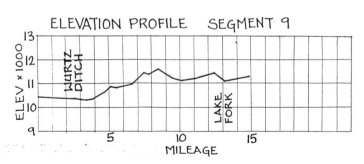

ELEVATION PROFILE   SEGMENT 9

WURTZ DITCH

LAKE FORK

ELEV × 1000

MILEAGE

This segment ends on the road where John J. Hagerman's Colorado Midland Railway once struggled to cross the Continental Divide at Hagerman Tunnel. Tennessee Pass, a somewhat inconspicuous but no less important crossing, was discovered by Col. John C. Frémont in the summer of 1845, when he was on his way to California. William Henry Jackson, with his portable darkroom in tow on his trusted mule Hypo, used the pass in August of 1873 on his epic quest to find and photograph the rumored mountain with the cross of snow. The D&RG built a narrow-gauge railroad over the pass in 1881, then standardized the line and built the tunnel under the pass in 1890. It is still in use today.

Trailheads/Access Points

Tennessee Pass Trailhead: Travel north from Leadville on US 24 approximately nine miles to the top of Tennessee Pass. A parking area on the left (west) side of the road provides adequate parking here. A trailhead bulletin board marks the CT. Don't be misled by the Powderhound Trail, which starts here also.

Wurtz Ditch Road (FS-100) Trail Access: Travel north from Leadville on US 24 approximately 7.5 miles to Wurtz Ditch Road (FS-100), which leaves the highway on the left (west). Go one mile on the dirt road and bear to the right as the road forks. Proceed 0.3 mile further, to a point where the CT crosses the road. There is room for only a few small cars here.

St. Kevins Trailhead (FS-107): This isolated portal into the Holy Cross Wilderness is ideal for those wanting to escape the crowds along most sections of the CT in the Sawatch Range. A high-clearance or 4WD vehicle is necessary for the last several miles on FS-107.

Travel south from Leadville on US 24 approximately 3.5 miles, turn right (west) onto Colorado 300 and proceed a half mile on the paved road. Turn right (north) onto the road, which is marked as the way to Turquoise Reservoir. Drive 1.8 miles north to a skewed three-way intersection. Go left onto the intersecting paved road (avoid the gravel road which also intersects here) and ascend 1.2 miles west to Sugarloaf Dam. Continue on the reservoir road nine miles, rounding the south, west and north sides of the reservoir, until you come to the somewhat obscure FS-107, which takes off to the left (north). Avoid the side roads and respect the nearby private property as FS-107 passes through the old St. Kevins mining district. Continue ahead a total of 2.4 miles on the rough road, until it ends at a small parking area at the edge of Holy Cross Wilderness.

Old Hagerman Road Trail Access: See Segment 10.

Supplies, Services and Accommodations
Available in Leadville (see Segment 10).

Maps
USGS Quadrangles: Leadville North, Homestake Reservoir. USFS Maps: San Isabel National Forest. CT Series: Maps 8 and 9.

Trail Description
From the parking area on the west side of Tennessee Pass, traverse just below the Continental Divide, bearing generally west to southwest. Note the blue diamonds high up in the lodgepoles, for use by skiers in deep snow. In a few places the thick forest allows views to the south of the upper Arkansas Valley. Cross the sturdy Wurtz Ditch footbridge at mile 2.5 (10,400). This artificial creek bed, which might be either gushing with water or completely dry, is a conduit that diverts water from the west side of the divide to the Arkansas River via Tennessee Creek.

Ascend 0.2 miles further to Wurtz Ditch Road, where the trail, somewhat obscure in places, continues on the opposite side. Pass through a clear-cut to Lily Lake road at mile 3.0 (10,350). Cross the road and pick up another that heads south to a meadow. Ford North Fork Tennessee Creek at mile 3.4 (10,320), then proceed south on the road 200 feet and ford West Tennessee Creek. Just beyond West Tennessee Creek, rejoin the faint trail ahead as the road curves to the left. The trail curves around to a westerly heading and joins an old road at mile 3.7 (10,360). The road becomes more trail-like as it ascends steadily west, paralleling West Tennessee Creek through a lodgepole forest. At mile 4.7 (10,760) you will join up with another old road, whose unused portion has been well barricaded to prevent confusion, and continue bearing generally southwest. Cross over a broad ridge at mile 5.1 (10,840), then descend slowly through a lodgepole/spruce forest. Enter the elongated meadow of Longs Gulch one mile beyond and pass the ruins of an old cabin.

A sign announces your entrance into Holy Cross Wilderness at mile 6.5 (10,920). Cross to the south side of the creek 400 feet beyond and begin a serious ascent to the southwest. Top a broad saddle at mile 7.4 (11,480), where the ponds of upper Porcupine Creek are nestled into spectacular alpine scenery. Descend 0.3 mile on the sometimes faint trail and cross Porcupine Creek. Follow the trail through a spruce/fir forest, then switchback up to tundra at 11,600 feet and enjoy views east and north of the Tenmile and Mosquito ranges. Reenter the trees at mile 8.5 (11,680) and then descend south to an old road. Continue the descent southward 0.6 mile, following an unnamed drainage that opens up into a meadow.

Briefly leave the wilderness at mile 9.4 (11,240), where FS-107 ends at the primitive trailhead parking area. A sign here marks the wilderness boundary. Cross the small stream behind the sign, reentering the wilderness, and proceed northwest on an abandoned road at the edge of the meadow. In 800 feet the old road becomes a rocky trail as it enters the forest and descends into Bear Creek drainage. The terrain is so rocky around here that the trail seems to vanish at times into the surroundings. The CT passes above Bear Lake at mile 10.1 (11,120), in rugged country which might make a usable but uncom-

fortable campsite. Continue past the shores of the last picturesque lake and ascend to a timberline ridge at mile 11.0 (11,280), where Mt. Massive and Hagerman Pass come into view.

Descend steadily through lodgepole forest to mile 12.4 (10,440), where the trail passes under a powerline at the southern boundary of Holy Cross Wilderness. Pass under the powerline again a half mile beyond and continue 600 feet to a convenient but unpretentious bridge at Mill Creek. Descend a few steps from Mill Creek to the lower part of a meadow near the Lake Fork at mile 13.1 (10,040), where a bulletin board has been erected for hikers. This junction is 300 feet west of the switchback on the paved reservoir road, just beyond May Queen Campground. It doesn't make a good trail access point because parking is very limited.

Back at the bulletin board in the meadow, cross the swiftly-flowing Lake Fork on a long footbridge and continue a few steps uphill on a jeep road, until the trail resumes at left. Pass under the powerlines again at mile 13.4 (10,120) and continue to Glacier Creek, which is crossed on a corduroy bridge. Traverse southeast beyond the creek in a cool spruce/fir forest. The Charles H. Boustead Tunnel, which channels water from the head of the Fryingpan River, is 150 feet below your feet as you approach Busk Creek. After Busk Creek, the trail ascends to the old Hagerman Road, which has been only slightly widened for temporary parking, at mile 14.9 (10,360).

Segment 10
Old Hagerman Road to Halfmoon Creek

Introduction

Old Hagerman Road is named after John J. Hagerman, builder of the Colorado Midland Railway, which followed the grade here to its Continental Divide crossing several miles up the road at 11,528-foot Hagerman Tunnel. The Midland then continued down the Fryingpan River to tap the Roaring Fork's profitable coalfields and silver mines. The right-of-way was abandoned by the railroad in 1920 and has been a dirt road ever since. It even served as an official state auto route in the 1920s, before more adequate highways were built over the Continental Divide.

This segment travels almost entirely within the boundaries of Mt. Massive Wilderness. The wilderness gets its name from the 14,421-foot mountain, second highest in the state, which is easily climbable from the CT. Mountain cyclists must detour around this segment (see the Mountain Bicycle Route).

In the early 1860s, placers flourished in the upper Arkansas country, and Abe Lee is credited with the original discovery of gold in California Gulch, now known as Leadville. The gold soon played out, but then silver was discovered in the surrounding hills and by 1879 Leadville was a rip-roaring boomtown which lasted until the demonetization of silver in 1893. In later years, and today as well, the Climax Molybdenum Mine contributed to the local economy. At several points along this trail segment, hikers can view Cloud City, its surrounding tailings and Mosquito Pass, over which many of the hopeful filtered into the valley.

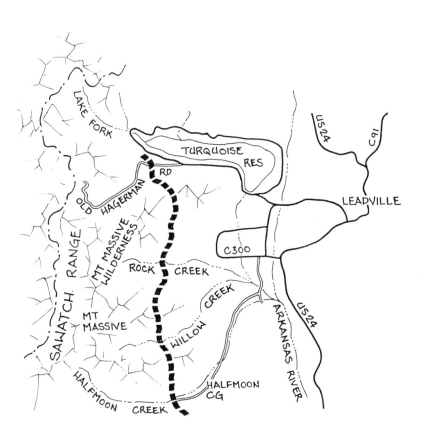

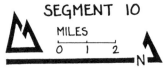

SEGMENT 10

MILES

0 1 2

N

MAP LEGEND

COLORADO TRAIL ████ ██

PAVED ROADS ══════

UNPAVED ROADS ══════

CONTINENTAL DIVIDE ──·──·──

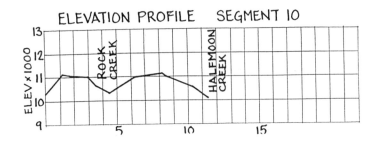

ELEVATION PROFILE   SEGMENT 10

ELEV ×1000

13

12

11

10

9

ROCK CREEK

HALFMOON CREEK

5   10   15

Trailheads/Access Points

Old Hagerman Road Trail Access: Travel south from Leadville on US 24 approximately 3.5 miles and turn right (west) onto Colorado 300. Proceed a half mile west on the paved road, then turn right (north) onto the road marked as the way to Turquoise Reservoir. Drive 1.8 miles north to a skewed, three-way intersection. Go left onto the intersecting paved road (avoid the gravel road which also intersects here) and ascend 1.2 miles to Sugarloaf Dam. Continue on the reservoir road 3.1 miles beyond the dam and go left onto a dirt road, which is nicknamed Old Hagerman Road. Continue 0.9 mile up the road to the point where the CT crosses it. No parking area is provided.

If you would like off-road parking, continue 1.4 miles past Old Hagerman Road on the paved reservoir road to the fisherman's parking area at the Boustead Tunnel outlet. To find the CT from this parking area, continue on the reservoir road 0.6 mile to a sharp switchback. Leave the road and continue several hundred feet up the rough side road, which is partially flooded by Mill Creek. The CT is marked by a bulletin board just ahead.

Halfmoon Creek Trailhead: See Segment 11.

Supplies, Services and Accommodations

Leadville is about eight miles east from the Old Hagerman Road trail access point via the reservoir road. The town, which has been restored to its original Victorian grandeur, has a grocery, sporting goods and hardware stores, and overnight accommodations.

Maps

USGS Quadrangles: Homestake Reservoir, Mount Massive. USFS Maps: San Isabel National Forest. CT Series: Maps 9 and 10.

Trail Description

If it weren't for the sign pointing out the CT intersection on the Old Hagerman Road, this inconspicuous crossing might be missed altogether. In early summer, lingering snow banks also make this point difficult to spot. From the road, the CT climbs steadily through a lodgepole forest. Several open areas along the way afford great views to the north of Galena Mountain and the Continental Divide. Reach the saddle just west and below Sugarloaf Mountain at mile 1.2 (11,080), where the trail crosses a logging road. Continue south of the road and pass underneath a powerline into a clear-cut area. The area around Leadville was heavily logged during the boom days to provide structural material for the town, mines and railroads. Perhaps this forest succumbed to that fate. You will encounter several areas where the trail has suffered severe erosion because of the timbering activity here, although the clear-cut does provide unparalleled views east and south across the upper Arkansas Valley.

Enter Mt. Massive Wilderness 700 feet south of the road crossing, then descend slightly and reenter the forest at mile 1.6 (11,040), where the trail crosses a small stream. The trail traverses across several small gullies populated by spruce and fir, in the cool, damp recesses, and lodgepole, on the exposed, drier ridges. Top the saddle west of Twin Mounts at mile 3.0 (11,000), then begin a descent south into Rock Creek drainage. Toward the end of the descent, the trail takes on a road-like appearance. Bear to the right on the trail at mile 3.6 (10,600), as the old road continues straight ahead. The CT crosses another road 250 feet beyond. Continue ahead (west) as the trail bends around the southern edge of Kearney Park. After briefly leveling out, the trail continues its descent and temporarily leaves the wilderness to enter Leadville National Fish Hatchery.

The trail descends to the north bank of Rock Creek at mile 4.4 (10,280), where you intersect a jeep road leading to the hatchery buildings to the east. Continue on the trail 200 feet beyond the jeep road and cross the creek on a sturdy bridge. The trail ascends 0.3 mile from Rock Creek to South Rock Creek, which is spanned by a corduroy bridge. Reenter the wilderness area in a somewhat spooky lodgepole forest, where the ground is pitted with large potholes that are likely to be filled with water early in the season.

At mile 6.2 (10,960), the CT intersects the Highline Trail, which continues three steep miles northwest to Native Lake, a popular angler's refuge. The CT proceeds south and crosses North Willow Creek at mile 7.2 (11,040). A few steps beyond this point the trail crosses another small stream on a dirt bridge over a metal culvert, a tasteless combination in a wilderness area. Ascend to a level spot south of North Willow Creek, beyond which you traverse into a sunny, open area with views east to the Mosquito Range.

Pass the cutoff trail to Mt. Massive's summit at mile 8.1 (11,240). On this side trail, it is approximately 3.5 miles and 3,180 vertical feet to the summit of the 14,421-foot mountain, the second highest in Colorado. The CT traverses south from the Mt. Massive summit trail, then suddenly descends to cross Willow Creek at mile 8.4 (11,000). Cross South Willow Creek 0.6 mile beyond and continue to mile 10.4 (10,600), where a steep cross-country ski trail descends abruptly to the left. Continue ahead on the CT, which gradually descends to the trailhead parking area on Halfmoon Creek Road at mile 11.4 (10,080), where you exit Mt. Massive Wilderness. The trail continues on the opposite side of the road, south of Halfmoon Creek.

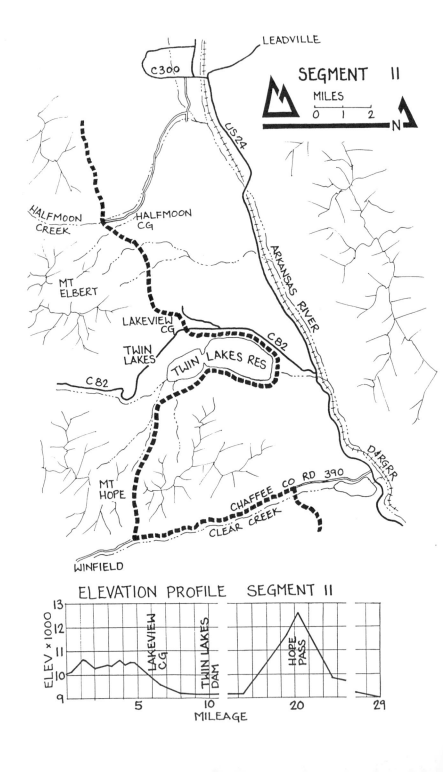

LEADVILLE

SEGMENT II

MILES
0   1   2

N

C300

US 24

HALFMOON
CREEK

HALFMOON
CG

ARKANSAS RIVER

MT
ELBERT

LAKEVIEW
CG

C 82

TWIN
LAKES

TWIN LAKES RES

C 82

D4RGRR

MT
HOPE

CHAFFEE CO RD 390

CLEAR CREEK

WINFIELD

ELEVATION PROFILE   SEGMENT II

ELEV × 1000

13
12
11
10
9

LAKEVIEW CG

TWIN LAKES DAM

HOPE PASS

5   10   20   29

MILEAGE

Segment 11
Halfmoon Creek to Clear Creek Road

Introduction

On your way to the trailhead on Halfmoon Creek, take notice of the water diversion structures which are part of the Pan-Ark Project. Twin Lakes Reservoir is also part of this immense project, which diverts water from the west slope under the divide to the east slope via the Arkansas River. Twin Lakes was enlarged in 1972 to serve the Mt. Elbert powerplant. This pumped storage station generates electric power in high demand periods by using water stored in a forebay above the plant.

At the head of the reservoir is the village of Twin Lakes. Twin Lakes was first established as Dayton and got its start, as did most of the towns in the upper Arkansas, in the brief but energetic gold placer boom of the 1860s. After the boom, the people of Dayton recognized their town was unique because of the incredible mountain scenery and the two lakes at their doorsteps. As early as 1866 Bayard Taylor was informing the world of the beauty of the area.

By the late 1870s Dayton and the Twin Lakes had become a popular resort area. One hotel, run by John Stanley and Charles Thomas, was established on the south shore of the lower lake and was known as Lakeside House. James Dexter acquired the property in 1883 and transformed it into an impressive resort. After improvements, the complex consisted of a dance pavilion, stables, the main hotel and an annex, storage building, laundry and a complete water system. Dexter was so enchanted with the location that he built himself a private, two-story log cabin with Victorian trim. To fit the mood of the expansion, the isolated retreat was renamed Interlaken.

The resort was very popular with anglers, tourists and nature lovers of the late 1800s, and it is a pity that the picturesque refuge went into a decline after the turn of the century. The main culprit in that decline seems to have been the transformation of the lakes into a reservoir, which backed up water over the stage road serving the complex.

When Twin Lakes was further enlarged in the 1970s, the Department of Reclamation decided to save the dilapidated buildings from inundation. The buildings were moved slightly uphill from their original foundations and given a fresh coat of paint. Thus the remains of Interlaken still exist for us to ponder today.

Probably no other section of the CT gives such an obvious view of glacially-deposited debris as the stretch from Twin Lakes to Clear Creek. The parallel ridges bordering the lower valley are lateral moraines, debris deposited by advancing glaciers. The original configuration of Twin Lakes, slightly altered because of its enlargement into a reservoir, was the result of damming by terminal, or end, moraines, deposited at the glaciers' snouts. These unconsolidated deposits, which included gold gouged out of the Sawatch Range and transported into the valley by water and ice, made possible the placer boom of the 1860s. The Arkansas River was pushed against the east side of the valley by the ancient ice flows, so that it now runs in a tight channel between the glacial debris and the hard, ancient core of the Mosquito Range. Those wishing to inspect the 1.7-billion-year-old Precambrian crest of the Sawatch Range can do so here by following a side trail to the top of 14,433-foot Mt. Elbert, the highest point in Colorado.

Hikers in this segment during the first weekend in August will be sharing the route with hardy runners participating in a torturous annual marathon called the Leadville 100.

Trailheads/Access Points

Halfmoon Creek Trailhead: Travel south of Leadville on US 24 approximately 3.5 miles and turn right (west) onto Colorado 300. Drive 0.8 mile and turn left (south) on a dirt road at the sign which marks the way to Halfmoon Campground. Continue another 1.2 miles and turn right. It is an additional 5.5 miles on the bumpy road to the trailhead parking area, which is on the north side of the road just beyond an earth-fill bridge creek crossing.

Lakeview Campground Trailhead/Twin Lakes Reservoir Trail Access: Travel south of Leadville and go west on Colorado 82 for approximately 4.0 miles. Turn right (north) on Lake County Road 24 and continue one mile to Lakeview Campground. A trailhead parking area is provided within the campground.

You can also park at the Mt. Elbert power station parking area, whose entrance is on Colorado 82 a half mile beyond Lake County Road 24. The CT runs right next to the parking area adjacent to the power station.

Finally, several parking areas convenient to the CT are provided on the north side of Twin Lakes Reservoir.

Clear Creek Road Trailhead: See Segment 12.

Supplies, Services and Accommodations

Twin Lakes is approximately one mile west of the CT crossing on Colorado 82. The village has a tavern and a small general store.

Maps

USGS Quadrangles: Mount Massive, Mount Elbert, Granite, Winfield, Mount Harvard. USFS Maps: San Isabel National Forest. CT Series: Maps 10 and 11.

Trail Description

From the trailhead parking area, cross the road to the south side of Halfmoon Creek and immediately intercept the CT as it heads south through a lodgepole forest. This trail is popular because it is one of the most direct routes up Mt. Elbert, which was named for territorial governor Samuel Elbert. Ford Elbert Creek at mile 0.4 (10,160) and notice how the creek has been diverted from its original streambed as shown on the topographical map. Terminate your ascent at mile 1.0 (10,600) and begin a gradual descent. (In 0.3 mile you will pass a right-branching spur trail which leads to the summit of Mt. Elbert.) Continue downhill a half mile to Box Creek and proceed beyond the intersection of an old path which ascends at right. The Mill Creek bridge keeps your feet dry at mile 2.0 (10,280). The trail joins an old road 0.3 mile beyond and begins an ascent to the southeast. The road splits at mile 2.8 (10,400); the right fork is barricaded, so follow the left, which leads past a campsite and a ford of Herrington Creek. Ascend the opposite side of the creek to mile 3.2 (10,320), where the trail improves a bit. Bear to the right 600 feet beyond, at a messy junction, and then resume ascending south on the old road. At the upper end of the road, enter the west edge of an elongated meadow and continue to a broad saddle at mile 3.8 (10,600) where, if you look closely, Turquoise Reservoir is visible to the north.

Descend from the saddle through an aspen forest to a meadow at mile 4.1 (10,440) where the CT veers to the right off the old road and reenters the forest. The trail stays to the right (west) and above several small ponds on Corske Creek. Bear to the right at a trail junction above the ponds at mile 4.5 (10,520) and continue uphill 100 feet to another trail junction. The trail which climbs steeply ahead is another route to Mt. Elbert's summit. The CT leaves the ascending path here, leading squarely to the left. Continue south on the CT and bear right on a jeep track at mile 4.8 (10,520), then cross the fast-flowing creek 150 feet beyond. Begin a steady descent on the jeep road, heading southeast through an aspen forest. Recross the creek at mile 5.2 (10,280). Keep descending on the road to mile 6.5

The Arkansas Valley and the Mosquito Range

(9640), where the trail resumes on your right. Just ahead is Lake County Road 24, which leads from Colorado 82 to the Mt. Elbert forebay and Lakeview Campground.

The trail next drops through an aromatic sagebrush field which affords views south into the basin of Twin Lakes. Pass the trailhead parking area within Lakeview Campground at mile 6.7 (9560) and continue descending beyond the campground to mile 7.1 (9320), where a pedestrian underpass at Colorado 82 insures safe passage. South of Colorado 82, the trail leads east and dips briefly into a cheerful ponderosa grove that blooms with an understory of pasque flowers in spring. The trail here was constructed with the help of Governor Richard Lamm in September of 1985. When the trail breaks out of the scattered ponderosa, the Mosquito Range and a huge lateral moraine that extends east are visible. The century-old buildings of Interlaken are barely visible on the south shore.

Pass the Mt. Elbert powerplant at mile 7.7 (9280) and continue east along the treeless north shore, where the reflection of Mt. Hope sparkles on the water's surface. Cross the lake's earthen dam at mile 10.9 (9200) and continue south on the gravel road until you can skirt the southeast edge of the reservoir using a dirt road which forks to the right (southwest). This road should be marked with a cairn. Follow the dirt road 0.4 mile west along the fluctuating shoreline until the trail peels to the left off the road in a field of sagebrush near the forest's edge. The south shore has a maze of roads and paths, created over the years by countless campers and anglers. If you lose the CT in the confusing labyrinth, stay close to the shore line and continue west; you will eventually pick up the correct trail. (When the water level in the reservoir is low, hikers might be tempted to use the rocky, exposed beach as a more romantic route. The rounded boulders, however, demand a balancing act that becomes nervewracking after only a short time, especially if you are carrying a full backpack.) From the south shore, the recessional moraine across the lake is very obvious. The huge undulations created by the receding glaciers are more fully revealed in the setting sun.

Continue west along the south shoreline, using in part the historic old stage road, to mile 13.9 (9200), where you pass right through the old Interlaken complex. Take a few minutes to look around at the numerous old buildings. Beyond Interlaken, the CT heads southwest for approximately 0.2 mile, crossing a small sagebrush meadow and gradually distancing itself from the reservoir. The trail becomes faint and difficult to follow at times after it enters a lodgepole/aspen forest. Continue 1.5 miles, bearing generally west and southwest, to a series of bridges over the fast-flowing stream at Boswell Gulch. Follow the obscure trail to a junction made obvious by the heavy, boiler-plate "Closed To All Vehicles" sign at mile 16.4 (9280). Go left (south-southwest) here on an intersecting trail which has the appearance of an old road. Ascend south on the rocky, abandoned road 0.3 mile and notice that the trail resumes at left (east). Continue less steeply, with the help of a switchback which returns you to a southerly bearing near the banks of Willis Gulch Creek.

When the trail splits at mile 17.6 (10,280), ignore the right fork and continue straight ahead (south) into Little Willis Gulch. Approximately 0.2 mile beyond, cross a large diversion ditch which clings awkwardly to the steep mountainside and might present some difficulty if flowing with water. The CT breaks out of the trees at mile 19.5 (11,760), near a protected alpine lake at the head of Little Willis Gulch. This lake would make a pleasant camping area. Continue ahead through the tundra, in the shadow of towering, 13,933-foot Mt. Hope, and top out on Hope Pass at mile 20.2 (12,520). Views to the south are of some of the less noticeable of the Collegiate Peaks: Oxford, Belford, Missouri, Huron and Ice Mountain.

From the pass, the CT continues south and drops quickly into the protection of the trees. At the end of its long, steep descent down Sheep Gulch, the trail joins a short, dead-end side road. Continue 800 feet ahead (south) and join up with Chaffee County Road 390 at mile 22.6 (9880). Bear to the left (east) on the county road and continue 6.3 miles down the valley of Clear Creek to the obscure CT trailhead on the dusty road at mile 28.9 (8960).

Segment 12
Clear Creek Road
to North Cottonwood Creek Road

Introduction

The noblest section of the Sawatch Range is the part known as the Collegiate Peaks, a collection of 14,000-foot mountains rising above high, extended ridges and deep valleys. The CT continues southward in this segment along the eastern slopes of the Collegiates, ascending and descending the magnificent terrain like a giant roller coaster. The backpacker will find exceptional campsites all along the way, as well as side trails leading to alpine lakes and isolated niches. The mountain climber will be challenged by several high peaks that rise near the trail, including 14,420-foot Mt. Harvard, 14,153-foot Mt. Oxford and 14,073-foot Mt. Columbia.

This portion of the CT begins in private property at Clear Creek Road but soon rises out of the valley and enters the Collegiate Peaks Wilderness, where it remains for most of the segment. Mountain cyclists are reminded that they will need to detour this segment, as well as Segment 13 (see Mountain Bicycle Route).

The stunning Collegiate Range was first surveyed in 1869 by a university team, thus accounting for the range's unique designation. It was Professor Josiah Dwight Whitney, the head of the Harvard School of Mining and Geology, who led a group of science students into Colorado Territory to give them experience and also to compare the heights of the Colorado Rockies with those of California's Sierra Nevada. The group climbed and named Mt. Harvard to honor their institution. Mt. Yale was named after Whitney's alma mater. Mt. Columbia didn't join the roster of the distinctive group of Ivy League fourteeners until 1916, when it was named by Roger Toll, an official of the Colorado Mountain Club.

Trailheads/Access Points

Clear Creek Road Trailhead: Travel north from Buena Vista on US 24 and turn left (west) on Chaffee County Road 390. Drive 3.0 miles to the informal trailhead parking area on the north side of the dirt road. The CT goes south from here.

To find the CT where it heads north to Twin Lakes, proceed west up County Road 390 an additional 6.3 miles to where the county road makes a wide bend just beyond the restored town of Vicksburg. A side road goes to the right (north) here for several hundred feet, to where the trail begins its steep ascent to Hope Pass.

North Cottonwood Creek Road Trail Access: See Segment 13.

Supplies, Services and Accommodations

Available in Buena Vista (see Segment 13).

Maps

USGS Quadrangles: Granite, Mount Harvard, Harvard Lakes, Buena Vista West. USFS Maps: San Isabel National Forest. CT Series: Maps 11 and 12.

Trail Description

The CT immediately enters private property at the trailhead on the south side of Chaffee County Road 390. Latch the gate behind you and continue among barns and outbuildings along the road, which crosses to the south side of Clear Creek. Pass through a barbed wire gate, then turn to the left at mile 0.2 (8960) and continue east on the road, passing the donkeys and cattle which will likely be grazing in the field. Just before you would pass through a fence and under a power line at mile 0.6 (8960), turn onto the faint road which heads to the right (south). Six hundred feet beyond, top a small, bald rise which till now has concealed from view a gateway in the fence and a

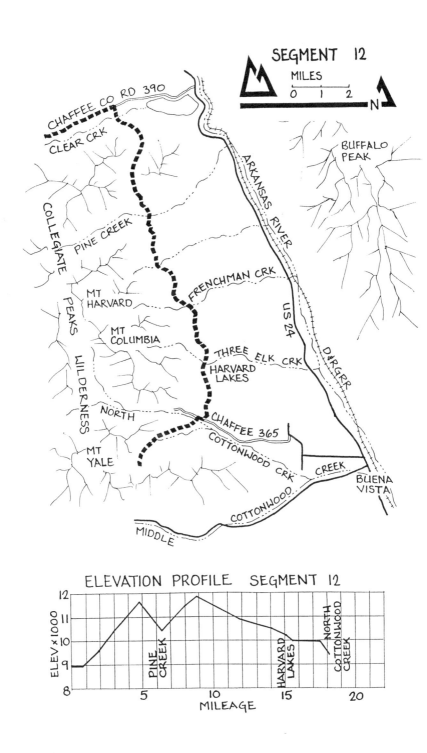

broken-down CT sign. From this point, continue a few more steps south to the edge of the trees, where a sturdy boiler-plate "Closed To All Vehicles" sign at mile 0.8 (8960) marks the trail, where it begins its ascent out of the valley.

Pass through a burned-out lodgepole forest which is slowly coming back to life and switchback uphill in the vicinity of the powerline. Enter damp but usually waterless upper Columbia Gulch at mile 1.9 (9640), where the CT crosses an old road in a sagebrush meadow encircled by aspen and lodgepole. As the trail reenters the trees, it crosses the boundary into Collegiate Peaks Wilderness and resumes its ascent southward in an aspen forest. Lodgepole begin to outnumber aspen as the trail rises onto the rocky mountainside above the gulch. The trail switchbacks to the right at mile 2.9 (10,040) and moves onto a sunnier exposure. Continue the serious ascent, crossing several small streamlets which form the headwaters of Columbia Creek. Mount the ridge extending east of Waverly Mountain at mile 4.8 (11,640). From here Mt. Harvard's impressive crest is dominant on the southern skyline.

The CT drops quickly through a lodgepole forest to its intersection with the Pine Creek Trail, down in the valley at mile 6.4 (10,400). Here there is a well established campsite. Follow the Pine Creek Trail 500 feet downstream to a bridge which crosses to the south side of the creek. The fork to the left continues downstream, parallel to Pine Creek, to a trailhead on US 24. Continue straight ahead on the CT and begin a long ascent out of Pine Creek valley.

At mile 8.1 (11,520), pass an unmarked and indistinct side trail to the right, which leads in 0.3 mile to ideally-sited Rainbow Lake. Continue climbing through a ghost forest and proceed to a windy, exposed point with a line of sight north up the Arkansas Valley. Duck back into the trees and climb to a ridge extending northeast from Mt. Harvard at mile 8.8 (11,800). For the next mile the CT traverses through alpine flowers and grasses with stands of spruce and bristlecone growing at the upper limit of their life zones. The open tundra areas provide tremendous views across the valley to the Buffalo Peaks, which are the southernmost mountains in the Mosquito Range. Even Pikes Peak is visible as a broad purple hump on the far eastern skyline.

Descend to the crossing of Morrison Creek at mile 9.8 (11,560), where several campsites are available. Approximately 0.7 mile beyond, pass the Wapaca Trail, which descends to the left. Continue through a spruce forest to Frenchman Creek at mile 11.8 (10,960) and cross the Harvard Trail 500 feet beyond. The CT continues southeast from this trail intersection and rises slightly to cross a ridge at mile 12.6 (11,160). At mile 14.1 (10,640) pass above a neglected mine whose operator left in such a hurry that he forgot his ore cart.

Just beyond the mine, pass an old road which is more steeply inclined than the CT. Descend to Three Elk Creek at mile 15.1 (10,280) and, 300 feet further along, pass at a right angle the trail which ascends to a cirque formed by Mt. Columbia's southeast face. Here the trail leaves the wilderness area and continues south to Upper Harvard Lake, which is more like a pond, and Lower Harvard Lake at mile 15.4 (10,280). Descend 0.2 mile from the lakes and ford a stream; then begin a traverse at about 10,000 feet through a lodgepole forest which has, in places, a lush understory of purple lupine.

Pass over a ridge at mile 17.5 (9880) and switchback down into an area of mountain mahogany that allows views west up the Horn Fork Basin to the Continental Divide and east into the Arkansas Valley. End this segment at the North Cottonwood Creek Road trailhead area, in a lodgepole/fir forest at mile 18.2 (9400). If you are continuing on the CT, hike approximately 0.1 mile west down the road and look for the trail where it resumes at left (south).

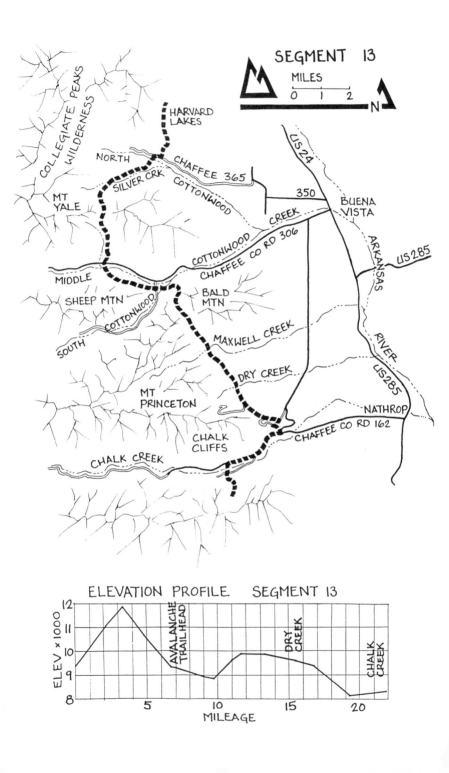

Segment 13
North Cottonwood Creek Road to Chalk Creek Trailhead

Introduction

Near the end of this segment, the CT traverses Mt. Princeton's lower eastern flank and descends into Chalk Creek, which was named for the white, crumbly pillars that support the mountain's southeast ridge. This unusual formation is the result of granitic rock which was kaolinized (altered) by hydrothermal solutions rising from cooling magma along fault and fracture zones in the area. Chalk Creek has always been popular for its hot springs and remains well known today. Trail crews working in this location always had plenty of volunteers, who were typically released by their team leaders early in the afternoon — only to reconvene a few minutes later at the hot springs.

Completion of the last five miles of this segment is still awaiting the acquisition of rights-of-way, so the CT route currently uses an assortment of county roads to reach the trailhead at Chalk Creek. The trail between North and Middle Cottonwood creeks crosses the southeast corner of the Collegiate Peaks Wilderness and passes within two miles and 2,300 vertical feet of 14,196-foot Mt. Yale. Mountain bicyclists are reminded that they must detour around this segment (see the Mountain Bicycle Route).

Mt. Princeton, which is known for the magnificent, symmetrical profile it displays to motorists descending Trout Creek Pass, is a large body of relatively young, 30-million-year-old quartz monzonite porphyry intruding into ancient Precambrian metamorphic rocks. It was originally named Chalk Mountain by the Wheeler Survey. Henry Gannett of the Hayden Survey gave the mountain its present title.

Trailheads/Access Points

North Cottonwood Creek Trail Access: This approach begins with a left turn (west) onto Crossman Street (Chaffee County Road 350) from US 24 at the north end of Buena Vista. Proceed two miles and turn right (north) onto Chaffee County Road 361. After 0.9 mile make a sharp left turn (south) onto Chaffee County Road 365, which may not be suitable for some conventional cars. Continue 3.5 miles on the rough road to a small parking area at an obscure trail access point, from which the northbound CT heads north to Harvard Lakes and eventually Clear Creek. One tenth of a mile beyond is the trailhead for the southbound CT. Parking at both places is extremely limited.

Avalanche Trailhead (Cottonwood Pass Road): From US 24 in Buena Vista, turn west at the stop light onto Main Street, which becomes Chaffee County Road 306 as it leaves the city limits. Travel approximately 9.5 miles west from Buena Vista on Chaffee County Road 306 to Avalanche Trailhead. The CT is marked where it crosses the trailhead area.

Chalk Creek Trailhead: See Segment 14.

Supplies, Services and Accommodations

Buena Vista, as might be inferred from its name, is a beautiful place to visit because of its mild year-round climate and striking

location on the Arkansas River, between the mineralized Mosquito Range and the towering Sawatch. The town is an ideal resupply point for long-distance trekkers because the CT through here is approximately halfway between Denver and Durango. The town has regular bus service, as well as grocery, hardware and backpacking stores and overnight accommodations. The most direct way to reach Buena Vista from the CT is to follow Chaffee County Road 306 9.5 miles east from Avalanche Trailhead.

Maps

USGS Quadrangles: Buena Vista West, Mount Yale, Mount Antero. USFS Maps: San Isabel National Forest. CT Series: Maps 12 and 13.

Trail Description

This segment of the CT begins approximately 0.1 mile west of the trailhead point at the end of Segment 12. Parking here is limited and usually crowded with the vehicles of those climbing Mt. Yale.

Proceed south from the road, cross North Cottonwood Creek and sign in at the register. Ascend in a lodgepole forest on the north side of Silver Creek, passing outcrops of banded, Precambrian metamorphic rock. Continue to a valley meadow, where a large beaver pond backs up Silver Creek at mile 2.2 (11,040). Campers here will be bedding down in the shadow of Mt. Yale, which is visible to the southwest. Continue 0.2 mile up the valley and cross to the creek's south side. Ascend the north slope of Mt. Yale's east

ridge, passing through a spruce/fir forest, and enter the Collegiate Peaks Wilderness. Top the pass between Silver Creek and Middle Cottonwood at mile 3.3 (11,880). This is the trail's closest approach to Mt. Yale. The spruce trees at the saddle are sparse enough to allow a striking and rarely-seen view of Mt. Princeton and its long, elevated western ridge.

Descend south from the pass through a stately bristlecone forest. Pass a good campsite on flat ground, situated in a lodgepole forest, at mile 4.8 (10,640). Hughes Creek is just a short walk down into the gully west of here. Next, curve to the left into a dry ravine at mile 5.3 (10,560) and continue descending through a sparse limber pine and Douglas-fir forest that allows a view up the valley of Middle Cottonwood Creek. In another 0.4 mile you will drop to an area too low for these trees to survive, where only mountain mahogany and similar bushes cling to a tenuous existence on the rocky hillside. Notice also the obvious avalanche chutes across the valley.

Exit the wilderness area at mile 6.3 (9400) and bear to the right, off the barricaded old trail and onto a newly-built tread. Pass the register in 700 feet and go right (west) a short distance beyond on the intersecting, abandoned road. Bear left (southwest) off the old road to the Avalanche Trailhead parking area at mile 6.6 (9360). Continue south-southwest across the large parking area and pick up the trail on the opposite side. The trail parallels Chaffee County Road 306 going east for 200 feet before it crosses to the south side of the paved road and continues another 200 feet down an obscure side road. This leads to an informal car camping area on the north shore of Middle Cottonwood Creek. Bend to the left here, toward the east end of the car camping area, and pick up the CT, which parallels the creek before crossing it on a bridge at mile 6.8 (9320). The trail is carved deeply into the side of the steep south bank of Middle Cottonwood Creek, and fireweed grows profusely in the disturbed soil.

Continue east 250 feet beyond the bridge crossing and enter the bottom of the avalanche chute which was seen during the descent on the opposite side of the valley. Notice how the aspen have all been knocked down in the direction of the avalanche's flow. The chute can be seen to extend all the way to the top of Sheep Mountain. At this point you will also notice a somewhat obscure and overgrown trail which proceeds west above and parallel to the CT and the creek. This old trail was the original route of the CT through here, but was rerouted after an avalanche wiped out part of the trail and a bridge west of the present crossing.

The trail ascends and then traverses the north slope of Sheep Mountain, providing views of Rainbow Lake through a thick, cool forest. Descend gradually to the eastern foot of Sheep Mountain, just west of the confluence of South and Middle Cottonwood creeks, where the trail opens up into a sunnier and less dense forest. Fork to the left where the trail splits, near the entrance to some private property at mile 8.9 (9000). Continue 400 feet downhill and cross to the east side of South Cottonwood Creek Road (Chaffee County Road 344). Follow a side road which leads first to an informal car camping site and then to a bridge across South Cottonwood Creek. Turn left immediately after the bridge and parallel the creek downstream. The trail slowly pulls away from the creek and crosses a dirt road at mile 9.6 (8880), then maneuvers through a series of switchbacks which take you out of the valley.

Cross an abandoned road at mile 10.8 (9440). About 350 feet beyond, turn right (south) onto another abandoned road and follow it uphill through an aspen forest. In another 350 feet, turn to the left where the road splits. Proceed another 350 feet past the fork and leave the abandoned road where the trail resumes to the left at mile 11.0

(9560). The trail continues its ascent to a point slightly above the saddle west of Bald Mountain at mile 11.6 (9880) and then begins a long traverse bearing generally southeast, dipping in and out of several drainages. Cross the meager flow of upper Silver Prince Creek at mile 13.3 (9840) and continue a half mile further to an established campsite near Maxwell Creek.

The trail descends gradually through a varied forest of fir, pine and aspen to Dry Creek at mile 15.5 (9600). A log bridge and a horse ford are provided at the creek, which, contrary to its name, usually has a good, swift flow. Continue on the CT to FS-322 at mile 16.7 (9480). An information board here explains the route the CT will follow on county roads for the next 5.2 miles.

Descend 0.9 mile on the rough dirt road. Where FS-322 splits, continue straight ahead (east), ignoring the right fork, which leads to private property. The Forest Service road joins up with Chaffee County Road 322 approximately 0.2 mile beyond. Follow the gravelled county road 0.6 mile east to where it begins to make a bend to the left (north). Make a sharp, 180-degree turn here to your right, which quickly leaves you heading west on an abandoned shelf road that descends the steep, dry slope inhabited by a community of piñon pines. This vantage point offers a fine, unobstructed view of the Chalk Cliffs ahead and Mt. Antero across the valley. In 0.4 mile turn left (east) from the abandoned road, back onto Chaffee County Road 322, and continue a half mile to paved Chaffee County Road 321. Descend south on the latter for 0.1 mile to an intersection with Chaffee County Road 162 at mile 19.4 (8160). For those requiring a pause to soak their bones before continuing, Mt. Princeton Hot Springs is immediately south across the road.

Proceed 1.4 miles west and southwest on paved Chaffee County Road 162, then veer to the left (west-southwest) onto Chaffee County Road 291. Continue 1.1 miles down this quiet, tree-lined dirt road to the trailhead parking area on Chalk Creek. This segment ends here at mile 21.9 (8360), where the trail resumes its southerly course at the footbridge over the creek.

Segment 14
Chalk Creek to US 50

Introduction

The southernmost peaks of the Sawatch Range honor the memory of the once mighty Ute Indian nation. Starting at Chalk Creek, the trail rounds the eastern flank of 14,269-foot Mt. Antero, which is named after a Ute chief of the Utah-based Uintah band. The trail then continues south to 14,229-foot Mt. Shavano and its western twin, 14,155-foot Mt. Tabeguache. Shavano, spelled "Chavanaux" in Indian treaty documents, was a medicine man and chief of the Ute Tabeguache band. On the southern horizon rises the broad, impressive Mt. Ouray and smaller Chipeta Mountain, connected to Ouray by a ridge. These landmarks are named for the last great Ute chief, who was the diplomatic spokesman for the Ute nation, and his wife.

Mt. Antero and its neighbor to the south, 13,667-foot Mt. White, are popular with the rockhounding crowd. Gemologists have been flocking to the peaks ever since Nathaniel Wannemaker discovered aquamarine near the 14,000-foot level on Mt. Antero in the 1880s. The crest of the mountain was designated as Mt. Antero Mineral Park in 1949, and the bronze plaque set on that date still greets peak baggers just below the summit.

As with previous segments in the Sawatch, this stretch subjects the traveler to a fair amount of elevation gain, especially in the northern portion. However, your efforts are rewarded with grand panoramas of the lower Arkansas Valley and the northern Sangre de Cristo Range. Mountain cyclists who want to avoid a lot of handlebar-pushing should refer to their special section for an optional route past this segment. Backpackers will find many campsites, as well as lots of gushing creeks to satisfy thirsts produced by the warmer temperatures of the lower elevations here. A side trail leads to the summit of Mt. Shavano for those so inclined.

Trailheads/Access Points

Chalk Creek Trailhead: Travel south from Buena Vista on US 285 to Nathrop. Go right (west) onto Chaffee County Road 162. Proceed approximately six miles into Chalk Creek Canyon and bear to the left on Chaffee County Road 291. Continue up the tree-lined dirt road 1.1 miles to the trailhead parking area near the footbridge over Chalk Creek.

Browns Creek Trailhead: Travel south from Nathrop on US 285. Go right (west) on Chaffee County Road 270; proceed 1.5 miles up this dirt road. Continue straight ahead on Chaffee County Road 272 as Road 270 bears to the right. Drive ahead on Road 272 approximately two miles and bear to the left (south) at an intersection. From this intersection it is 1.6 miles further south on Road 272 to Browns Creek Trailhead. From here follow the Browns Creek Trail west 1.4 miles to where it joins up with the Colorado Trail.

Angel of Shavano Trailhead: From the intersection of US 285 and US 50 at Poncha Springs, go west approximately six miles on US 50 to Chaffee County Road 240 (North Fork South Arkansas River Road). Go right (north) on 240 and proceed along the dirt road 3.8 miles to the trailhead parking area opposite Angel of Shavano Campground.

US 50 Trail Access: See Segment 15.

Supplies, Services and Accommodations

Available in Poncha Springs and Salida (see Segment 15).

Maps

USGS Quadrangles: Mount Antero, Maysville. USFS Maps: San Isabel National Forest. CT Series: Maps 13, 14 and 15.

Trail Description

Hikers going north from this trailhead point should note that a

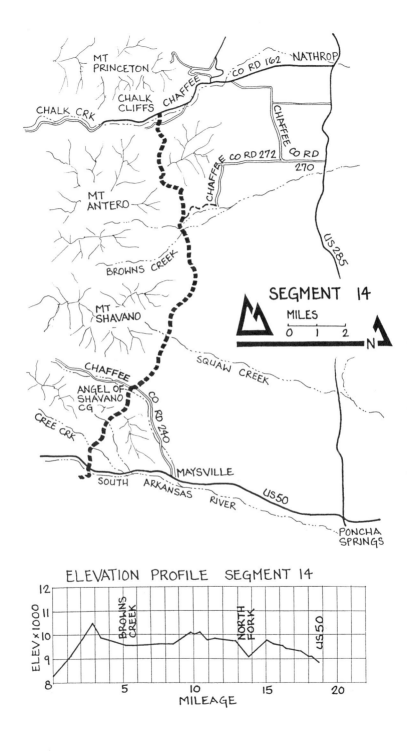

MT PRINCETON

CHALK CLIFFS

CHALK CRK

CHAFFEE

CO RD 162   NATHROP

CHAFFEE CO RD 270

CHAFFEE CO RD 272

MT ANTERO

BROWNS CREEK

MT SHAVANO

US 285

SEGMENT 14

MILES
0   1   2

N

SQUAW CREEK

CHAFFEE

ANGEL OF SHAVANO CG

CO RD 240

CREE CRK

MAYSVILLE

SOUTH   ARKANSAS   RIVER   US 50

PONCHA SPRINGS

ELEVATION PROFILE   SEGMENT 14

ELEV ×1000

12
11
10
9
8

BROWNS CREEK

NORTH FORK

US 50

5   10   15   20

MILEAGE

temporary detour will have them walking on county roads for the next 5.2 miles. From the bridge over Chalk Creek at the trailhead parking area, the trail resumes for southbounders and begins a gradual ascent out of the broad valley. The CT continues 0.4 mile southeast beyond the creek and joins up with an old road. Proceed a few steps up the road and join Chaffee County Road 290, which is the abandoned railroad grade of the DSP&PRR. Go right (west) on 290 for just a hundred feet and notice that the trail resumes again to the left on the south side of the road. Sign in at the register and angle uphill slightly to mile 0.6 (8640), where you join a jeep road which continues south up a ravine. Stay on the jeep road for 300 feet, where the trail resumes at left as the road continues ahead to a quarry. The delicate trickle of a small stream can be heard below as you ascend the trail, which clings to the steep side of the ravine. Curve to the left (east) at mile 0.9 (8840) and enter a small, grassy side canyon which might make a good campsite if the little stream here is still flowing. Aspen, fir and spruce inhabit the cool, north-facing slope of the canyon, while the sunny, south-facing slope can support only piñon pine and mountain mahogany.

Continue east to the head of the canyon and maneuver through a series of switchbacks which have been seriously eroded by motorized dirt bikes using the trail illegally. Top the sandy saddle above the side canyon at mile 1.3 (9200) and take a few minutes to enjoy a seldom-seen view of the Chalk Cliffs to the north. Continue an ascent south from the saddle and slowly merge with the upper drainage of Eddy Creek. Cross to the opposite side of the creek and continue to the forested saddle at mile 2.8 (10,520), where you join up with an old road which ends at a mining prospect on the summit to the east.

Descend steeply south on the old mine road from the saddle, in a mixed forest of limber pine, lodgepole and Douglas-fir, to a junction in Raspberry Gulch at mile 3.4 (9880). Here the route bends to the left (east) and continues following the road downhill through the gulch. A short, deadend side road here continues up the gulch to the right (west), leading to several established campsites near the creek. As the summer advances, this Raspberry Gulch creek gradually dries up, and late-summer campers may not find water downstream from this point in the gulch.

Follow the jeep road 0.4 mile east down Raspberry Gulch, where the trail resumes at right (south) and crosses the presumably dry streambed in 200 feet. Keep traversing and join up with the Browns Creek Trail at mile 5.1 (9600), just above the ponds on Little Browns Creek. Ascend southwest past an old fork to the left, which dead-ends at a beaver pond, and continue to a trail junction at mile 5.3 (9640). Go left at the junction and continue 400 feet to Little Browns Creek. Six hundred feet further the trail crosses Browns Creek.

Continue on the wide trail 700 feet past Browns Creek to another trail intersection, where you continue straight ahead on the CT and ignore the fork leading downhill to the left. Ascend slightly and then traverse through a lodgepole forest to Fourmile Creek at mile 7.5 (9680). The trail grazes a jeep road 0.7 mile beyond here and continues to Sand Creek at mile 8.7 (9600).

The trail ascends to a gravelly ridge at mile 9.8 (10,160), then descends into a wet gully 0.4 mile beyond. The trail then ascends to another high point, where Mt. Ouray and Chipeta Peak can be distinguished to the south through the fir/lodgepole forest. Descend to Squaw Creek at mile 10.9 (9760) and continue 0.2 mile further to a trail register. The CT joins a jeep road here and proceeds south. The Mt. Shavano trail ascends to the right at mile 11.4 (9880). Cross a cattle guard 0.2 mile beyond and leave the jeep road as it descends to the left. Notice that the rather obscure trail continues ahead (south-southwest) through a grassy meadow ringed with aspen. Pick up an obvious trail in 400 feet on the opposite side of the meadow and cross a jeep road at mile 11.9 (9800). About 0.4 mile beyond, pass through a meadow well trampled by cattle; the trail might be a little hard to spot here, but becomes easier to follow once it reenters the aspen. Not long after reentering the forest, the CT crosses two old roads and descends into a lodgepole forest.

Pass through a gate and ascend slightly to a ridge at mile 12.9 (9640), where the forest stops abruptly. Descend a sunny slope and reenter the trees just before the cul-de-sac parking area on the north side of Chaffee County Road 240, at mile 13.6 (9160). Continue northwest on the road, toward the entrance of Angel of Shavano Campground. The trail resumes to the left just beyond the campground sign and continues 800 feet to the footbridge over the fast-flowing North Fork. Steer through several switchbacks, then ascend to a lodgepole-forested ridgetop at mile 15.2 (9760). The trail then descends 0.3 mile in a pronounced ravine, after which it bends to the right and begins a traverse. Join up with another trail at an obscure intersection at mile 15.7 (9600) and continue 600 feet to a more obvious trail junction. Continue straight ahead on the CT here, ignoring the prominent fork to the left. The trail continues around the northwest side of Dry Lake, an isolated pond with no inlet or outlet.

Continue west beyond the pond, staying on the well-blazed main trail and avoiding the several spurs which split off to either side. Beyond mile 16.2 (9560), the trail has been obscured by a logged and burned area. Notice how aspen are coming up to take the place of the destroyed lodgepole forest. Continue bearing generally south along the east edge of the burned forest, following a set of jeep tracks. Approach the southern edge of the burned area in 0.1 mile, where the jeep tracks end at an intersection of three dirt roads which lead east, west and south. Follow a very indistinct route which proceeds west-southwest between the roads leading west and south. This obscure spur leads in 150 feet to a sharp left back onto the CT, in a healthy forest.

Descend to Lost Creek at mile 16.5 (9400) and cross a jeep road just west of the creek. Proceed south and west to a small, open area at mile 17.5 (9360). The sometimes faint trail proceeds 0.1 mile around the north and west perimeter of this open area and crosses a dirt road. Descend to Cree Creek at mile 18.0 (9200); backpackers should note that this is the last camping opportunity north of US 50. Next, the trail ascends south from Cree Creek to the edge of a lodgepole forest, where the South Arkansas Valley and US 50 come into view. Continue south underneath a powerline tower and descend an exposed, south-facing slope on a rocky old road. Cross the abandoned D&RG railroad grade at mile 18.6 (8880), then enter a ponderosa forest and continue 450 feet to US 50. This trail segment ends here on the highway at mile 18.7 (8840).

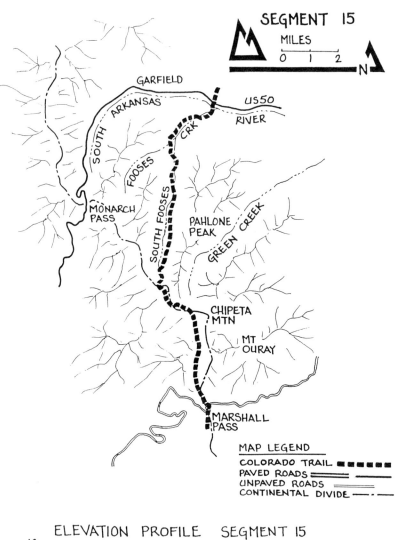

SEGMENT 15

MILES

0 1 2

N

GARFIELD

US50

SOUTH ARKANSAS

RIVER

FOOSES CRK

MONARCH PASS

SOUTH FOOSES

PAHLONE PEAK

GREEN CREEK

CHIPETA MTN

MT OURAY

MARSHALL PASS

MAP LEGEND

COLORADO TRAIL ■ ■ ■ ■
PAVED ROADS ══════
UNPAVED ROADS ═════
CONTINENTAL DIVIDE ─ · ─

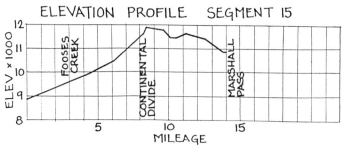

ELEVATION PROFILE   SEGMENT 15

ELEV × 1000

12

11

10

9

8

FOOSES CREEK

CONTINENTAL DIVIDE

MARSHALL PASS

5   10   15

MILEAGE

Segment 15
US 50 to Marshall Pass

Introduction

Long-distance trekkers will want to make sure they are well supplied before progressing south of US 50. The next supply point is Creede, nearly a hundred miles away.

The CT mounts the Continental Divide in this segment and wanders along one side or the other of its crest for the next 130 miles. The trail from the head of South Fooses Creek to Marshall Pass traverses the first portion of this high-altitude route, offering views of the Cochetopa Hills and the Gunnison Basin.

Just before the trail drops down to Marshall Pass, it skirts the western ridge which connects 13,971-foot Mt. Ouray and 12,850-foot Chipeta Mountain. These mountains are named for the Ute chief who represented the Ute nation during the disastrous treaty negotiations of the late 1880s, and for his wife. Mt. Ouray is the southernmost peak of the Sawatch Range, although it can also be thought of as a giant hub around which spokes fan out to form the Sawatch to the north, the Sangre de Cristo to the southeast and the Cochetopa Hills and La Garita Mountains to the southwest.

The rocks in the Mt. Ouray area are ancient sedimentary and metamorphic Precambrian, mostly derived from ancient volcanoes. Interestingly, these 1.7 billion year old rocks underlie adjacent and similar 30 million year old volcanic rocks in the next trail segment, southwest of Marshall Pass.

Trailheads/Access Points

US 50-Fooses Creek Trail Access: From the intersection of US 285 and US 50 at Poncha Springs, drive west approximately nine miles on US 50 to Fooses Creek Road. A widened shoulder on the highway provides temporary parking for those going north on the trail toward Angel of Shavano Campground.

The CT crosses the highway here and follows primitive Fooses Creek Road, which continues southwest from US 50. If you choose to drive up the road, a high-clearance vehicle is recommended. It is 2.9 miles up the rough road to the trail access point on Fooses Creek. Be aware that the first 0.7 mile is on private property. After you reenter public lands, go left at each of three consecutive forks in the road. The last left will take you in 0.1 mile to the obscure trail access point on Fooses Creek. There are no facilities here, though there is room to set up a primitive car camp.

Marshall Pass Trail Access: See Segment 16.

Supplies, Services and Accommodations

Poncha Springs is located approximately nine miles east of the CT crossing on US 50. A general store here provides the basics.

Salida is approximately 13 miles east of the CT crossing on US 50. The town has hardware and sporting goods stores, a grocery, overnight accommodations and regular bus service.

Garfield is located approximately three miles west of the crossing on US 50. A small general store here in the past has provided some basic items.

Maps

USGS Quadrangles: Maysville, Garfield, Pahlone Peak, Mount Ouray. USFS Maps: San Isabel National Forest. CT Series: Maps 15 and 16.

Trail Description

Starting on US 50 just east of Garfield, follow Fooses Creek Road 2.9 miles to the primitive trailhead point. The road crosses private property for the first 0.7 miles, passes a small reservoir and then forks to the left at junctions located at miles 1.7, 2.0 and 2.8. The trail resumes at mile 2.9 (9560), where it crosses Fooses Creek. Continue up South Fooses Creek 300 feet, where a section of forest has been burned. The blue diamonds here indicate a cross country ski route and not necessarily the CT.

Cross over to the east side of South Fooses at mile 3.4 (9720) and ascend through a lodgepole forest. After fording the creek to the west side at mile 4.3 (9840), continue 0.4 mile to a very labor-intensive section of turnpike tread constructed specifically to help keep your feet dry in marshy terrain.

Cross to the east bank on a wobbly bridge at mile 5.0 (10,160). Continue to a meadow in the shadow of Mt. Peck and negotiate a quick double switchback, which helps ease the ascent, at mile 6.2 (10,520). Enter another grassy area 0.4 mile beyond and begin to rise higher on the mountainside. The trail here is rough and rocky at times. As the CT gains elevation, it crosses several streamlets which form the headwaters of South Fooses Creek.

At mile 8.3 (11,600) the trail enters the tundra, where the receding blanket of snow reveals a field of marsh marigold. Top out on the Continental Divide at mile 8.5 (11,920). Angle left (southeast), following the sign which points the way to Marshall Pass. Look closely for the tiny alpine forget-me-nots which carpet the gravelly ridge. The trail, although obscure for several hundred feet, soon

Pahlone Peak and the southern Sawatch Range

resumes and traverses the southwest slope of a minor summit, Point 12,195, then continues due south on the divide ridge, passing impressive cairns constructed from white quartz. Mounts Ouray and Chipeta can be inspected closely from here, and farther to the south rises 13,269-foot Antora Peak.

The trail next descends through a spruce forest, then opens into a small meadow on the divide at the head of Green Creek at mile 10.1 (11,480). The trail in this small opening is somewhat overgrown with grass. A lean-to shelter at the edge of the trees here can provide a bit of shelter from afternoon showers. For those contemplating an overnight stay, the headwaters of Green Creek are not more than an 0.3-mile walk from here.

The CT reenters the trees on the east side of the meadow, and is pointed out by a sign showing the way to East Agate Creek. Continue south and reenter the tundra at mile 10.4 (11,480). The trail crosses a small seep here, then passes into a ghost forest. The tundra foliage is lush and colorful and contrasts sharply with the gray, rocky slopes of Mt. Ouray to the east. The Agate Creek Trail descends to the right at mile 11.2 (11,720); just beyond, the CT enters a spruce forest and begins a gradual descent. The trail crosses a rockslide in 0.3 mile, where thistles and columbine grow out of the jumbled, rocky terrain. Continue past a small stream and pick up a jeep road at mile 12.6 (11,400). From the site of an old quarry, this road descends south past a miner's cabin and a spring that gurgles out of a pipe. Cross a cattle guard at mile 13.4 (11,000) and continue 0.4 mile through two switchbacks down to the Marshall Pass Road. Ascend 0.2 mile south on the road to the deep roadway cut, which is the summit of the pass and the end of this segment at mile 14.0 (10,880). The CT leaves the main pass road just before the cut and continues south on a logging road.

Segment 16
Marshall Pass to Sargents Mesa

Introduction

This segment enters the Tertiary lava flows, volcanic tuffs and breccias of Colorado's southwestern mountains. Before making the transition to the dramatic scenery of the San Juans, the CT continues south from Marshall Pass through the more mellow Cochetopa Hills, providing glimpses of the La Garita Mountains ahead and the Sawatch Range behind.

Because the trail remains near the crest of the Continental Divide, water may be a concern for backpackers looking for a campsite. The only place you will find running water along this segment of the trail is on the headwaters of Tank Seven Creek, although it is feasible to detour into upper Silver Creek, closer to Marshall Pass, in order to resupply. Logging activity which obscures the route can be a problem just south of the pass and also around Cameron Park. In addition to possible route problems where logging activity occurs, portions of the trail in this segment are faint or otherwise difficult to follow. Therefore, it is highly recommended that you carry topo maps and a compass and that you have some knowledge of orienteering.

The lands west of the divide here made up part of the huge Ute Indian Reservation of 1865, which was moved further west three years later. Marshall Pass was discovered in 1873 when a bad toothache persuaded Lt. William Marshall of the Wheeler Survey to take a shortcut from Silverton to the dentist in Denver. It was Otto Mears who built the toll road over the pass and who later sold it to the D&RG. Rails were laid over Marshall Pass in 1881 to connect the mineral-rich Gunnison country to the east slope.

Trailheads/Access Points

Marshall Pass Trail Access: Travel approximately five miles south of Poncha Springs on US 285 and turn right (west) at the Marshall Pass and O'Haver Lake Campground turnoff. Proceed on Chaffee County roads 200 and 202 for 13.1 miles to the roadway cut at the top of the pass. The CT bends to the left here, off of the main road, and continues south on a logging road. The trail heading north to Fooses Creek leaves the pass road 0.2 mile before the roadway cut at the top of the pass.

Sargents Mesa Trail Access (FS-855): See Segment 17.

Supplies, Services and Accommodations

No convenient supply points.

Maps

USGS Quadrangles: Mount Ouray, Bonanza, Chester, Sargents Mesa. USFS Maps: San Isabel National Forest, Rio Grande National Forest. CT Series: Maps 16 and 17.

Trail Description

From the roadway cut at the top of Marshall Pass, the CT bears to the left off the main road. Avoid the left fork 300 feet beyond, which descends east into Poncha Creek. Follow the logging road south to a gate at mile 0.3 (10,880). This gate will admit only foot traffic or two-wheeled vehicles. Continue south and take a side road which ascends to the left at mile 1.5 (10,880). Stay on the main logging road as it ascends, levels out, and then resumes climbing to the broad, forested ridge of the divide. An old Forest Service directional sign on the road has somehow survived all the logging activity. Continue climbing along the road, until it levels out beyond mile 2.3 and leaves the logging area behind. The Silver Creek Trail descends to the left at mile 3.1 (11,240). If you need water, the headwaters of the creek are only a short hike down into the valley, which also makes a nice camping spot at the foot of 13,269-foot Antora Peak.

The CT ascends a jeep track southwest through a meadow of blue flax and enters the trees at mile 3.8 (11,440). A less obvious trail

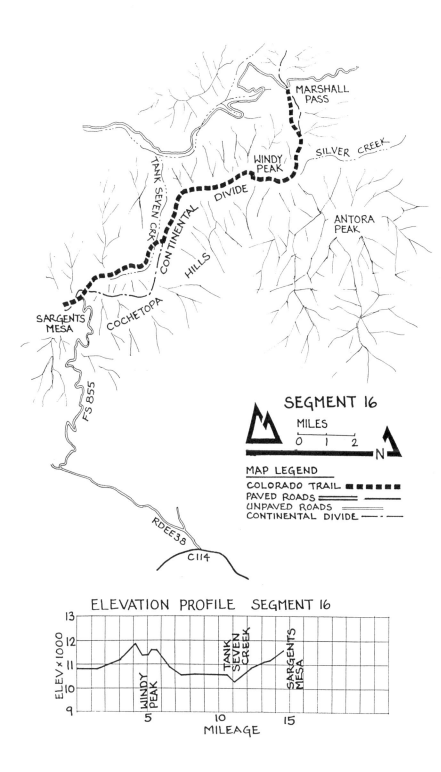

MARSHALL PASS

SILVER CREEK

WINDY PEAK

TANK SEVEN CRK

CONTINENTAL DIVIDE

ANTORA PEAK

HILLS

SARGENTS MESA

COCHETOPA

FS 855

RDEE38

C114

SEGMENT 16

MILES
0 1 2

N

MAP LEGEND
COLORADO TRAIL ▬▬▬▬
PAVED ROADS ═══════
UNPAVED ROADS ═════
CONTINENTAL DIVIDE —·—

ELEVATION PROFILE   SEGMENT 16

ELEV × 1000

13
12
11
10
9

WINDY PEAK

TANK SEVEN CREEK

SARGENTS MESA

5   10   15
MILEAGE

contours to the left here as the CT continues a steep ascent 0.2 mile to a gate, which signals your passage from San Isabel National Forest into Rio Grande National Forest. Continue a steady ascent to just short of Point 11,862, on the divide at mile 4.1 (11,840). A curious cairn of fire bricks here marks the descent west, where the trail ends on the saddle southeast of Windy Peak at mile 4.6 (11,440). Here the trailless CT route, which is well marked with blazes and cairns, begins a traverse west along the south side of Windy Peak. An important, and somewhat inconspicuous, sharp right turn in 0.4 mile takes you up the peak's forested south ridge to mile 5.3 (11,680), where the blazed route bends to the left (northwest) and levels out just below the summit. Follow a series of cairns 0.3 mile to where the trail reemerges, and begin a descent west along the broad, forested ridge of the Continental Divide.

Cross Jay Creek Road at mile 6.6 (10,880) and continue descend-

ing west, through a lodgepole forest. The trail ends its long descent at mile 7.4 (10,560) and begins a series of minor ups and downs on the crest of the divide, still heading west. Join up with a swath cut through the forest for a natural gas pipeline at mile 8.4 (10,640), and follow the swath 200 feet south to where the trail resumes at right. Continue on the divide 0.2 mile beyond, as the CT makes a rapid turn from west to south, and continue along the broad ridge past occasional small knobs.

Make a sharp right at mile 10.6 (10,560) and descend to the ford on Tank Seven Creek, which received its unusual name from a D&RG water stop downstream from this point.

Backpackers should be aware that Tank Seven Creek is the last water until Baldy Lake, 11 miles to the west. Join up with the old road on the west side of the creek at mile 11.1 (10,280). Proceed south and then west up the old road, which parallels Tank Seven Creek, to grassy Cameron Park at mile 12.3 (10,800). A couple of dilapidated cabins here might provide minimal protection in a downpour.

An improved road which serves the logging industry leads across Cameron Park. A Forest Service road leaves the logging road near the cabins and progresses north and then west into the forest. Heavy logging activity here makes it necessary to remain as close as possible to upper Tank Seven Creek in the elongated meadow, so as not to get lost in the maze of roads on either side. Therefore, head a few steps west from the cabins in Cameron Park to the faint trail which begins between the roads. Ascend generally west-southwest in and out of the trees on the north side of the elongated meadow. Cross a logging road at mile 13.2 (11,080) and continue 0.2 mile west to the lower portion of the large park which covers much of Sargents Mesa. Proceed west across the marshy meadow to a post on the opposite side at mile 13.6 (11,240), then continue a hundred feet beyond (west) to FS-486. Follow FS-486 uphill (south then southwest), mostly in an alpine meadow, to mile 14.5 (11,600), where FS-855 dead-ends into FS-486 at the edge of the trees. Segment 16 comes to an end here, at this obscure Forest Service road intersection on Sargents Mesa.

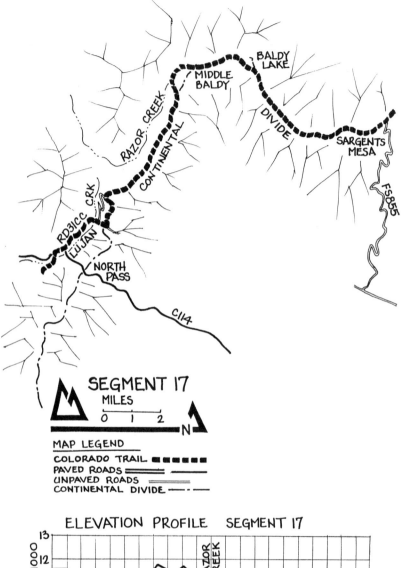

SEGMENT 17

MILES

0 1 2

N

MAP LEGEND

COLORADO TRAIL ▰▰▰▰▰

PAVED ROADS ══════ ───

UNPAVED ROADS ══════

CONTINENTAL DIVIDE ─ ∙ ─ ∙ ─

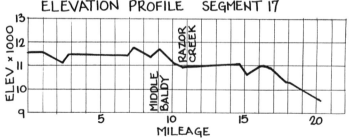

ELEVATION PROFILE   SEGMENT 17

Segment 17
Sargents Mesa to Colorado 114

Introduction

This segment continues through the Cochetopa Hills and, with the exception of a short bypass into upper Razor Creek, remains on the broad, forested crest of the Continental Divide until reaching Lujan Creek Road. The Cochetopa Hills are composed of the relatively recent (Tertiary age) lava flows, volcanic ash and breccias that form much of the San Juan Mountains.

Introspective backpackers will love the isolation of the Cochetopa Hills, but should be aware that no drinking water is available along the first seven miles of this segment. Not until reaching Baldy Lake, which is a half mile off the trail, can you be assured of water. Upper Razor Creek is an ideal place to camp, and you are likely to see elk grazing there.

As in the previous segment, the trail in this segment is rarely used and is obscure in places. It is possible that map and compass readings might be necessary from time to time to confirm your location.

Trailheads/Access Points

Sargents Mesa Trail Access (FS-855): From Saguache on US 285 in the San Luis Valley, drive west on Colorado 114 for 10.5 miles and turn right (north) onto County Road EE38. Proceed 0.8 mile to a fork and bear to the left. Approximately five miles beyond, make a sharp right onto Road 32JJ, also marked as FS-855. Continue approximately ten miles on FS-855, then go left at a fork (the right fork here enters a confusing labyrinth of logging roads which eventually passes through Cameron Park). Proceed on the left fork 0.4 mile to the end of the improved road. FS-855 continues as a jeep road another 0.7 mile, where it dead-ends into FS-486, which is the CT route in the upper park on Sargents Mesa.

Lujan Creek Road Trail Access: From Saguache on US 285 in the San Luis Valley, drive west on Colorado 114 approximately 30 miles to the summit of North Pass. Descend 1.1 miles from the pass to Lujan Creek Road (Road 31CC), which ascends to the right (northeast). Follow this dirt road, which is an impassable quagmire in rainy weather, two miles to a switchback. The left fork is the official CT, which here utilizes existing logging roads. If you wish to use an alternate trail connector which avoids the logging roads, bear to the right at the switchback and proceed 0.1 mile to a cattleguard at the top of the Continental Divide. Immediately you will face a fork in the road; go left and continue east 0.1 mile to where a CT marker identifies the alternate trail connector.

Colorado 114 Trail Access: See Segment 18.

Supplies, Services and Accommodations

No convenient supply point.

Maps

USGS Quadrangles: Sargents Mesa, West Baldy, North Pass. USFS Maps: Rio Grande National Forest. CT Series: Maps 17 and 18.

Trail Description

From the upper end of the Sargents Mesa park, the CT follows FS-486 from the spot where FS-855 dead-ends into it. Enter a patchy spruce forest and follow the road southwest as it levels out on the large, rolling summit of the mesa. The La Garita Mountains are visible ahead, just above the forested horizon. The road skirts around the north side of a burned-out knob on the west end of the mesa at mile 1.0 (11,640) and descends 1.3 miles beyond to the saddle between Long Branch and Jacks Creek. Here the obscure CT leaves the road, which descends to the left (south). Continue 800 feet west, across the gravelly saddle, to mile 2.4 (11,160), where you will cross a faint trail which leads north down into the Long Branch. Ascend west a half mile to a minor summit, Point 11,547. Descend slightly from the summit and begin a stroll northwest along the broad, undulating Continental Divide ridge, on a trail which is sometimes rocky and hard to spot but usually well blazed.

Intersect the Baldy Lake Trail at mile 6.9 (11,480). The lake, which is located in a cirque below Long Branch Baldy, is a half mile down this side trail to the right (north). From this trail intersection, ascend 0.4 mile west to a high point south of Long Branch Baldy. Slowly descend 1.2 miles to the saddle, then ascend to the large summit of Middle Baldy at mile 9.2 (11,680). After observing the huge Gunnison Basin from the treeless west side of Middle Baldy,

Baldy Lake

pass the trail which descends north into Dutchman Creek at mile 9.8 (11,480). Enter upper Razor Park 0.2 mile beyond, where the trail disappears in the grass. Descend south-southwest across the park, and aim for the funnel formed by the trees in the lower part of the meadow which drops into the distinct draw above the mouth of Razor Creek. A faint trail emerges at mile 10.4 (10,920) and crosses to the left (east) side of the creek in 250 feet. Continue south and ford to the right (west) side of Razor Creek at mile 10.7 (10,880). Immediately a sign directs you back to the east side of the creek. The trailless CT now continues eastward away from the creek 200 feet across a meadow, then enters the trees, where a marker confirms the route. Continue southeast, where a swath has been cleared but no trail built.

The CT next aligns itself again on the wide crest of the divide, passing the Razor Creek Trail at mile 12.3 (10,960). Trail conditions improve as you progress south to south-southwest on the divide. Ascend to a minor summit, Point 11,017, at mile 14.4, then descend 0.7 mile to a forested saddle. Ascend steeply from the saddle on several poorly built switchbacks to a logging road at mile 16.1 (11,000). The original route of the CT followed the logging road downhill to the right, but in 1988 volunteers rebuilt a seriously neglected footpath giving hikers the opportunity to remain on trail for another mile and a half.

Bear left (south) on the logging road and follow it a few steps to a broad, forested ridge, which is again the crest of the Continental Divide. The old logging road here changes into a sometimes difficult-to-follow trail and begins a descent to the south, still on the ridge of the Continental Divide. The trail swings through several long switchbacks on its way to Lujan Creek Road at mile 17.8 (10,320), passing through an alternating forest of aspen, lodgepole and bristlecone.

Bear right (west) on the road and continue several hundred feet to a cattleguard. Follow the road approximately 500 feet and bear downhill to the left (southwest) at the switchback. Avoid the logging road which continues north from this switchback.

Follow Lujan Creek Road downhill (southwest) and join up with Colorado 114 at mile 20.0 (9680). Continue 0.3 mile southwest on Colorado 114 to the widened shoulder on the south side of the road at mile 20.3 (9600), where this segment comes to an end.

Segment 18
Colorado 114 to Saguache Park Road

Introduction

Cochetopa Gap has been used for centuries by humans and animals shuttling between the San Luis Valley and the Gunnison Basin. In fact, "Cochetopa" is a Ute word meaning Pass of the Buffalo. Few other Continental Divide crossings in the state have such an impressive background, probably because the Cochetopa Gap extends for miles, providing several relatively easy passages rather than a single, isolated notch, as is characteristic of most Colorado passes.

The gap was already well trampled by the Utes and buffalo when the Spanish governor of New Mexico, Juan Bautista de Anza, led his army into the San Luis Valley in 1779. De Anza's object was the Comanche Greenhorn, but during his pursuit he did not fail to notice the long, low point in the mountains to the west, which he correctly deduced was the divide between the Rio Grande and the western San Juan country, which had been explored by Father Escalante two years before. By 1825, Antoine Rubidoux was directing pack trains over the gap, after first entering the San Luis Valley via Mosca Pass in the Sangre de Cristo Range.

Probably the area's most dramatic event took place just southwest of here in the winter of 1848-49, when Colonel John Charles Frémont led a party into the region to explore potential railroad routes. Unfortunately, guide Bill Williams aimed in the wrong direction and the expedition ended up somewhere on the high ridges of the La Garita Mountains. A fierce blizzard resulted in the deaths of 11 of the original 35 men. Some of the survivors were accused, but never formally charged, with cannibalism.

A more infamous cannibal, Alferd Packer, made his way over the gap in April of 1874, after having survived the winter by murdering and devouring his five fellow travelers. Packer was later arrested in Saguache. Quite perversely, Packer's name has been immortalized by at least one eating establishment in the state, as well as by a society of tongue-in-cheek admirers whose motto is "Serving our Fellow Man for 114 Years."

Otto Mears and Enos Hotchkiss built a toll road from Saguache to Lake City over Cochetopa Pass in 1874. Today, the rarely-used, historic Cochetopa Pass Road and the more recent North Pass (Colorado 114) are only minor crossings of the divide when compared to other Colorado passes. This seems odd, considering the relative ease of passage through here, but travelers will find that the area's resulting quiet generates an appropriately mystical feeling of antiquity.

Backpackers will find meager water supplies along this segment. Lujan, Pine, Archuleta and Los Creeks all have small but steady flows. Special measures may have to be taken during dry years or in late summer. A small spring at Luders Creek Campground could be detoured to in emergencies. The CT in this segment uses a curious assortment of logging, jeep, Forest Service and county roads, relying on its own trail for only a few stretches. A map and compass would come in handy to help decipher the maze.

Mountain cyclists should refer to their chapter for a description of the long detour, starting on Cochetopa Pass Road, that will take them around the La Garita Wilderness.

Trailheads/Access Points

Colorado 114 Trail Access: From Saguache on US 285 in the San Luis Valley, go west on Colorado 114 approximately 30 miles to the summit of North Pass. Descend 1.1 miles on the west side of the pass to Lujan Creek Road (Road 31CC), which ascends to the right (northeast) and is the route of the CT in Segment 17. Continue on Colorado 114 for 0.3 mile to a widened shoulder of the highway, which is not graded for parking. The CT continues south from here across the meadow of Lujan Creek.

A better trail access point, away from the activity of the highway,

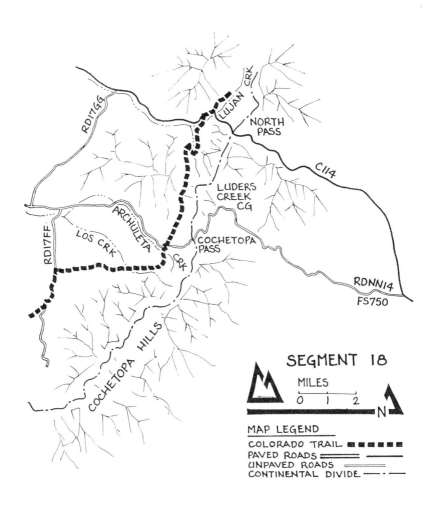

SEGMENT 18

MILES
0   1   2

N

MAP LEGEND

COLORADO TRAIL ■ ■ ■ ■ ■
PAVED ROADS ══════
UNPAVED ROADS ═════
CONTINENTAL DIVIDE — · —

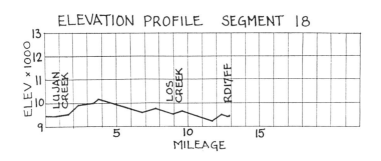

ELEVATION PROFILE   SEGMENT 18

is up Lujan Creek Road (Road 31CC). Refer to Lujan Creek Road Trail Access, described in Segment 17.

Cochetopa Pass Road (Road NN14 and FS-750) Trail Access: From Saguache on US 285 in the San Luis Valley, go west on Colorado 114 approximately 21 miles and bear to the left on Road NN14 (FS-750), which is the historic route of the original Cochetopa Pass Road. Follow the road to Luders Creek Campground, then ascend on FS-750 approximately 1.8 miles to the summit of Cochetopa Pass. Descend 1.2 miles west of the pass to FS-876 (Corduroy Road), which leaves FS-750 to the right (north) and is the route of the CT. From this point, the CT follows FS-750 for the next half mile as it descends through two switchbacks. No parking is provided at this trail access point.

Saguache Park Road 17FF: See Segment 19.

Supplies, Services and Accommodations

No convenient supply point.

Maps

USGS Quadrangles: North Pass, Cochetopa Park. USFS Maps: Gunnison National Forest. CT Series: Maps 18 and 19.

Trail Description

At the widened shoulder 1.4 miles west of North Pass on Colorado 114, proceed southwest through the gate and drop down slightly into the lush meadow of Lujan Creek. Ford the creek at mile 0.2 (9560) and rise above the marshy lowlands surrounding it. Follow the trailless route, which is marked with flimsy carsonite posts that wave pitifully in the breeze, in a more westerly direction. Curve to the left (south) and follow the posts into Pine Creek drainage. Join up with a logging road at mile 0.8 (9560). Continue south up the valley and ignore the fork to the left 0.1 mile beyond. Cross over to the west side of the creek at mile 1.6 (9680) and take time to admire the cinquefoil and sego lily which adorn the area. Go right at the fork 0.1 mile beyond, where the logging road splits and begins an ascent out of Pine Creek Valley. Continue along the road as it bends around, until the road assumes a northerly direction. Then switchback to the left at mile 2.4 (9920) and resume a southerly bearing.

The logging road ends in a cul-de-sac at mile 3.4 (10,000). Continue ascending south from the road, following a route that has been cleared but as yet has no trail. Reach the saddle between Lujan and Archuleta creeks at mile 3.7 (10,240) and pass through a gate. Descend 0.1 mile on a cleared route to another logging road. Go left on the logging road (FS-876), which descends south in the upper drainage of Corduroy Creek. Reach the Cochetopa Pass Road at mile 6.4 (9760).

Follow the pass road downhill to the right a half mile, through two switchbacks, to where a jeep track leaves the graded road to the left (south). Cross over to the south side of Archuleta Creek on a dirt-fill bridge and continue on the jeep track, which parallels the pass road and the tiny flow of the creek upstream for several hundred feet. Bend slowly to the right as the jeep track angles south up a shallow, intersecting valley. Ignore the fork to the right, which cuts up into the hillside, and continue a slow bend to the southwest at the edge of the meadow. Pass through a gate at the indistinct divide between Archuleta and Los Creeks at mile 7.7 (9800) and descend west into the wide, grassy valley. Begin paralleling the main flow of Los Creek a half mile beyond. Continue west on the north side of the creek, which is almost hidden by willows and cinquefoil.

Cross Los Creek as it turns north at mile 8.9 (9560), just above a stock pond. Ascend west out of Los Creek drainage on a jeep track. Top a grassy saddle a half mile beyond and descend, bearing generally west, on the jeep track, which parallels a fence. A full view of broad Cochetopa Dome dominates the scenery to the north. Level out as the jeep track enters the edge of immense Cochetopa Park at mile 10.4 (9400). Go right 0.8 mile further, where the jeep track forks, and continue to Saguache Park Road (Road 17FF) at mile 11.4 (9340). Turn left (south) onto the road and continue to a cattleguard at a wooded saddle. Descend west along the road, then bend back to the south and ascend slightly to mile 12.9 (9520). This segment terminates here, as the CT route joins a jeep track to the right and leaves the Saguache Park Road in a meadow at the edge of the forest.

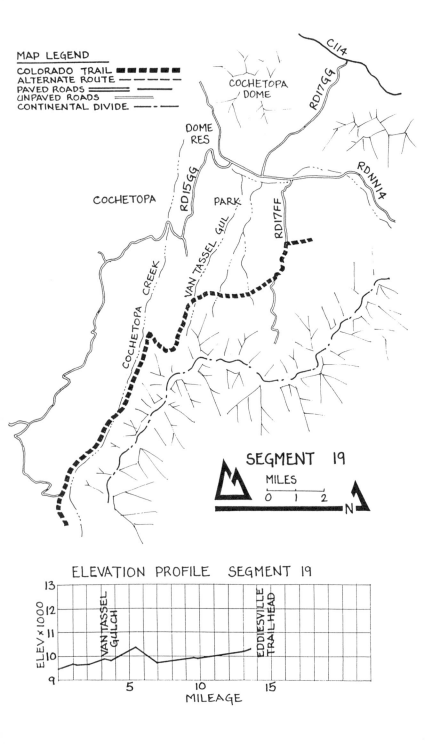

MAP LEGEND

COLORADO TRAIL ▆▆ ▆▆ ▆▆
ALTERNATE ROUTE ― ― ― ―
PAVED ROADS ════════
UNPAVED ROADS ════════
CONTINENTAL DIVIDE ―·―·―

C114

COCHETOPA DOME

RD17GG

DOME RES

RDNN14

COCHETOPA

RD15GG

PARK

RD17FF

VAN TASSEL GUL

COCHETOPA CREEK

SEGMENT 19

MILES
0   1   2

N

ELEVATION PROFILE   SEGMENT 19

VANTASSEL GULCH

EDDIESVILLE TRAILHEAD

ELEV × 1000

13
12
11
10
9

5   10   15

MILEAGE

Segment 19
Saguache Park Road
to Eddiesville Trailhead

Introduction

The CT in this segment crosses several small drainages while skirting the southern boundary of Cochetopa Park on existing jeep tracks. Backpackers will find many campsites once in the isolated valley of Cochetopa Creek, but may experience some aggravating moments if they unintentionally stray off the obscure trail which parallels the creek to Eddiesville Trailhead.

The last several miles of the segment take you into La Garita Wilderness, where mountain bicycles are not allowed (refer to the Mountain Bicycle Route).

Trailheads/Access Points

Saguache Park Road Trail Access: From Saguache on US 285 in the San Luis Valley, go west on Colorado 114 approximately 30 miles to the summit of North Pass. Continue on Colorado 114 west of the pass approximately 5.2 miles and go left (south) on County Road 17GG. Continue on the dirt road approximately 5.2 miles around the southwest side of Cochetopa Dome. Go left (east) onto County Road NN14, the Cochetopa Pass Road. Drive 1.1 mile east on the pass road and go right (south) on Road 17FF (FS-3088, also called the Saguache Park Road). Continue up Road 17FF to the cattleguard, which signals your entry into Gunnison National Forest. The CT takes off immediately to the left (east) at this point, following a set of jeep tracks.

Continue ahead (south) 1.5 miles on Road 17FF to where the CT, using another set of jeep tracks, veers to the right (southwest) off the Saguache Park Road. No parking area is provided at either of these access points.

Eddiesville Trailhead: See Segment 20.

Supplies, Services and Accommodations
No convenient supply point.

Maps
USGS Quadrangles: Cochetopa Park, Saguache Park, Elk Park. USFS Maps: Gunnison National Forest. CT Series: Maps 19 and 20.

Trail Description
The CT leaves the Saguache Park Road and joins up with a jeep track at right, which proceeds southwest through the meadow. At mile 0.1 (9520), continue straight ahead on the less obvious track and ignore the fork to the right. Ascend in a small gully of scattered spruce and aspen. The CT forks at mile 0.5 (9600) and, although these two forks reconverge in 0.2 mile, the right-hand and less obvious fork here appears to be the official route. Continue to a small rise, where the two forks come back together, and descend slightly into the dry gully of Sunshine Creek, where fields of sego lily bloom. Ascend to a low, open ridge dividing Ant and Sunshine Creeks, then descend to the tiny flow of Ant Creek at mile 1.2 (9720). Pass through a gate on each side of the creek. Avoid the left fork, which goes south and uphill after crossing Ant Creek, and instead continue west at the edge of the forest along the southern boundary of the park. The rounded, smooth profile of Cochetopa Dome dominates the foreground, while the Elk Mountains provide a snowy backdrop far to the north.

Descend slowly, entering the Quemado Creek drainage, to a confusing junction at mile 2.2 (9760), where several jeep tracks come together. Continue 0.2 mile northwest from this junction on an obscure jeep track, then bear to the left (west) on another set of tracks, which take you to the opposite side of the boggy creek in 150 feet. Climb west out of the drainage to a high point, where you pass through a gate at mile 3.2 (9960). Descend west and then south into Van Tassel Gulch. Cross the tiny stream at mile 3.7 (9840) and continue 500 feet to a jeep road. Turn left (south) onto the road and ascend on the west side of the wide gulch through a sparse aspen forest.

Top the saddle at mile 5.4 (10,400), in a small clearing ringed with aspen. Follow the jeep road as it descends and slowly bends to the right (west). As the road continues to drop, it slowly assumes a more northerly direction and eventually breaks out of the trees and switchbacks to the left (southwest) at mile 6.5 (9960). Continue 0.2 mile southwest to a pond, where the CT briefly leaves the jeep track. Proceed between the west shore of the pond and a small knoll. Pick up the jeep track again southwest of the pond and descend to mile 7.0 (9720), where the trail resumes at left and begins a long, gradual ascent south and southwest up Cochetopa Creek.

Cross a small stream just as the trail leaves the jeep track and continue south on the east side of the broad valley. Cochetopa Creek meanders through the grassy valley bottom, which offers many campsites for backpackers. The sometimes obscure trail bears generally south-southwest and begins to take on the character of a jeep track in 0.7 mile. Ascend to a high point in the surrounding aspen at mile 9.5 (9960), then descend quickly 0.1 mile to a small side stream. Continue on the jeep track a hundred feet beyond the side stream, where the trail bears to the right (southwest). This short section of trail is only about a hundred feet long and joins another jeep track that continues southwest on a grassy, elevated bench above and parallel to Cochetopa Creek.

Toward the southern end of the grassy bench at mile 10.2 (9960), the trail descends quickly to the level of the creek and disappears in a sand bar. Bear to the right through a tangle of willows and carefully ford Cochetopa Creek at a deep, precarious crossing. Once across the creek, head south-southwest to an enormous cairn on the west bank, just above the level of the willows. The trail is indistinct in places until you rise above the creek. Ascend southwest from the cairn to the grassy bench on the west side of the creek, then join up with the trail again at mile 10.5 (10,000). From here, another trail (not shown on the maps) continues downstream (northeast). Because this junction is obscure, it could be a problem for hikers headed for Saguache Park

Road.

Continue along the trail south-southwest up the west side of Cochetopa Creek and ford the rushing side drainage of Nutras Creek at mile 10.8 (10,000). Enter La Garita Wilderness just beyond. Ascend near the banks of the creek on a mostly treeless slope with a southern exposure, which can be uncomfortably warm on summer afternoons. The trail levels out on a rolling, grassy bench well above the creek at mile 12.1 (10,240). Take the right fork where the trail splits at mile 13.0 (10,280). Continue to the isolated Eddiesville Trailhead parking area at mile 13.5 (10,320), where the CT briefly leaves the wilderness.

Segment 20
Eddiesville Trailhead to San Luis Pass

Introduction

This segment traverses stunning alpine country on the old and appropriately-named Skyline Trail. It also has the honor of making the CT's closest approach to a 14,000-foot peak, passing just 1,400 feet below and within 1.3 miles of 14,014-foot San Luis Peak. This mountain was probably christened by members of the Hayden Survey, who were no doubt influenced by the huge valley to the east.

Stewart Creek gets its name from the mountain on whose slopes it begins. Stewart Peak (13,983 feet), which is not visible in this segment, was named by the Wheeler Survey for Senator William M. Stewart of Nevada, who was an advocate of the free coinage of silver. Having this man's name attached to a prominent peak is evidence of the strong feelings Coloradans had for free silver. Stewart Peak also has the dubious distinction of having been demoted from its previous 14,000-foot stature, which occurred when inaccurate, early-day surveys were superseded by more accurate, modern ones. Though only a mere 17 feet shy of the "magic number," this noble mountain is now virtually ignored by the peakbaggers who flock into the area to climb San Luis Peak.

From San Luis Saddle west to San Luis Pass, the CT stays at or above 12,000 feet and only once barely grazes the upper limits of a spruce forest, at the head of Spring Creek. With the exception of the last mile as you approach San Luis Pass, the trail is generally continuous, although obscured at times by talus or thick tundra grasses. Hikers should be aware that snowfields often linger well into the summer on the north slopes beyond San Luis Saddle, and mountain bicyclists are reminded that their wheels are not allowed within the wilderness.

Backpackers will certainly want to tarry in this segment, which remains almost entirely within La Garita Wilderness, and set up camp anywhere along the upper course of Cochetopa Creek or in the headwaters of Spring Creek further west. The interesting gnome-like figures, or "hoodoos," that decorate the mountainsides through here have been eroded out of volcanic ash.

Trailheads/Access Points

Eddiesville Trailhead: From Saguache on US 285 in the San Luis Valley, travel west on Colorado 114 approximately 30 miles to the summit of North Pass. Continue on Colorado 114 west of the pass approximately 5.2 miles and go left (south) on County Road 17GG. Continue on the dirt road approximately 5.2 miles around the southwest side of Cochetopa Dome and go right (west) on County Road NN14, which is the Cochetopa Pass Road. Drive west 1.3 miles on the pass road and go left on Road 15GG (FS-3086). Follow this main road, which is marked as "Stewart Creek," approximately 21 miles to the Eddiesville Trailhead parking area near the end of the road.

San Luis Pass Trail Access: See Segment 21.

Supplies, Services and Accommodations

Available in Creede (see Segment 21).

Maps

USGS Quadrangles: Elk Park, Halfmoon Pass, San Luis Peak. USFS Maps: Gunnison National Forest, Rio Grande National Forest. CT Series: Maps 20, 21.

Trail Description

From the Eddiesville Trailhead parking area head south on the road, which dips slightly to cross Stewart Creek. Leave the road as it enters private property at mile 0.2 (10,320) and continue to the right (southwest) 500 feet on a trail which parallels a barbed wire fence to a gate. Pass through the gate and briefly enter private property. The

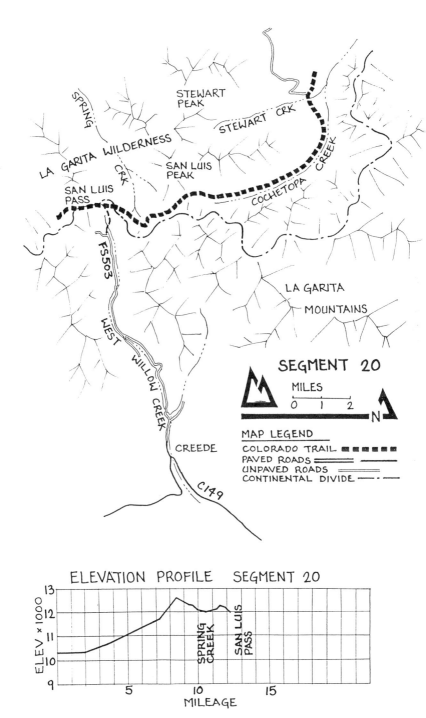

STEWART
PEAK

SPRING

STEWART CRK

LA GARITA WILDERNESS

SAN LUIS
PEAK

CRK

SAN LUIS
PASS

COCHETOPA

CREEK

FS503

LA GARITA

MOUNTAINS

WEST WILLOW CREEK

SEGMENT 20

MILES
0   1   2

N

CREEDE

C149

MAP LEGEND
COLORADO TRAIL ■ ■ ■ ■ ■
PAVED ROADS ═══════
UNPAVED ROADS ════════
CONTINENTAL DIVIDE ─ · ─ · ─

ELEVATION PROFILE   SEGMENT 20

ELEV × 1000

13
12
11
10
9

SPRING
CREEK

SAN LUIS
PASS

5   10   15
MILEAGE

Cañon Hondo Trail ascends to the right 300 feet beyond. Proceed south at the western edge of the broad Cochetopa Creek valley; a small homestead is visible at left. The trail joins a set of jeep tracks in 0.3 mile and continues south. At mile 1.1 (10,360), a trail separates just briefly from the jeep tracks to pass through a gate and reenter the La Garita Wilderness. It then immediately rejoins the jeep track and continues south along the west bank of Cochetopa Creek.

The CT bends southwesterly at mile 2.0 (10,400) and begins to encounter clumps of spruce. Pass through a gate at mile 3.5 (10,640) and continue through a forest, then pass the obscure cutoff to Stewart Creek at mile 7.2 (11,720) and ford the headwaters of Cochetopa Creek 200 feet beyond. Beyond timberline now, follow the trail through willows and enjoy a grand view of Organ Mountain. The trail is engulfed by tundra grasses just short of San Luis Saddle. Continue to the saddle at mile 8.4 (12,600). The summit of 14,014-foot San Luis Peak is only a 1.3-mile ridge walk north of this point.

Pick up the trail again on the opposite side of the saddle and traverse south, then west, into a cirque at the head of Spring Creek. Climb slightly to another saddle at mile 9.6 (12,360), then descend on the trail, which disappears 200 feet beyond in the grass. A post visible just west of the saddle marks where the trail resumes. Descend slightly into another alpine cirque. An old sign at mile 10.0 (12,080) identifies where the obscure Spring Creek Trail intersects the CT. Cross a small stream 200 feet beyond and continue to mile 10.5 (12,000), where the trail briefly enters an upper-limit spruce forest.

Proceed 0.4 mile on the trail to another small stream and begin a long ascent. Climb west to mile 11.3 (12,200), where the trail disappears. Continue northwest and aim to the right (north) of the rocky crest which extends above the grassy ridge of the Continental Divide. Top the divide north of the rocky crest at mile 11.6 (12,360). No trail is apparent from here to San Luis Pass, and posts and claim stakes make the descent confusing. From mile 11.6, descend 0.3 mile to the northwest, staying above the willows below. Continue your slow descent until San Luis Pass comes into view below, then descend steeply west to the pass at mile 12.2 (11,920). Creede is about 10 miles distant on the trail which descends south down the valley.

San Luis Peak

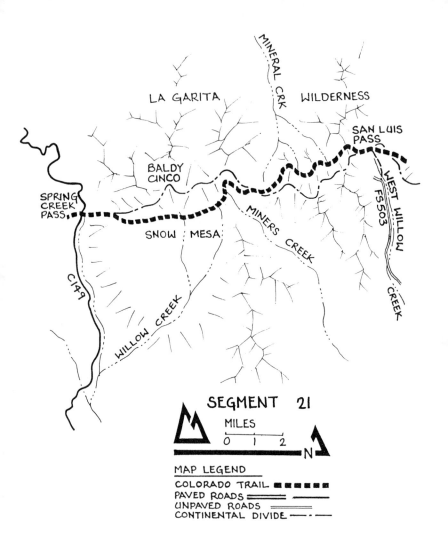

SEGMENT 21

MILES

0 1 2

N

MAP LEGEND

COLORADO TRAIL ■■■■■■
PAVED ROADS ═══════
UNPAVED ROADS ═════
CONTINENTAL DIVIDE ─·─·─

LA GARITA

MINERAL CRK

WILDERNESS

SAN LUIS PASS

BALDY CINCO

SPRING CREEK PASS

WEST WILLOW

FS 503

C149

SNOW MESA

MINERS CREEK

WILLOW CREEK

CREEK

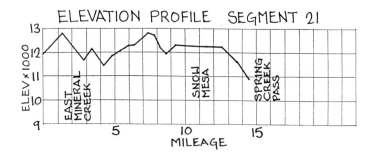

ELEVATION PROFILE SEGMENT 21

ELEV × 1000

13
12
11
10
9

EAST MINERAL CREEK

SNOW MESA

SPRING CREEK PASS

5   10   15

MILEAGE

Segment 21
San Luis Pass to Spring Creek Pass

Introduction

This segment continues a challenging, but exceedingly rewarding, portion of the CT along the old Skyline Trail, which began in the previous segment. The high-altitude route is sometimes poorly identified and the short sections of trail that do exist are too infrequent. Map and compass are a must, as is a knowledge of orienteering. North slopes on the route are likely to be snowed in until mid-July, and you might encounter significant lightning hazard on the many exposed ridges and on Snow Mesa.

Much elevation is gained and lost as the CT mounts high ridges and then dives into the headwaters of East and Middle Mineral creeks, where campsites can be found in the protection of upper-limit spruce forests. Snow Mesa provides an alpine experience unlikely to be forgotten, as the CT makes its way along an old stock driveway whose cairns and posts still remain. Mountain bicyclists should refer to their chapter for the mandatory detour around the wilderness area.

There is something magical about hiking through the La Garita Wilderness, something almost spiritual in its primeval isolation. The Spanish term means "The Lookout" and conjures up visions of conquistadors probing uncharted territories, though the area was very likely named by Indians who used the mountains as signal stations. It was probably among the high ridges of the La Garita Mountains that Frémont's expedition met disaster during the winter of 1848-49, although no one knows for sure.

Nicholas Creede probably never dreamed of the rowdy town that would spring up after he staked out his Holy Moses Mine on East

Willow Creek in 1889. Creede, like other high-spirited mining communities, had its share of riffraff. The most notorious were Soapy Smith and Bob Ford. Ford, the killer of Jessie James, was himself shot to death while residing in Creede. The town was made famous by Cy Warman's poem of the day, which could have typified many of Colorado's mining towns:

Here's a land where all are equal
Of high or lowly birth
A land where men make millions
Dug from the dreary earth
Here meek and mild-eyed burros
On mineral mountains feed
It's day all day in the day time
And there is no night in Creede.

The cliffs of solid silver
With wondrous wealth untold
And the beds of the running rivers
Are lined with the purest gold
While the world is filled with sorrow
And hearts must break and bleed
It's day all day in the day time
And there is no night in Creede.

Trailheads/Access Points

San Luis Pass Trail Access: Travel on Colorado 149 to Creede and go north on the town's main street. At the north edge of town, proceed into a dramatic, steep-walled, narrow canyon. One half mile beyond Creede, continue straight ahead on FS-503 as a side road forks to the right. Your car will need a good first gear and a little extra ground clearance to negotiate these extremely steep roads. Follow the Forest Service road north approximately 6.5 miles to the end of the improved dirt road at the entrance to the Equity Mine. A small parking area is provided here for conventional cars. FS-503 continues as a 4WD road, which you should follow north up the valley for another 1.6 miles, either on foot or in an appropriate vehicle, until it bears to the left (west) and climbs steeply over the high ridge. On foot, continue northward on the sometimes obscure trail in the narrowing valley bottom another 1.5 miles to San Luis Pass.

This access point is popular with people setting off to climb San Luis Peak, so you will probably have lots of company.

Spring Creek Pass Trailhead (Colorado 149): See Segment 22.

Supplies, Services and Accommodations

It is a 10-mile side trip into Creede from San Luis Pass. Descend on the trail south along the headwaters of West Willow Creek until you meet up with FS-503, then continue into town, where there is a backpacking store, grocery and various watering holes which recall the town's rip-roaring past. A Rio Grande National Forest district office is located here as well.

Maps

USGS Quadrangles: San Luis Peak, Baldy Cinco, Slumgullion Pass. USFS Maps: Gunnison National Forest, Rio Grande National Forest. CT Series: Maps 21, 22.

Trail Description

From the low point at the directional signs on the grassy saddle at San Luis Pass, ascend slightly, without the aid of any visible trail, a little south of west, entering a mass of willows after 500 feet of easy tundra walking. Fight your way through the willows until you reach the trail, visible ahead, which bends to the left (south) and ascends the steep hillside southwest of the pass. Follow the trail south while scraping against overgrown willows to mile 0.3 (12,080), where a post marks the end of the path from the pass. Make a sharp right (west) here and mount the top of a somewhat broad ridgeline, which becomes more defined as you gain elevation. Follow the ridge west toward the base of a rocky summit, Point 13,111, at mile 1.1 (12,760). A weathered post here signals the beginning of a short segment of trail and entry into the La Garita Wilderness.

Proceed northwest on the rocky trail to the east side of a long, grassy ridge which extends north from the steep slopes of Point 13,111. The trail disappears here, near a post on the grassy ridge at mile 1.3 (12,840). Massive San Luis Peak dominates the eastern horizon from this vantage point. Continue west over the ridge and descend southwest on the wide, grassy slope. Stay close to the slope's high point at right if you want to follow the dotted route shown on the USGS topo map. Bear to the left (south) at mile 1.6 (12,520) and cross a wide erosion course approximately 600 feet beyond. Don't be tempted to follow this channel downhill, but instead cross it and continue south until you pick up the beginning of a deeply eroded trail at mile 1.8 (12,320). Follow the trail as it leaves the grassy slopes to descend the steep walls of an amphitheater and continue to the alpine meadow below. Ford an upper tributary of East Mineral Creek at mile 2.0 (12,120), where an alpine camp could be set up. Descend slowly another 0.2 mile, where the trail fades out in thick tundra grasses.

Continue west, following a posted route which picks up the trail again at mile 2.4 (11,920), then traverse generally southwestward across a rockfall which is home to a variety of alpine flowers. Enter the trees at mile 2.5 (11,880) and continue several hundred feet on a descending trail to the lower end of a small open area. The trail continues to be obscure through here; it descends diagonally through the open area on an east-west axis until it reenters the trees on the opposite side, about 200 feet beyond. Proceed on the faint trail through a spruce forest to mile 2.6 (11,840), where the trail again opens out onto an inclined, linear clearing. At the eastern edge of this opening, an ancient directional sign confirms the intersection of the obscure East Mineral Creek Trail with the old Skyline Trail. Continue west 150 feet across the clearing and pick up the faint trail at the edge of the trees.

At mile 2.7 (11,800), the trail abruptly leaves the trees at the edge of a massive rockslide. Bear to the right (north) here and descend steeply to a stream crossing 250 feet beyond. Make a short but steep ascent after the ford and continue around the foot of the rock avalanche to mile 2.8 (11,720). Here the trail enters the trees and begins an ascent out of the East Mineral Creek drainage. Exchange the spruce forest for tundra and continue to mile 3.3 (12,160), where the trail fades out just below the saddle. Bear to the right (west-southwest) here and head for the post 200 feet beyond. This post marks the saddle between East and Middle Mineral creeks.

From the saddle, descend west through a few willows on a faint trail, which gives out after a few hundred feet. Continue the steep descent westward on a grassy slope, following a posted route which enters the trees just before the crossing of an intermittently-flowing streambed. Head southwest across the normally dry streambed at mile 3.6 (11,760), then continue descending to the southwest through an opening in the trees for about 200 feet and look for a blaze which marks the beginning of an old trail through the thick woods.

Proceed through a spruce forest to the edge of another clearing at mile 3.7 (11,720), where the trail fades away again. Descend diagonally west across the inclined meadow, following a posted route, and cross a small stream near the middle of the opening. Continue west and enter the trees at mile 3.8 (11,680), where the trail gradually reappears. If you plan to camp, consider using the established, convenient campsite here to help reduce your impact on the wilderness.

Cross the main drainage of Middle Mineral Creek 0.1 mile past this point, just downstream from a large beaver dam. A few steps beyond, the trail becomes indistinct for about 50 feet as it bears to the right (northwest) near the remains of a collapsed log cabin. Cross another tributary stream and continue to the trail's low point in this valley at mile 4.2 (11,480). Ascend through several switchbacks to the saddle between Middle and West Mineral creeks at mile 4.8 (11,840). Notice the evidence of a forest fire which burned long ago in the vicinity.

Continue southwest across the saddle, keeping a sharp eye out for the obscure trail, which is marked by old blazes. From the saddle, the path continues to ascend, bearing generally southwest through a spruce forest. Cross a prominent avalanche chute at mile 5.2 (12,000). A snowfield here usually lingers well into the summer. Continue west 0.1 mile, to a point where the trail exits the cool, north-facing spruce forest onto a west-facing, exposed rock face which can be uncomfortably warm on sunny summer afternoons.

The trail crosses a rockslide area just below some impressive cliffs and continues an ascent to the saddle visible ahead. In a north-facing gully just before the saddle, you may find that you have to cross a steep snowfield if hiking before late summer. Cross over the saddle at mile 5.7 (12,240) and continue on the faint trail, which generally follows the contour around an upper side-drainage of West Mineral Creek onto another north-facing slope with a potential steep snowfield crossing.

Enter a field of willows at mile 6.0 (12,280) and maneuver between the bushes, bearing generally west-southwest on a vague path which eventually is engulfed by the willows. A directional sign at mile 6.1 stands alone in a sea of willows and points out the junction of the obscure West Mineral Creek Trail and the Skyline Trail. From the sign, continue west through the willows to the grassy saddle between West Mineral Creek and Miners Creek at mile 6.3 (12,280). The saddle is marked with a solitary post. Ascend west-northwest on the broad ridge which extends upward from the saddle, following a posted route. Navigate as necessary through the willow patches and pick up the trail again at mile 6.7 (12,480), near the bottom of a talus slope. Bear to the left and continue ascending generally southward on a reemerging trail marked with posts. As the trail bends to the right (west) and levels out, it fades away at mile 7.1 (12,680), but a posted route continues northwest through lush alpine tundra just below the crest of the broad Continental Divide ridge.

At mile 7.4 (12,760), pick up a faint but recognizable trail which descends gradually to the west-northwest. The distinctive profile of Uncompahgre Peak is visible through the notch ahead. On the opposite side of the valley, to your left and below, is a curious rock formation reminiscent of the Wheeler Geologic Area. Continue a descent to mile 7.8 (12,600), where the CT obscurely but sharply forks to the left, off the old Skyline Trail, and descends into the split-level headwater bowl of Miners Creek below. The Skyline Trail continues west across a rockslide and through the notch ahead.

Without the aid of a trail, following cairns which define two long switchbacks, descend grassy slopes into the upper floor of the bowl at mile 8.2 (12,240). Continue down the cairned route, making a steep diagonal descent to the east-southeast, to the lower level. Follow the marked route around the left side of the lower level, staying up high enough to avoid a marshy area. Slowly bend to the right (south then south-southwest) around the perimeter of the bowl to the crossing of upper Miners Creek, near the edge of the lower level at mile 8.6

(11,920).

Begin a steep ascent southwestward out of Miners Creek, following a poorly-marked route through numerous rocks. At mile 8.9 (12,120), near the bottom of a long, inclined valley with a high ridge at right and a much lower, grassy ridge to the left, the route opens up. Angle to the left (south) briefly and ascend to the lower ridge, which is marked with stock driveway posts. Continue climbing to the south-southwest along the grassy ridge to mile 9.3 (12,360). This high point, just east of the pond at the head of Willow Creek, is on the extreme eastern portion of Snow Mesa. Continuing to follow the stock driveway cairns, bend to the right here and assume a more westerly bearing toward the south side of the pond.

Continue west across expansive Snow Mesa, following the infrequent driveway cairns as you gently dip into and out of several shallow branches of Willow Creek. If the weather is clear at mile 11.5 (12,360), the cairns and posts marking the southern boundary of the stock driveway and the route of the CT can be seen to stretch westward in front of you for more than a mile. A large rock cairn, barely visible at the western edge of the mesa, identifies the northern line of the driveway and should be ignored.

Continue west, following the southern line of the stock driveway cairns, to mile 12.6 (12,280), where a final cairn marks your approach to the western edge of Snow Mesa. Do not be misled by the large rock cairn to the north. Proceed west-southwest to the head of a prominent drainage which plunges off the western edge of the mesa. An obscure but important post at mile 12.7 (12,240) signals the beginning of a trail which descends into the drainage. The rocky trail makes a gradual bend to the right (west), then rises slowly on the north side of the drainage and enters the trees at mile 13.0 (11,840). Next, it descends through the spruce forest, bearing generally west to west-northwest, on an obscure trail marked with old blazes.

Angle to the right (northwest to west-northwest) and leave the old trail shown on the USGS topo map at mile 13.4 (11,640) as it exits the forest and enters a meadow dotted with a few stands of spruce. Views ahead are of Jarosa Mesa and the lopsided summit of Uncompahgre Peak. Continue cross country across the meadow, following blazes on occasional trees. The route enters a stand of spruce at mile 13.6 (11,600). Bend to the right here and take on a more northerly bearing for approximately 200 feet as the obscure route dips slightly into a shallow gully. Bear to the left (west) and descend in a small clearing ringed with spruce to mile 13.7 (11,560). Enter the trees again and follow the route as it bears to the right (west-northwest) and traverses approximately 200 feet to the Continental Divide, which is forested here and barely recognizable as the backbone of the continent. Descend on the crest of the divide due west, on a route that has been cleared and blazed but which might be difficult to spot in places.

As you approach Spring Creek Pass, Colorado 149 is visible below through the spruce and aspen. Exit the trees just above the highway and cross the diversion ditch ahead. The ditch sends water from the headwaters of Cebolla Creek to the eastern slope. End this segment at mile 14.5 (10,898), where Colorado 149 tops the Continental Divide at Spring Creek Pass.

Segment 22
Spring Creek Pass to Carson Saddle

Introduction

With an average elevation in excess of 12,000 feet, this segment has the distinction of being the loftiest single portion of the CT. Not surprisingly, it also tops out at the trail's high point, 13,334-foot Coney Summit. The trail winds its way along the broad, grassy, alpine ridges of the Continental Divide and only twice drops down to suitable camping areas, once at Big Buck Creek and again at Ruby Creek. Otherwise the entire route is waterless. (If necessary, you can find water by descending from the saddle between Jarosa Mesa and Antenna Summit to the north into Rambouillet Park, or to the south into the headwaters of Buck Creek.)

This segment, like the previous one, is a challenging alpine route. Although a well-defined jeep road does exist for the first ten miles, the next seven miles to Coney Summit are entirely without trail, with only an occasional stock driveway cairn to mark the way. Map and compass are essential, as is a knowledge of orienteering. Mountain bicyclists are given the option of detouring around this segment on a 4WD Forest Service road.

Hiking on this segment's grassy, rolling highlands and extensive rockfields is not particularly dangerous in itself. But late-lingering snowfields, which may not melt until well into July, can turn the route into a threatening obstacle course. Likewise, frequent summer thunderstorms pose a significant lightning hazard.

On the positive side, this exposed ridge walk abounds with views nearly every step of the way. To the southwest are the Needle Mountains and Grenadier Range, while to the west, in a confusing

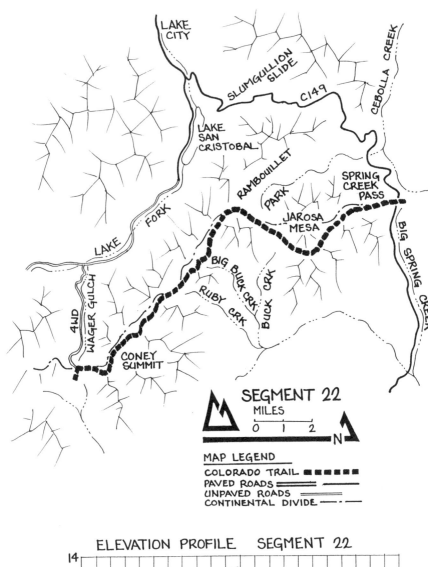

LAKE CITY

SLUMGULLION SLIDE

C149

CEBOLLA CREEK

LAKE SAN CRISTOBAL

RAMBOUILLET

PARK

SPRING CREEK PASS

JAROSA MESA

LAKE FORK

4WD WAGER GULCH

BIG BUCK CRK

RUBY CRK

BUCK CRK

BIG SPRING CREEK

CONEY SUMMIT

SEGMENT 22

MILES

0 1 2

N

MAP LEGEND

COLORADO TRAIL ■■■■■■
PAVED ROADS ══════
UNPAVED ROADS ══════
CONTINENTAL DIVIDE ─·─·─

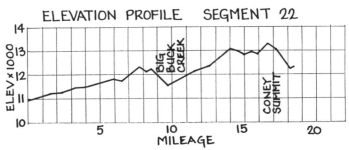

ELEVATION PROFILE SEGMENT 22

BIG BUCK CREEK

CONEY SUMMIT

ELEV×1000

14
13
12
11
10

5 10 15 20

MILEAGE

jumble of summits, are three popular fourteeners, Handies, Redcloud and Sunshine peaks. To the north, down in the valley of the Lake Fork, is Colorado's second-largest natural body of water, Lake San Cristobal.

Although there is some controversy over the naming of the lake, there is no question as to how it was formed. Somewhere between 700 and 350 years ago, the still-active Slumgullion Earthflow (a massive landslide-earth-mud-flow complex, called "Slumgullion" because its brightly colored, mineralized contents reminded New Englanders of the discarded entrails of a slaughtered whale) detached itself from the Cannibal Plateau and flowed down to dam the valley, creating emerald-green Lake San Cristobal. The great, cliff-forming escarpments through here were formerly thought to be lava flows extruded on the surface, but are now recognized to have been formed out of airborne ash so hot that it was welded together upon deposition, forming a dense, crystalline rock layer.

The most likely, if not the most romantic, explanation for the naming of Lake San Cristobal holds that it was named by the engineers of the H.G. Prout Ute Reservation survey of 1873. It seems one of the engineers, a Cornishman, was a great admirer of Tennyson, and one night around the campfire persuaded his colleagues to bestow on the lake the name of one of the poet's fictional landscapes.

Trailheads/Access Points

Spring Creek Pass Trailhead (Colorado 149): This obvious trailhead is located where Colorado 149 tops out on the Continental Divide at Spring Creek Pass. The pass is approximately 17 miles southeast of Lake City and 33 miles northwest of Creede. A few picnic tables and a pit toilet are the only facilities you will find here. A jeep road, FS-550, continues west from the top of the pass along the Continental Divide and serves as the CT route for the first several miles of this segment.

Carson Saddle-Wager Gulch Road Trail Access: See Segment 23.

Supplies, Services and Accommodations

It is 17 miles to Lake City on Colorado 149 from Spring Creek

Pass. The town has a grocery, a few local pubs and cabins which are usually full during the tourist season.

Maps

USGS Quadrangles: Slumgullion Pass, Lake San Cristobal, Finger Mesa. USFS Maps: Gunnison National Forest, Rio Grande National Forest. CT Series: Maps 22, 23.

Trail Description

Begin at the cul-de-sac pullout on the west side of Colorado 149 at Spring Creek Pass (10,898). This is not an official campground and no services, other than picnic tables and a pit toilet, are available here. The CT follows FS-550 as it ascends steeply west from the cul-de-sac, then levels off in a spruce forest punctuated with meandering meadows. Continue on the jeep road and notice the headwaters of Rito Hondo Creek off to the left (south) and below at mile 1.6 (11,040).

Cross a small stream at mile 2.5 (11,320) while ascending toward Jarosa Mesa on the jeep road through a wide corridor in the spruce forest. Notice the old stock driveway signs posted on tree trunks on either side of this elongated, ascending meadow. Top out on a grassy field at mile 2.7 (11,480), east of wide, rolling Jarosa Mesa, which appears emerald green because of its extensive covering of willows. Bear to the left (southwest) as the sometimes indistinct jeep track continues around the perimeter of the mesa. Snow Mesa and Bristol Head can be identified to the east, and the unique cone of Rio Grande Pyramid is visible ahead.

The jeep track penetrates the willows at mile 3.3 (11,520) and continues its traverse around the southeast side of Jarosa Mesa. Exit the willows at mile 4.1 (11,480) as the jeep track gradually ascends west, then northwest. Take the right fork (north-northwest), marked as FS-550, at mile 5.8 (11,840). The summit of Jarosa Mesa east of here appears nearly flat. Those considering camping in this area will have to descend into Rambouillet Park to the north or into the headwaters of Buck Creek to the south in order to find water.

Descend slightly to another jeep track junction at mile 6.5 (11,720), where an unmarked fork goes to the left. FS-550 continues its descent north into the willows, drops into Rambouillet Park and continues on to rejoin Colorado 149. The unmarked jeep track at left traverses around the south side of Antenna Summit (12,305), so called because of the radio tower at its top, and rejoins the official CT route in 1.4 miles. To continue on the official route, head northwest on the grassy tundra between the two jeep tracks, toward a very obvious swath cut in the willows. This swath ascends to the smooth, rounded top of Antenna Summit. Climb northwest, then west, to the summit at mile 7.8 (12,305), using the convenient corridor cleared through the willows. The photovoltaic antenna array on top seems strangely out of place here in the wilds. Five fourteeners are visible from here (can you identify them?), as well as the path of Slumgullion Slide, which dammed Lake San Cristobal in the valley below.

To continue, bear generally south-southwest from the summit and pick up the route of the stock driveway as it descends to the saddle at mile 8.2 (12,040). Join up with the jeep track which traverses the south side of Antenna Summit, and follow it 0.2 mile uphill (southwest) to another grassy knob on the divide. Begin a slow descent southwest on the jeep track, which follows the rolling highland. As you approach timberline, the jeep track drops more

Hiker approaching 13,334-foot Coney Summit

quickly until it levels off at mile 9.8 (11,480), in a gently inclined meadow, ringed with spruce, on the headwaters of Big Buck Creek. The route here varies greatly from that shown on the USGS map.

Bear to the right (west) on the jeep track and ascend an elevated, marshy side drainage. Just before crossing the saddle visible ahead, leave the jeep track at mile 10.3 (11,720) and bear to the left (south), following a series of posts 600 feet across the grassy marsh. Pick up a set of jeep tracks as you enter a spruce forest and continue a sometimes steep ascent through the forest, bearing generally south.

At mile 11.0 (12,000), break out of the trees onto the lower end of a broad, slightly inclined, willow-covered ridge which extends west toward the grassy crest of the Continental Divide. Follow the indistinct jeep track in a more westerly direction through the willows. As you progress, an unmistakable swath develops in the willows. The swath slowly assumes a more southwesterly direction. As the willows become patchy and the swath less recognizable, the CT bears west again. Try to pick out two barely recognizable switchbacks beyond the willows on the grassy tundra ahead. The trail bears to the south as it exits the willows at mile 11.6 (12,200). Switchback to the right (northwest) in 200 feet, and then to the left (south) in 250 feet. The route through here, confirmed by carsonite posts, continues on an alpine footpath which bears generally south-southwest near the edge of the willows.

The route assumes a more southwesterly direction at mile 12.6 (12,440) as it heads for an indistinct, rocky saddle on the Continental Divide one half mile beyond. Pick up a short trail remnant at the saddle, then begin a curvilinear ascent into a grassy upper bowl to the right of the impressive cirque which forms the main drainage of Ruby Creek. Take advantage of a short section of trail which climbs steeply through several switchbacks to a rocky point on the Divide at mile 14.0 (13,040). Weather permitting, take a few minutes to observe the dramatic, rarefied surroundings and your route along the Divide to this lofty position. Follow the route marked with carsonite posts as it bears generally south-southwest, detouring around patches of talus and rock where necessary, near the crest of this huge, rolling highland. Views extend all the way to San Luis Peak on the northeast horizon. At mile 14.5 (13,000), the route bends to the southwest, then west, where a saddle becomes visible.

Descend to the saddle at mile 15.0 (12,840) and then immediately begin a diagonal ascent to the south-southwest, crossing an inclined rock field to the gentle slopes of another, though smaller and rockier, alpine highland. This ascent does have small pieces of trail near its top, which is marked with a cairn. Contour to the right (southwest), still following the route of the stock driveway. At mile 15.5 (12,960), yet another saddle comes into view to the southwest. Descend to this saddle at mile 15.9 (12,840) and then begin an ascent south-southwestward to the highest point on the entire CT, just below 13,334-foot Coney Summit.

Take a minute to ponder your route to Coney Summit from here. The route shown on the USGS map ascends a steep, north-facing talus slope, which levels out on the left (east) side a little below the top. Until midsummer, however, this route can be blocked by a steep and potentially dangerous snowfield. If the official route is snowed in, it is possible that a narrow, grassy corridor between the snowfield and a steep dropoff at the very crest of the divide (west of and above the official route) might be thawed out at an earlier date. If this alternative is also snowed in, it is much more dangerous than the official route, described below. If the entire face is snowed in, the only reasonable alternative for those without mountaineering skills would be a drastic descent into the headwaters of Kitty Creek.

To follow the official CT route to Coney Summit, ascend south-southwest from the saddle. Head slightly more to the south at the steep talus slope, then pass to the left (east) and a little below Coney Summit at mile 16.6 (13,280). This is the high point of the CT. Widely-spaced stock driveway markers identify this route. A few steps uphill lead you to the Divide at Coney's 13,334-foot summit.

From the top, an indistinct jeep track begins and descends south-southwest to a grassy saddle between Coney Summit and Point 13,277 at mile 17.1 (13,080). Bear to the right (west-northwest) on an obvious jeep road and descend steeply into the old Carson mining district. Go right (west-northwest) on an intersecting jeep road at mile 18.1 (12,320). Continue to a three-cornered jeep-road intersection in Carson Saddle, where this segment ends at mile 18.3 (12,360). One jeep road descends from this saddle northward into Wager Gulch, while the route of the CT bends to the left (south) and descends into the headwaters of Lost Trail Creek.

reasonable alternative for those without mountaineering skills would be a drastic descent into the headwaters of Kitty Creek.

If you wish to follow the official CT route to Coney Summit, ascend south-southwest from the saddle. Head slightly more to the south at the steep talus slope, then pass just to the left (east) and a little below Coney Summit at mile 17.0 (13,280). This is technically the high point of the CT. Widely-spaced stock driveway markers identify this route. A few more steps uphill to the west will put you on the crest of the divide at Coney's 13,334-foot summit.

From the top, an indistinct jeep track begins and descends south-southwest to a grassy saddle between Coney Summit and Point 13,277 at mile 17.5 (13,080). Bear to the right (west-northwest) on an obvious jeep road and descend steeply into the old Carson mining district. Go right (west-northwest) on an intersecting jeep road at mile 18.5 (12,320). Continue to a three-cornered jeep-road intersection in Carson Saddle, where this segment ends at mile 18.7 (12,360). One jeep road descends from this saddle northward into Wager Gulch, while the route of the CT bends to the left (south) and descends into the headwaters of Lost Trail Creek.

Segment 23
Carson Saddle
to Rio Grande Reservoir-Stony Pass Rd.

Introduction

The challenging, high-altitude route of the CT continues into this segment, although now more of the way is on established trails which make the going a little easier. The only places you will have to bushwhack, through thick and sometimes marshy tundra grasses, are brief stretches on the upper parts of Lost Trail and Pole creeks. In the case of Pole Creek, it is important that you carefully maintain your bearings at the head of Cataract Gulch or you may find yourself incorrectly marching down the trail to Cataract Lake. As in the previous segments, you should have a map and compass handy to confirm your route.

Campsites abound along Lost Trail Creek and the broad, grassy meadows of upper Pole Creek, where trout splash in the meandering watercourse. Mountain bicyclists may opt to detour around this segment using the Cinnamon Pass Road (refer to Mountain Bicycle Route).

The old Carson mining district began when Christopher J. Carson discovered gold-bearing ores here in the early 1880s. The town of Carson, which still exists as a well preserved ghost town, developed at the head of Wager Gulch about a mile north of the mining district. Most of the supplies, however, were sent in from the south via the road, built in 1887, up Lost Trail Creek. The most prolific producers here were the Bonanza King and the St. Jacob's mines, but by the early 1900s even these once-fruitful mines had been abandoned.

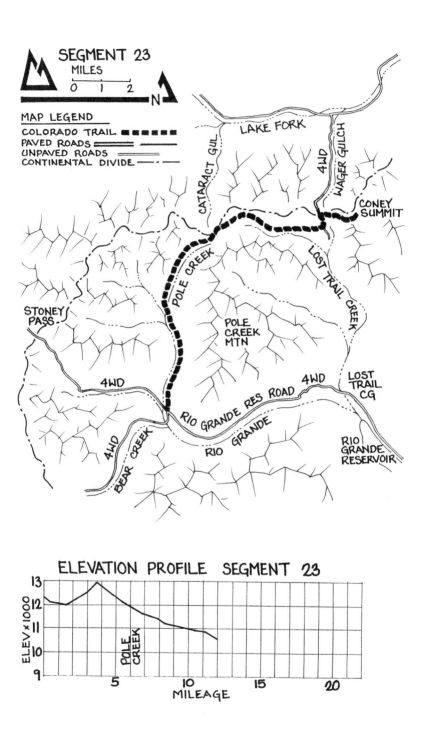

SEGMENT 23

MILES
0   1   2

N

MAP LEGEND
COLORADO TRAIL
PAVED ROADS
UNPAVED ROADS
CONTINENTAL DIVIDE

LAKE FORK

CATARACT GUL

4WD

WAGER GULCH

CONEY SUMMIT

POLE CREEK

LOST TRAIL CREEK

STONEY PASS

POLE CREEK MTN

4WD

4WD

BEAR CREEK

RIO GRANDE RES ROAD

4WD

LOST TRAIL CG

RIO GRANDE

RIO GRANDE RESERVOIR

ELEVATION PROFILE SEGMENT 23

ELEV×1000

13
12
11
10
9

POLE CREEK

5   10   15   20
MILEAGE

Trailheads/Access Points

Carson Saddle-Wager Gulch Trail Access: From Lake City travel south on Colorado 149 approximately 1.5 miles to a turnoff which leads right to Lake San Cristobal. Continue 9.3 miles on the road up the valley of the Lake Fork to the 4WD turnoff at left, which leads to Wager Gulch and Carson. It is approximately five miles up this rough road to Carson Saddle, so called because it is a low point on the Continental Divide about a mile beyond the old mining town of Carson.

Rio Grande Reservoir-Stony Pass Road: See Segment 24.

Supplies, Services and Accommodations

Available at Lake City (see Segment 22).

Maps

USGS Quadrangles: Finger Mesa, Pole Creek Mountain. USFS Maps: Gunnison National Forest, Rio Grande National Forest. CT Series: Maps 23, 24.

Trail Description

From the three-cornered jeep road at Carson Saddle, gradually descend southward on the road past the ruins of the old mining district. Be alert for the trail to bear obscurely off the jeep road at mile 0.5 (12,200) just before the road turns east for a steep descent into the valley ahead. The trail angles away from the road, then quickly rounds a ridge line and assumes a westerly heading high above Lost Trail Creek. The trail descends slowly to a side stream and a low point at mile 1.5 (12,000), though still well above the wide, marshy valley bottom of the main creek drainage. Dead ahead is a formidable-looking rock outcropping, through which the trail skillfully weaves its way for the next 0.3 mile. This area of rock and talus is notorious for remaining heavily snowed-in during early summer.

Once through the rocky obstacle course, the CT opens into the upper portion of a wide, gently inclined, grassy meadow at the head of Lost Trail Creek and trends a few degrees north of west. The trail, which is obscure at times in the thick alpine grasses, stays in the upper part of the meadow away from the tangled mass of willows closer to the creek and ascends to the right of the rather ominous cliffs visible at the head of the valley. As you progress, the CT bears west-northwest as it gains elevation on the hillside, pulling away from the wide valley floor. At mile 3.0 (12,560), the trail ties into a switchback, part of an older footpath that descended into the extreme upper end of the valley. Continue an ascent, past the rocky, gnome-like figures, so typical of the San Juans, and continue an ascent to the pass at mile 3.6 (12,920).

From the pass, the trail makes a gradual descent to the west, high above the headwaters of Pole Creek. Follow the trail southwest as it settles onto a broad, descending ridge of the Continental Divide and approaches a prominent cliff at the head of the cirque which forms Cataract Gulch. Reach an important saddle and trail intersection at mile 5.0 (12,360), near the cliff above Cataract Lake. The CT bears to the left (southwest) here as another trail continues ahead eventually to descend northward into Cataract Gulch. Proceed south-southwest, descending into the headwaters of Pole Creek on an intermittent trail across a broad, marshy alpine meadow. The trail reappears at mile 5.5 (12,120), on the north side of the creek, and continues a sometimes steep descent into the long and spacious upper valley, which is carpeted with fringed gentian in late summer.

Continue southwest to south-southwest on a nearly flat and sometimes faint trail which follows the meanderings of Pole Creek. The broad valley narrows into a tighter, V-shaped gap beyond mile 6.9 (11,680). Cross briefly to the east side of Pole Creek at mile 7.8 (11,480), then return to the west side 800 feet beyond. It is impossible to keep your feet dry at these crossings unless you are on horseback.

The trail leaves the narrow gap at mile 8.3 (11,280) and leads into another rolling meadow at timberline. A side trail forks sharply to the right (northwest) here and ascends North Fork Pole Creek. Continue south-southeast 150 feet beyond the trail junction and make a final ford to the east side of Pole Creek. The trail follows a grassy bench south-southeast slightly above the creek, passing many campsites.

Another intersecting side trail at mile 9.0 (11,200) forks sharply to the right (west) and ascends West Fork Pole Creek. Continue south 400 feet beyond the trail junction, and be sure to take a short walk off the trail to view scenic Pole Creek Falls.

The trail continues a gradual descent to the south, staying on a grassy, spruce-lined bench while Pole Creek drops off further and further below. Several intersecting side streams provide water for those wishing to camp along the way. The trail drops to the level of Pole Creek at mile 10.4 (10,960) and enters another long, grassy meadow ringed with willow and spruce.

Pass through a gate at mile 11.1 (10,920) and pause briefly to check out the CT's route up the valley of Bear Creek, visible extending for several miles to the south-southwest. Begin a short but steep descent from the elevated meadows. Pole Creek roars as it accelerates in the gorge at right. Ignore an intersecting trail which forks to the right at mile 11.7 (10,600) and continue ahead (south) through a grassy meadow. This segment ends as the trail intersects the Rio Grande Reservoir Road (Stony Pass Road) at mile 12.0 (10,560). A sign here indicates that the reservoir is down the road to the left (southeast and east) and Stony Pass to the right (northwest and west).

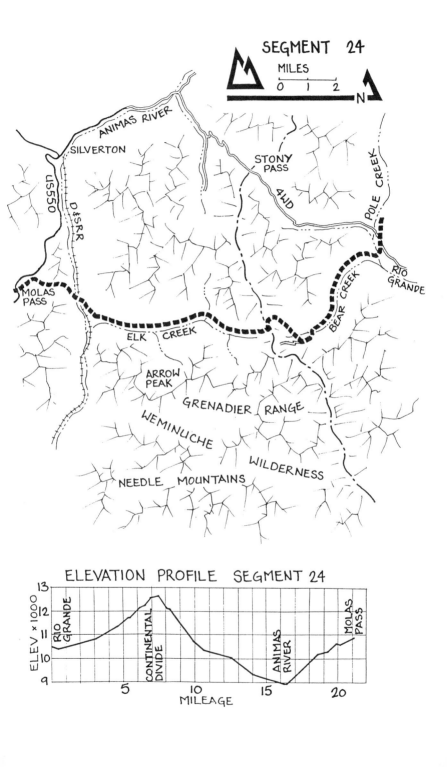

SEGMENT 24

MILES
0 1 2

N

ANIMAS RIVER

SILVERTON

US550

D&SRR

STONY PASS

4WD

POLE CREEK

RIO GRANDE

MOLAS PASS

ELK CREEK

BEAR CREEK

ARROW PEAK

GRENADIER RANGE

WEMINUCHE

WILDERNESS

NEEDLE MOUNTAINS

ELEVATION PROFILE SEGMENT 24

ELEV × 1000

13
12
11
10
9

RIO GRANDE

CONTINENTAL DIVIDE

ANIMAS RIVER

MOLAS PASS

5   10   15   20
MILEAGE

Segment 24
Rio Grande Reservoir-Stony Pass Road to Molas Pass

Introduction

The mystical San Juan Mountains reach a crescendo in the rugged and beautiful Needle District and Grenadier Range. This 21.1-mile segment penetrates much of this spectacular scenery and, for the last time, crosses the Continental Divide. Mountain bicyclists will have to bypass this segment, because the CT passes through part of the Weminuche Wilderness.

Hikers have plenty of challenges in this segment, starting with the crossing of the Rio Grande. This is the widest ford on the entire CT, and is precarious, deep and frigid. Keep your boots and socks on; you will never make it barefoot in the numbing waters. Bring an extra pair of dry socks along as a favor to your feet.

For the first five miles of this segment, the CT follows a 4WD road up Bear Creek. Kite Lake, at the head of the creek, is a popular destination for jeepers and you may be able to hitch a ride across the Rio Grande, and perhaps all the way to Beartown, in a 4WD vehicle. With the exception of a few mine dumps, nothing remains today of Beartown, which was a bustling mining community in the 1890s.

Another challenge to hikers is the extreme, almost dizzying, steepness of the headwaters of Elk Creek. Snowfields in Elk Creek's narrow gorge may linger well into July, and could be a hazardous obstacle, even for experienced mountaineers.

Once backpackers arrive at the Animas River, they will be confronted with a unique choice: either to finish the last 70 miles of the CT or take a nostalgic shortcut to Durango via the narrow gauge railroad. This curious remnant of the past was constructed in 1882 by the D&RG and remained part of the system into the early 1980s, when it was sold to a new company that maintains the line as one of Colorado's historical highlights. Don't be tempted to hike down the railroad tracks in the narrow Animas River canyon; locomotives can appear quickly around blind corners, and it's illegal anyway.

The enthusiasm which a certain Captain Charles Baker had for the San Juans was unfortunately never justified by the quantity of gold he panned from its rivers. But after the Confederate's untimely death – at the hands of the Indians on whose land he was trespassing – other prospectors discovered a bonanza in the area's silver lodes. Eventually, enough pressure was exerted on the Utes to force them to cede a large portion of their reservation in the infamous Brunot Treaty of 1873. Soon after, the valleys around Bakers Park echoed with activity. The little mining town of Silverton sprang up in the park and thrived for nearly 20 years, until the Sherman Silver Purchase Act was repealed in 1893, devastating the economy of the area. By then, however, the region had received its legendary nickname, by which it is still known by many today: the Silvery San Juan.

Trailheads/Access Points

Rio Grande Reservoir-Stony Pass Road: From Creede, drive west on Colorado 149 for 21 miles and turn left on the side road marked "Rio Grande Reservoir." Continue 19 miles to where the graded dirt road ends and the 4WD road begins. From here on, the road is rough, occasionally steep, often muddy and sometimes impassable. Continue seven miles to where the CT crosses the road at a sign reading "Pole Creek Trail."

US 550-Molas Pass: See Segment 25.

Supplies, Services and Accommodations

No convenient supply point.

Maps

USGS Quadrangles: Pole Creek Mountain, Rio Grande Pyramid, Storm King Peak, Snowdon Peak. USFS Maps: Rio Grande National Forest, San Juan National Forest. CT Series: Maps 24, 25.

Trail Description

Starting from where Pole Creek Trail joins the Rio Grande Reservoir-Stony Pass Road, go right (northwest) on the road about 150 feet, then make a sharp left (south) on the intersecting jeep road. A sign here marks this road as the way to Beartown. Gradually descend south on the jeep road to the difficult ford of the Rio Grande at mile 0.4 (10,440). If you are lucky, you will catch a ride across the river, which runs deep and cold, especially in early summer.

Once across the Rio Grande, follow the jeep road as it ascends west, then southwest, through a grassy, inclined valley bordered by a thick spruce forest. Pass through a gate at mile 3.1 (10,920) and ascend a half mile further to the lower end of a large meadow. As the jeep road enters several scattered groups of spruce and begins an ascent out of the upper end of the meadow at mile 4.5 (11,320), it passes through the townsite of Beartown. The only signs of human occupation here are a few long-abandoned mine dumps. Fields of columbine now bloom on these slopes, which were once trampled by the feet of fortune seekers.

Ford a tributary stream at mile 4.6 (11,360) and continue 500 feet beyond to a more challenging ford of Bear Creek's main flow. A trail which some backpackers use to continue along the Continental Divide via Starvation Pass peels off to the left (east) at mile 4.9 (11,400). To stay on the CT, proceed ahead (southwest) to timberline on the ascending jeep road. Here the remains of an abandoned mine are visible at left. Bear to the right at mile 5.3 (11,720), onto an old mine access road that has been closed to motorized traffic, then leave the jeeps behind on the dusty road, which continues straight ahead to Kite Lake. The trail which ascends Hunchback Pass is visible in places across the valley.

Continue through a wet alpine meadow blanketed with marsh marigold and willow, then cross to the north side of Bear Creek at mile 5.6 (11,720). Ford a tributary stream 80 feet beyond and ascend, steeply at times, into a higher alpine meadow just below the grassy ridge of the divide. The old road levels off briefly at mile 6.1 (12,080) and splits into two routes which roughly parallel each other for the next 0.4 mile. The official CT route follows the left fork. Across the valley are the remains of several cabins which might provide shelter during one of the frequent San Juan showers.

Ascend on the old road to a still higher alpine meadow, which is splashed with the colors of a thick carpet of wildflowers. The old road becomes more of a jeep track near the head of the valley at mile 6.5 (12,280), where the two paralleling routes diverge. The right-hand route continues north, up a narrow, V-shaped draw, and connects eventually with Stony Pass. The CT bears to the left (west), then quickly swings back to the north as it steeply climbs a rounded, grassy slope near the crest of the divide.

Follow the jeep track to the left as it bends to the west, then southwest, and slowly mounts the divide at mile 6.9 (12,600). Lingering snowfields here might obscure the route in places until mid-July. The jeep track bears due south as it follows the wide, rolling crest of the Continental Divide. The divide here is covered with marsh marigold that blooms where the tundra has been saturated by melting snowfields. On a clear day it is possible to pick out massive San Luis Peak and the long, horizontal profile of Snow Mesa to the east-northeast.

At mile 7.3 (12,680), the CT makes a sharp right (west), leaving the jeep track. The latter continues south along the divide, while the CT begins the descent to Elk Creek. The trail immediately loses 500 feet of elevation as it maneuvers through nearly 30 switchbacks, on an extremely steep mountainside seemingly held in place by the intertwining roots of an exquisite alpine flower garden.

The trail levels out briefly near an old mine cabin in the headwaters of Elk Creek at mile 8.3 (12,080), where a convenient camp could be set up. Below the cabin, the valley narrows dramatically into a tight gorge, bordered by sheer cliffs which feature numerous waterfalls. The descent from the Continental Divide through this gorge could be dangerous if blocked by snowfields in early to mid-summer.

The trail briefly crosses to the south side of Elk Creek at mile 8.6 (11,800), then returns to the north bank 0.2 mile beyond. As you continue, the creek plunges further down the gorge, leaving the trail perched a dizzying distance above. Enter the security of a spruce forest at mile 9.3 (11,400) and continue a steep descent, bearing generally west. The trail levels off and takes on a northwesterly heading somewhat nearer the creek at mile 9.8 (10,720). Campsites become more frequent here in the roomier valley below the gorge.

Ford a large side stream at mile 10.7 (10,320) as the CT swings to the west and gradually pulls away again from the creek. Descend a rocky trail in a sunny Douglas-fir and aspen forest at mile 12.6 (10,000), where the impressive faces of Vestal and Arrow Peaks are reflected in a picturesque but stagnant pond at trailside. The trail continues its descent, steeply at times, to mile 14.0 (9360), where it parallels the creek in a narrowing canyon. Listen for the whistle of the narrow gauge locomotive as the CT ascends slightly and pulls away from Elk Creek.

A sign and register at mile 15.5 (9040) mark your exit from the Weminuche Wilderness. There are two trails to choose from here. The lower, left-hand fork descends to a whistle stop siding on the D&SRR at Elk Park for those who would like a short cut to Durango. If you are continuing on the CT, take the right fork, which traverses northwest slightly above the Animas River and Elk Park. Cross the tracks at mile 16.1 (8940) and continue north 700 feet to a large, convenient bridge spanning the river.

About 600 feet beyond the bridge, ford Molas Creek and begin a monotonous, 1,300-foot ascent on a zigzagging trail with more than 30 switchbacks. One benefit of this ascending section is watching the spectacular Animas Canyon and Grenadier Range come into perspective. Notice the dramatic metamorphic folds in the huge rock wall just opposite the trail.

The trail tops out finally at mile 18.6 (10,280) and leaves the trees behind in a gently sloping meadow. Climb steeply through two vague and eroded switchbacks at mile 19.3 (10,360) as Molas Creek rushes down a nearby deep ravine. Take the left fork as the trail levels off just beyond. Ascend to the edge of a spruce forest at mile 19.8 (10,600), where the trail splits. The right (north) fork goes 0.2 mile further to the trailhead parking area just off US 550. To stay on the CT, bear to the left (west) and follow the trail as it curves around nearly 180 degrees and assumes a southerly bearing. Then ford Molas Creek at mile 20.1 (10,520). The trail makes several wide, meandering switchbacks underneath a powerline as it ascends, at times following a posted route through an alpine meadow. This segment ends at mile 21.1 (10,880) as the CT crosses US 550 just 600 feet north of that highway's summit on Molas Pass.

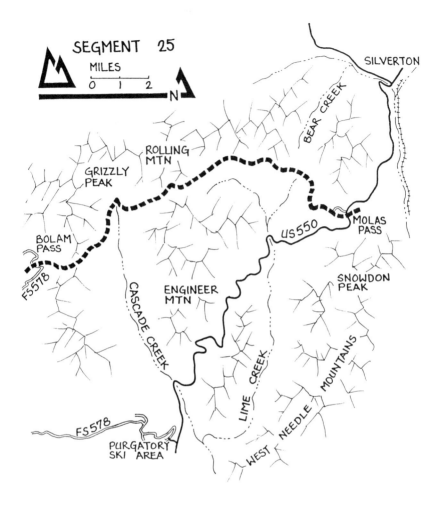

SEGMENT 25

MILES

0   1   2

N

SILVERTON

BEAR CREEK

ROLLING MTN

GRIZZLY PEAK

BOLAM PASS

FS578

US550

MOLAS PASS

CASCADE CREEK

ENGINEER MTN

SNOWDON PEAK

LIME CREEK

WEST NEEDLE MOUNTAINS

FS578

PURGATORY SKI AREA

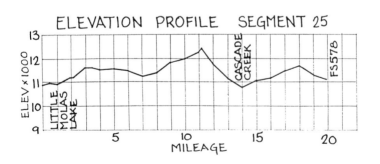

ELEVATION PROFILE   SEGMENT 25

LITTLE MOLAS LAKE

CASCADE CREEK

FS578

ELEV × 1000

13
12
11
10
9

5   10   15   20

MILEAGE

Segment 25
Molas Pass to Bolam Pass Road

Introduction

From US 550 westward the CT traverses a unique, rolling highland. Once heavily forested, the terrain was cleared by a devastating fire in 1879 and has not yet recovered, despite efforts at reforestation. One result of the fire is the unequalled panorama afforded by this highland segment, with views extending south to the La Plata Mountains and west to the Needles and Grenadiers. Prominent along this stretch of trail are 12,968-foot Engineer Mountain, known as Station 31 to the Hayden Survey, and 13,077-foot Snowdon Peak, which was named after the founder of Silverton, Francis Marion Snowdon. Approximately ten miles of the CT between Molas Pass and Rolling Mountain were built in 1987 by volunteer crews.

From US 550, the CT gradually climbs and then contours above Lime, North Lime and West Lime Creeks under a pediment of cliffs high above the trail. Large portions of this section have no forest cover, and snowfields may linger here until early July. Backpackers will want to tarry in this segment and perhaps set up a high-altitude camp in the shadow of Twin Sisters Peaks. Mountain bicyclists can rejoin the official route of the CT at Molas Pass after their long detour.

Trailheads/Access Points

US 550-Molas Trailhead: From Silverton, drive south on US 550 for 5.5 miles to a dirt drive on the left marked "Molas Lake-Molas Trail." An unmaintained road leads south from the parking area 0.2 mile to the CT.

Little Molas Lake Trail Access: From Molas Pass on US 550, go north 0.4 mile and turn left (west) on a dirt road. Continue one mile to Little Molas Lake. The CT is just northwest of the lake.

Supplies, Services and Accommodations

Silverton has groceries, accommodations and regular bus service. Molas Lake Campground, near Molas Trailhead, has limited supplies, as well as cold beer and hot showers.

Maps

USGS Quadrangles: Snowdon Peak, Silverton, Ophir, Engineer Mountain, Hermosa Peak. USFS Maps: San Juan National Forest. CT Series: Map 25.

Trail Description

This segment begins about 600 feet north of the sign which reads "Molas Pass Summit — Elev. 10,910" on US 550. Look for the trail on the west side of the highway. The CT soon crosses a cut in an old snow fence and meanders through gently rolling terrain, at times following a posted route, toward Little Molas Lake a little less than a mile away.

The trail goes to the west of and slightly above the lake. For the next mile or so the route is not adequately marked, and it will require a little care to stay on the trail. When you can see a small parking area by the lake, watch for the trail to bear left through a small wooded area; it does not go to the parking area. After coming out of the woods, the trail hits a road. Turn left here, go a hundred feet down the road and look for a blazed post on your right.

The CT now begins a series of gentle switchbacks through terraced terrain. Follow blazed posts in areas where the tread is not obvious. Notice the lodgepole pines planted after the 1879 fire. These trees do not appear to have done well as reforestation plantings. In 0.7 mile you will come to an old road. Stay right and go uphill on the road. In a half mile the CT turns a sharp 135 degrees to the right (northeast) onto another old road, which continues uphill along a broad ridgeline. The next 0.6 mile follows blazed posts. If you cannot see the posts, follow the old road uphill and eventually the posts will show on your left. Soon you'll see newly built trail ahead.

For the next several miles the CT follows the approximate route of an old pack trail. To stay on the new trail, follow blazed posts and avoid the old trail, which has been barricaded with rocks, stumps and logs. Approach the saddle between North Lime and Bear Creeks at mile 4.0 (11,520). To the north there is a nice view of Bear Mountain on the left and Sultan Mountain on the right. At mile 4.5 (11,560) a pack trail comes in from the right, although it is difficult to find. This side trail will take you down Bear Creek to US 550 northwest of Silverton.

At mile 5.0 (11,520) you get a 270-degree panorama of peaks. As you face the valley below, visible from right to left are Twin Sisters, Jura Knob, Engineer Mountain, Potato Hill, Twilight Peak, Snowdon Peak and the Needle Mountains.

Descend a few switchbacks and cross Lime Creek at mile 6.1 (11,340). For the next couple of miles you'll notice large conglomerate rocks that appear to have broken off the cliffs above. There are many, many cascades and waterfalls descending from above and lots of wildflowers everywhere. At mile 9.6 (11,920), just before you reach a small lake on your right, a stream comes out of the side of the mountain. This is a perfect place to fill water bottles.

At mile 10.3 (12,120) near a large lake, the CT joins the Engineer Mountain Trail. Make a sharp right turn here and begin following posts and cairns. At mile 11.0 (12,320) you'll turn left at the obvious trail intersection of the old Rico-Silverton Trail. To complete a loop hike, you can go right on the Rico-Silverton Trail to South Mineral Creek Campground.

Staying on the CT, cross the pass south of Rolling Mountain at mile 11.2 (12,490). On clear days this spot affords a view of Uncompahgre Peak to the northeast and the La Platas to the southwest. There is also a fantastic view of Grizzly Peak from here.

The CT now descends a series of steep switchbacks into the Cascade Creek drainage. This area has a variety of paintbrush and yellow compositae. At mile 12.3 (11,640) there are two trail intersections where care must be taken. The first is marked "Rico-Silverton Trail." Ignore the trail coming in from your right, and bear downhill to your left. In 200 feet a major intersection marked "White Creek Trail" requires a second decision. Turn right and follow the sign marked "Rico-Silverton Trail." For most of the next seven miles you'll see occasional Rico-Silverton Trail signs on the well-marked pathway. Cross Cascade Creek at mile 13.8 (10,820). During high water this crossing is hazardous to hikers, as the rocks are slippery and the water can be deep. There is a safer ford 400 feet upstream, where the creek is shallower and has a sandy bottom.

Continue on the CT to mile 14.2 (10,800), where the Cascade Creek Trail comes in from the left. Stay right on the Rico-Silverton Trail. If you take the Cascade Creek Trail, it will lead you down the valley to US 550 just north of Purgatory Ski Area. The CT now begins an ascent on the west side of the valley, then contours in and out of several side drainages. For the next few miles the trail affords views of the Cascade Village complex down the valley on the highway. You will also see some large areas logged by the clear-cut method, but fortunately the trail does not pass through any clear-cuts for another 15-20 miles.

At mile 18.1 (11,760) the trail crosses a saddle and drops into the upper part of Tin Can Basin and the Hermosa Creek drainage. In front of you, about two miles distant to the west, is Hermosa Peak, a prominent landmark visible for the next ten miles. To the north are the peaks of Lizard Head and the Wilson group. Descend to the north, following posts across the meadows. These will soon lead to an old road that is closed to vehicular traffic; turn left here and follow the posted road downhill into the timber. Very soon you will come to a road which allows vehicles. Turn left on this road and enjoy the views of the La Plata Mountains 20 miles distant. In 0.6 mile, be on the lookout for a large cairn on your left, which marks the CT as it goes into the trees. (If you miss this turn the road will take you to the unnamed lake mentioned below.) From the cairn, the trail goes into deep woods for less than 0.3 mile and emerges on FS 578 (Bolam Pass Road) at mile 19.9 (11,120), near the south end of an unnamed lake.

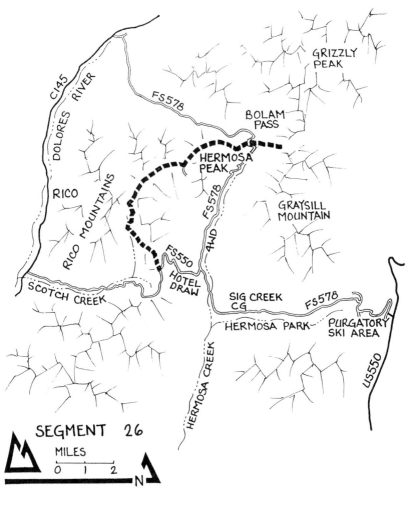

SEGMENT 26

MILES

0 1 2

N

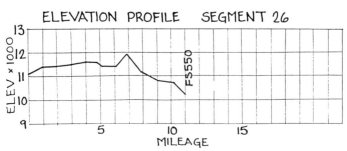

ELEVATION PROFILE   SEGMENT 26

ELEV × 1000

13
12
11
10
9

FS550

5   10   15

MILEAGE

Segment 26
Bolam Pass to Hotel Draw

Introduction

Hikers along this segment will continue to enjoy exceptional views, but will not encounter as many water stops as in the previous segment, primarily because the trail now stays near the crest of the range. Here, also, snowfields may linger well into July. The well-planned trail, built by volunteer crews in 1986, travels around Hermosa Peak and through the Rico Mountains before descending into the headwaters of Straight Creek to reach the end of the segment on FS-550.

From the start of this segment, the CT follows the scenic divide between the Animas and Dolores Rivers. These isolated ramparts were explored by a Hayden Survey team in 1874, one year after the Utes ceded a large part of their mineral-rich reservation. The expedition, led by the well respected geographer Allen Wilson and the articulate topographer Franklin Rhoda, ascended many peaks in the area, including Hermosa Peak, Blackhawk Mountain, Mount Wilson, Engineer Mountain and Vermillion Peak. This early team of surveyors can at least be partially credited with making sense out of the rugged jumble of mountains and valleys in southwestern Colorado.

Trespassing prospectors were testing the soil in the headwaters of the Dolores River long before the Brunot Treaty actually wrested the land from the Utes. But the boom didn't come until 1879, when lead carbonates rich in silver were discovered. So optimistic were the miners that they named their town and the surrounding mountains Rico, which means "rich" in Spanish.

Trailheads/Access Points:

Bolam Pass Trail Access (From US 550): Travel approximately 28 miles north of Durango on US 550 and turn into the Purgatory Ski Area entrance. At the upper parking area, bear right onto FS-578, a gravel road. At the top of the ridge the road heads north briefly; this approach then takes the left fork, marked with signs, to Sig Creek Campground and Hermosa Park. Follow FS-578 west, then north, being careful to take the right fork about a mile after the ford at Hermosa Creek (which requires 4WD or high-clearance vehicles during high water). Continue approximately seven miles up the rough road to a small lake. The CT skirts the southeast end of the lake. To the east the trail is marked with a cairn; to the west you will have to walk 300 feet into the woods to pick up the trail. There is room on the side of the road to park a few cars. The last mile of this approach may require 4WD vehicles.

Bolam Pass Trail Access (From Colorado 145): Travel approximately six miles north of Rico on Colorado 145 and turn right on FS-578, Barlow Creek Road. Climb steadily for seven miles. Soon after the road levels off, take a left where the road forks, then go another couple of miles until you come to the small lake mentioned above.

Hotel Draw Trail Access: See Segment 27.

Supplies, Services and Accommodations

Some supplies, but no groceries, are available at Purgatory Ski Area. Limited groceries and supplies are available in Rico.

Maps

USGS Quadrangles: Hermosa Peak. USFS Maps: San Juan National Forest. CT Series: Maps 25, 26, 27.

Trail Description

This segment begins at the south end of the small lake, just west of FS-578, mentioned in the trail access description. Walk toward the woods to the west and you should spot the trail in 100-200 feet. The trail here begins a gradual ascent as it goes around a steep ridge and heads for a saddle at the eastern edge of Hermosa Peak. There are excellent views of the La Plata Mountains to the south. In early

August this area is lush with red paintbrush.

After reaching the saddle, follow blazed posts and cairns along the edge of talus coming off Hermosa Peak. Soon you will come to a jeep track, where you turn right (northwest) and proceed for 0.1 mile to a 4WD road. Turn left (west) here and follow the road. As of 1988, the 4WD road was not marked with CT signs. Continue west on the road 1.3 miles around the north side of Hermosa Peak. The road begins to climb slightly and in about 0.3 mile the trail takes off to the right (west). The place where the CT leaves the road may not be clearly marked, but some cairns were placed at this point when the trail was constructed in 1986. The road continues past a nice meadow and heads south towards the Spanish King Mine.

The trail now generally follows the ridgeline for about three miles. Views abound in all directions, and include Grizzly Peak and San Miguel Peak to the north and the La Platas to the south. Just before Section Point, a snowfield may require an extensive detour in some years. As you enter the switchback at Section Point, don't be misled by a trail heading west to northwest down the ridge. The CT goes southwest after leaving the turn.

The trail soon enters a lush basin and begins climbing toward Blackhawk Pass. About 0.3 mile below the pass, and below a couple of switchbacks, is a nice spring coming out of a rock cliff. It may take a little looking for, but is a good place to fill water bottles. Top out on Blackhawk Pass at mile 6.9 (11,970). Take some time to enjoy the fine view from the pass. Nearby are dramatic red rock cliffs, while to the south are the La Platas and Indian Trail Ridge, which the CT follows. To the north is Lizard Head.

The CT now begins the descent into the Straight Creek drainage. The trail makes many wide, swinging switchbacks to maintain an easy, 7-8 percent grade. At mile 8.5 (10,980) the trail crosses Straight Creek. Just before the creek, a short 200-foot side trail leads uphill to a view of a nearby, six-cascade waterfall. This makes a nice rest stop.

The CT next follows the drainage downhill for about a mile and then bears southeast, away from the drainage, and heads for the top of a ridge. There are many nice meadows along the way. As you reach the ridge, at a point affording a view of Graysill Mountain a couple of miles to the east, the trail seems to end at a cairn. Look for a road which follows the top of the ridge southward. This road has now been closed to vehicles and reseeded. In a few years it may be overgrown and a new trail will be needed in this section. If you cannot follow the road, stay on top of the ridge for the next mile until you arrive at FS-550.

This segment ends here at mile 11.0 (10,400). The road you just descended is labeled 550-A and is blocked by a green Forest Service gate. Near the gate is a sign reading "Highline Trail." Just uphill from the gate you will find the benchmark noted on the USGS topographical map. (The map shows the elevation as 10,419 feet, but the benchmark itself shows 10,413 feet.) The CT continues south from here, following FS-550 along the ridge.

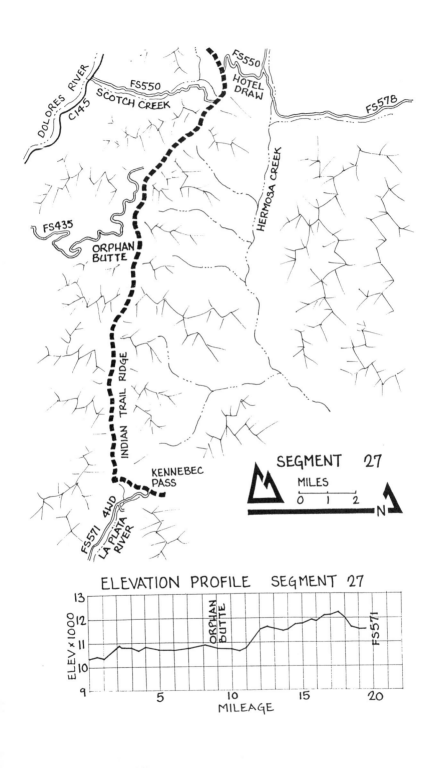

Segment 27
Hotel Draw to Cumberland Basin

Introduction

From the start of this segment at FS-550, the CT continues to follow the divide between the Animas and Dolores Rivers. Elevation is gained in a series of steps, with lots of mostly-level hiking in between. The trail is marked with numerous old blazes and cairns and labeled with old signs calling it either the Highline Trail or Trail 1520. There are, unfortunately, extensive areas of clear cutting where the old Highline Trail has been obliterated. Care must be used to follow the trail description to avoid getting lost or delayed in these areas, as they are not yet adequately marked or signed. To the relief of hikers who've been on this section, volunteers are scheduled to begin building new tread around these confusing logged areas in 1989.

Water may be difficult to find in this segment. Unless you're willing to scamper down off the ridge to find the headwater springs forming the considerable flows of Hermosa Creek or the Dolores River, you will have to content yourself with a few muddy springs between Orphan Butte and Indian Trail Ridge, or hold your thirst until reaching Taylor Lake at the end of this segment.

The first several miles of this segment follow FS-550 as it travels south on the ridge. This is the route of the historic Rico-Rockwood toll road. Completed in 1881, the latter connected the mining community of Rico to the smelter in Durango via Hermosa Park, and served the little town until Otto Mears built his Rio Grande Southern up the Dolores River in 1891. Weary travelers on the road at the mouth of Hotel Draw could rest at an inn operated by Hans Aspaas.

Evidence indicates that even these early-day pioneers were not the first to use the long Animas-Dolores divide. Indian Trail Ridge further south, as the name suggests, was very likely traversed not only by the Utes but perhaps even by people of pre-Columbian cultures.

Trailheads/Access Points

Hotel Draw Trail Access: Travel north from Durango on US

550 approximately 28 miles and turn into the Purgatory Ski Area entrance. At the upper parking area, turn right onto FS-578, a gravel road. At the top of the ridge follow the road as it turns north briefly, then take the left fork, which is marked with signs, to Sig Creek Campground and Hermosa Park. Follow FS-578 west and then north to the ford on Hermosa Creek, which requires a 4WD or high-clearance vehicle. About a mile after the ford, the road forks. At this point take a sharp left turn onto FS-550. The sign, which is sometimes shot full of holes, indicates Scotch Creek and Hotel Draw to the left. Go approximately 3.5 miles on FS-550, which is impassable if muddy, to a gate on the right (north), which is marked 550-A. There is room to park a few vehicles on the side of the road here. The CT leads north along the ridge beyond the gate; to the south, it follows FS-550.

This spot is also accessible from Colorado 145 by following FS-550, Scotch Creek Road, approximately seven miles.

FS-435 Trail Access: From Colorado 145 south of Rico, turn onto FS-435. When you reach a signed fork in the road take FS-564, which is complete all the way to FS-550. FS-564 is a good gravel road with gradual grades. It is a long drive, but does reach several access points along the CT (see trail description). Near Orphan Butte, there are numerous logging roads (closed to vehicles) that leave FS-564 and meander over to the CT.

Cumberland Basin Trailhead: See Segment 28.

Supplies, Services and Accommodations

Limited supplies are available at Purgatory Ski Area and Rico (see Segment 26).

Maps

USGS Quadrangles: Hermosa Peak, Elk Creek, Orphan Butte, La Plata. USFS Maps: San Juan National Forest. CT Series: Maps 27, 28.

Trail Description

From FS-550 and 550-A by the green gate, head south on FS-550, which follows the ridge. Within 0.7 mile the road begins a gradual climb and goes over a saddle. Do not make a left (east) turn on top of the saddle. Instead, bear right (west) and gradually descend. In a half mile be on the lookout for a fork marked with signs, and turn left (southwest) onto FS-564. FS-550 descends to the right (west-northwest) to Scotch Creek. Follow FS-564 for 350 feet and look for a sign reading "Trail" on your left. Pick up the trail on the left and begin a steep ascent. This section may be rebuilt in the future, using more gradual switchbacks and grades.

In about a mile, you will find a trail sign reading "Corral Draw Trail, Hermosa Creek—5" on the east edge of a small meadow. Ignore this side trail, which leads left (southeast), and continue ahead on the CT. Soon the trail leaves the Hermosa Peak USGS map and crosses a small corner of the Elk Creek map.

At mile 3.7 (10,800) the trail returns to FS-564 once again. For northbound hikers leaving the road, the trail is marked with large blazes on the trees at the edge of the forest. Southbound hikers follow the road to the left (south to southwest) 650 feet, where the trail leaves the road to the left and leads through the woods for a short 300 feet. Upon hitting the road again, turn left and continue on the road. (The 300-foot trail section just cuts across a hairpin turn in the road.) Follow the road for 550 feet (there are some blazed trees along this section). At another hairpin turn, the trail again leaves the road to the left (south) and begins a contour around the ridge. The trail here is narrow and goes through some high grass. Sheep graze in this area in summer.

The CT again hits FS-564 after 0.7 mile, traversing along the southeast side of the ridge. Turn left (south) on the road, follow it for 250 feet, and then turn left onto the trail again. Blazed posts mark trail intersections with the road in some cases. In 0.7 mile you'll find another intersection with FS-564. Turn left (south) onto the road for 300 feet and then look for the trail leaving the road to the left (south) again. All of these intersections provide good access points with some parking.

Continue southbound on the CT to mile 6.2 (10,620), where there is a signed trail intersection with the Big Bend Trail. If you leave the CT here and head uphill several hundred feet you'll come to FS-564 and a good off-road parking or camping area. In another half mile a side trail coming in from the right also leads to FS-564. Along this part of the ridge there are views of the spectacular Needle Mountains to the east.

At mile 7.6 (10,860) you come to a trail intersection which makes a "Y" in a meadow. Going to the left (east) is the Salt Creek Trail (Hermosa Creek 6). Continue on the right (south) fork to stay on the CT. Soon the trail emerges from the trees into a clear-cut area and joins an old logging road.

The next several miles will require some care to get through, as they lead through confusing, clear-cut logging areas. In general the trail stays on the ridge or slightly to the west of it. It alternates between trail and old logging roads. Look carefully for blazed posts, cairns and blazed trees next to the roads. A few small old signs are in use, too.

When you first reach the logging road a prominent landmark, Orphan Butte, is only a half mile ahead of you to the south. It is a small, 200-foot high, tree-covered knob, and has been clear-cut around its base, making it appear banded from a distance. Stay on the logging road, which goes around the butte on the east side. Northbound hikers should note that the point where the trail leaves the logging road north of Orphan Butte is marked by a blazed post in the flat area of a saddle. A few hundred feet past the butte, be alert to turn left (southeast then south) onto another logging road. Follow blazes on the trees and posts along the road for about 0.4 mile. Bear slightly left whenever there is a questionable turn. Watch for the trail to leave the road at around the 0.4-mile point. Where it leaves the road, turn left (south) and follow posts through a meadow. In 400 feet you'll enter the forest. In another 550 feet you'll leave the forest and enter a clear-cut area. For about a quarter mile more, follow blazes on old trees. The trail here is on the east side of the ridgetop and about 30 feet below it. After leaving the clear-cut area, the CT reenters the forest for 0.3 mile on an obvious trail. In this area you'll see a trail coming in from the left, but continue to the right (southeast).

Upon leaving the woods the trail enters another confusing area. The trail now bears southwest and starts to go slightly downhill, away from the top of the ridge. The clear-cut here is a conglomeration of high undergrowth, downed timber and dead stumps and snags. Look for blazed posts or blazes on trees and you can get through without climbing over downed timber. There is a cleared trail here, even though it's not always easy to see or follow. Within 700 feet you'll come to a logging road; bear left and follow it downhill. In just under 0.5 mile a road comes in from the left; ignore it and continue ahead downhill. In another 0.2 mile you'll come to a "T" intersection; turn left (south) and go uphill on a logging road. This 90-degree turn is marked with a sign high on a tree. In about 0.2 mile the road leaves the forest and enters another large clear-cut. Continue uphill. In 0.2 mile a road comes in from the left (east); ignore this and continue south-southeast. The trail heads for, and soon ascends, a rocky ridge. After passing the aforementioned road on the left, continue 700 feet and watch for a fork in the road. This inconspicuous point is marked by a blaze and an old sign high in a tree. Climb uphill on the left fork for a few hundred feet and look for the trail to begin at left, re-entering the trees. There may be cairns or flags hanging on branches to mark this turn. Once you find this entrance into the forest, the CT is easily followed for the next 10 miles.

The CT now climbs some steep switchbacks to the top of Indian Trail Ridge. At mile 12.6 (11,520), the trail intersects the Good Hope Stock Trail and Flag Point Trail (Hermosa Creek 12). This intersection is in a small meadow, where the trail almost disappears.

La Plata Mountains above Junction Creek Canyon

If you lose the trail in the meadow, you can pick it up at the far end where it reenters the forest. The Good Hope Stock Trail goes east over a rocky ridge called the Cape of Good Hope, then descends to Hermosa Creek. Stay on the CT by heading to the south end of the meadow.

After 1.7 miles of pleasant ridge hiking, with periodic views to the east, you'll arrive at the intersection with the Grindstone Trail at mile 14.3 (11,710). This intersection is well signed. The CT continues south and is marked with occasional signs as Trail 1520 or Highline Trail.

The next several miles are very scenic and the displays of wildflowers are spectacular. The CT begins a series of stair-like steps up the ridge. Every half mile or mile the trail dips to cross a saddle, then goes back up to a higher part of the ridge. A few places have steep dropoffs to the east side, but the trail is wide enough that it presents no real hazard, at least in good weather. This ridge walk would be very dangerous, however, during afternoon thunderstorms or high winds. It is best to plan to hike this stretch in the morning. Snowdrifts could hamper travel in this area until mid-July. On a clear day, seemingly all of the San Juan Mountains can be seen. The Wilson group, Lizard Head and Hermosa and Grizzly peaks are visible to the north, as are the Needle Mountains to the northeast. As you approach the highest point on the ridge, 12,338 feet in elevation, the views of the western La Platas are spectacular. Huge snowfields cover the north slopes above Bear Creek Basin, and Sharkstooth and Centennial Peaks are among the prominent landmarks.

After passing the spot on Indian Trail Ridge labeled on the USGS map as Point 12,258, you will come to an old sign reading "Trail 1520." Here the CT turns east and descends into Cumberland Basin. Below is Taylor Lake, and two miles beyond are three peaks of the eastern La Platas: Cumberland Mountain, Snowstorm Peak and Lewis Mountain. As you approach the lake, take the left (east) fork of the trail signed as "Highline Loop 520." This area is abundant with magenta paintbrush, columbine and delphinium at the end of July and in early August. At mile 19.7 (11,600) you'll reach the trailhead parking area, where an informational bulletin board is posted. FS-571, a 4WD road, descends south from here into La Plata Canyon.

Segment 28
Cumberland Basin
to Junction Creek Trailhead

Introduction

This segment is the final leg of the 469-mile trip from Denver. The trail tops out at scenic Kennebec Pass and begins its long descent to Durango. The drop from Kennebec Pass to Junction Creek Trailhead is 4,790 feet, the greatest single altitude change on the entire trail. In addition, there is a thousand feet of ascent to contend with along the way, making the total elevation drop in this segment nearly 5,800 feet.

The trail generally follows the canyon of Junction Creek, winding in and out of numerous steep side drainages, where setting up camp could be challenging. Beyond Walls Gulch, the trail clings to the side of the gorge far above the creek, and water is scarce for 12 miles, until you descend again into the canyon. Some construction work north of Sliderock Canyon must still be completed before the trail will be suitable for horse and mountain bicycle traffic.

Portions of the CT in the upper end of the canyon use the historic Oro Fino (Fine Gold) Trail, which supplied the mining district of the same name during the early 1900s. This trail was nearly overgrown and obliterated in spots when volunteer trail crews began working in the Junction Creek area in 1986. It took two difficult summers for the volunteers to build nearly 18 miles of new trail between Junction Creek Trailhead and FS-543 and to rejuvenate the dilapidated Oro Fino.

Trailheads/Access Points

Cumberland Basin Trailhead: From Durango, travel west on US 160 approximately a half mile beyond Hesperus and turn right (north) on FS-571. A sign here points out La Plata Canyon. The trailhead is approximately 14 miles from US 160. The last two miles follow an unmaintained 4WD road and may be snowed in until June.

Junction Creek Trailhead: Go north on Main Avenue in Durango and turn left (west) on 25th Street. Drive approximately three miles and go left at a "Y." Continue approximately 0.4 mile to a cattleguard and a sign announcing your entrance into San Juan National Forest. The CT begins on the left, a hundred feet past the cattleguard. There is room for a few cars here; there is more adequate parking 1.1 miles up the road at the switchback. The road continues beyond the cattleguard as FS-543.

Trail access to the upper part of this segment near Kennebec Pass is possible by continuing on FS-543 for 17.5 miles beyond the cattleguard to a side road to the left (west), whose portal is identified with two large-diameter wooden posts. Continue up the side road 0.7 mile to where the trail ascends at right toward Kennebec Pass.

Supplies, Services and Accommodations

Durango has all the amenities you would expect from a town of its size, including a variety of hotels and grocery, hardware and sporting goods stores. The town also has regular bus and airline service.

Maps

USGS Quadrangles: La Plata, Monument Hill, Durango West. USFS Maps: San Juan National Forest. CT Series: Maps 28, 29.

Trail Description

From the Cumberland Basin Trailhead, ascend southeast on the road for 0.2 mile and turn left onto another road, which has been closed to vehicular traffic. There is a sign here pointing to Kennebec Pass. In about a half mile you will arrive at the pass and have views toward Durango and the Junction Creek drainage. Paintbrush, bistort, marsh marigold and Old Man of the Mountains are abundant here. For an interesting side trip, with better views and more alpine flowers, hike up 12,388-foot Cumberland Mountain from its northwest ridge.

At Kennebec Pass the CT begins an immediate descent toward the east. (The road continues an ascent to the Muldoon Mine a short

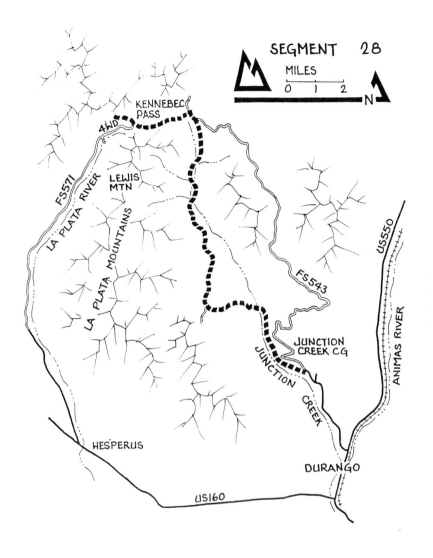

SEGMENT 28

MILES
0 1 2

N

KENNEBEC PASS

4WD

FS571

LA PLATA RIVER

LEWIS MTN

LA PLATA MOUNTAINS

FS543

JUNCTION CREEK C.G.

JUNCTION CREEK

US550

ANIMAS RIVER

HESPERUS

DURANGO

US160

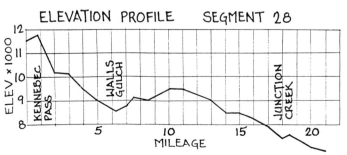

ELEVATION PROFILE   SEGMENT 28

ELEV × 1000

12
11
10
9
8

KENNEBEC PASS

WALLS GULCH

JUNCTION CREEK

5   10   15   20

MILEAGE

distance away.) The CT descends rapidly, with redrock cliffs above and the headwaters of Junction Creek below. Use caution when crossing lingering snowfields here, as the dropoffs are steep. The trail continues its steep descent and enters a spruce forest interspersed with meadows and lush vegetation. Ignore a side trail coming in from the right.

At mile 2.0 (10,340) the trail intersects a Forest Service road. A sign here reads "Sliderock Trail, Kennebec Pass." Don't be tempted to take the trail which is visible south of the road; it comes to a dead end in 0.7 mile. Until this trail section can be completed, you must use the Forest Service road for approximately one mile. Bear to the left (east) on the road and follow it 0.7 mile to the intersection of FS-543. Turn right (southeast) on FS-543 and walk 0.2 mile to a level, grassy area surrounded by aspens on your right (south). The trail, which is not obvious for several hundred feet, leaves the road here and continues south down the drainage. This is not an improved trail and is quite steep for a half mile, until it hits newly constructed trail. About 0.2 mile after leaving the road, there is a small spring on the right, under a cluster of pine trees about 20 feet from the trail. (The route just described, from mile 2.0 (10,340) to the point where the newly constructed trail begins, is a temporary detour to be used until new trail can be built to link the two points together.)

The newly constructed trail continues down Fassbinder Gulch on even grades past the confluence of the Flagler Fork. The CT makes a brief easterly turn into Leavenworth Gulch, passing a 50-foot waterfall and then a wide switchback which leads to the bottom of the canyon. It then crosses to the west side of the Flagler Fork. The next 1.5 miles will have about ten fords, which can be difficult during spring runoff or after rains. The crossings below the confluence of the Flagler Fork and Junction Creek are wide and have much heavier water flow. There are some areas where the trail may be in the flood plain and partially washed out.

The last ford of upper Junction Creek, at mile 6.4 (8520), is near the mouth of Walls Gulch. Here the trail crosses to the west side of the creek and begins a gradual, four-mile, thousand-foot ascent, winding endlessly in and out of side drainages. This is beautiful, rugged terrain with steep slopes and views down into the Junction Creek gorge. Water flow in these side canyons is variable, but First

Trail Canyon, Sliderock Canyon and the first drainage north of Sliderock all have minimal flows even in September. Road End Canyon and Chicago Gulch can be dry. Beyond Road End Canyon there is no water for six miles.

About a half mile before Road End Canyon, the CT tops out at one last rise and begins the final descent to the Junction Creek Trailhead. The trail gradually turns into an old 4WD road, which it follows for the next three miles. Notice the chalk-white cliffs visible below in Junction Creek Canyon. Shortly after passing the Ernest Canyon drainage there are panoramas of Lewis Mountain to the northwest.

As the road changes direction from southwest to due east, you will come to a red steel cattle gate. Continue 0.2 mile past the gate and leave the road as the trail begins again to the left (east). This point is difficult to spot and is marked only with a small, temporary sign. If you come to a drainage and the road starts heading more steeply downhill, you have missed the turn. Once leaving the road, the CT contours almost level for a mile through a sunny ponderosa forest, passing occasionally through gambel oak thickets. This is good elk habitat and if you walk quietly you might see some.

Upon leaving the ponderosa forest, the trail goes over a ridge and drops into a small drainage, then goes through another red steel cattle gate. Be sure to close the gate and not to disturb any livestock grazing in the area. If you need water and cannot wait until you reach Junction Creek, take a side trail to the left (northwest) just past the red gate and go a half mile to a spring in a clearing ringed with aspen. This is a good place to camp, though you may have to share it with grazing cattle.

Back on the CT, continue 400 feet down the trail through an aspen grove and pass through a third red gate. There are also remnants of an old brush fence here, which means the area must have been grazed for many years. The CT appears to be following an old existing road along here. Continue downhill; bear left at any questionable intersections. One mile beyond the last gate, watch for the trail to turn to the left and leave the old road. This may not be an obviously marked turn. At this point the trail should be heading first southeast, then east. In 0.3 mile you will come to an overlook at the edge of a rock cliff that gives a bird's eye view of the last few miles of the CT, descending Junction Creek Canyon, and Fort Lewis College on the mesa above Durango.

The trail now maneuvers through several switchbacks on its descent to Junction Creek. Building these switchbacks required five weeks of hard labor by volunteer trail crews in 1987. Please help preserve their hard labor and resist the temptation to cut across the switchbacks. Cross over to the east side of Junction Creek at mile 18.2 (7390) on a large fallen cottonwood. One hopes a bridge will be built here in the future.

Bear right (south) on the trail and continue to Quinn Creek, which is a small tributary stream, then begin a climb which takes you nearly 200 feet above Junction Creek. This area is lush with vegetation and hosts many birds. You may see a Western tanager here, or perhaps a dipper diving into the whirling pools along the creek.

Hikers should be aware of two major hazards along Junction Creek. First, the creek is subject to flash floods, and camps should not be set up in the flood plain. Second, the area contains a lot of poison ivy and poison oak, which at times is camouflaged on the sides of the trail. Some has even been sighted up on the switchbacks behind large boulders. Be careful where you walk and sit; trail crews learned about this hazard the hard way. There are also two areas where mudslides have wiped out the trail during spring rains and will probably continue to do so on an annual basis.

About 1.3 miles after crossing Junction Creek, you will come to a side trail on the left. This leads in 200 feet to a switchback on FS 543 (Junction Creek Road), where there is more adequate parking than at the official trailhead. The CT continues to the right at this fork, down Junction Creek. This is the final mile of the CT. Do not take any of the side trails leading uphill to the road above. Along this stretch are many water holes and several cascades in the creek. It is a summer paradise, with lots of shade, grasses, flowers, birds and, unfortunately, poison ivy. There are 200-foot cliffs on the southwest side of the canyon.

Soon the canyon widens and you cross an irrigation ditch which takes you through the flood plain for 0.3 mile to the trailhead and the official western terminus of the Colorado Trail at mile 20.8 (6960). Turn right (southeast) onto the road; it is 3.4 miles to town. Welcome to Durango!

Mountain Bike Route

Introduction

Mountain bicycles are allowed on almost all of the CT, the only exceptions being those sections that pass through wilderness areas. In addition, there are other areas where cyclists may end up pushing their bikes more than riding them, especially if they are loaded down with gear. These areas are most likely to be above timberline where no built trail exists and where the terrain is particularly rough. This special section identifies suitable detours, optional or mandatory, around these areas. If planning a mountain bicycle trip on the CT, it might be a good idea to contact the appropriate Forest Service district(s) to check if any further restrictions have been imposed.

The detours described here use primarily 4WD roads, Forest Service roads and county roads. However, it is sometimes necessary to use paved highways, where appropriate precautions should be taken to make yourself visible to motorists. Safety gear, which is also important on steep, narrow trails, is a must for maneuvering on curving mountain roads with blind corners. Cattle guards, an obvious hazard to bicycles, will be encountered often on Forest Service and county roads. Be aware that, in most cases, private property is immediately adjacent to county roads and highways but is rarely marked as such. Mountain bicyclists should not be disappointed by the fact that they are occasionally compelled to make detours, for the alternate routes hold as much fascination as the main CT corridor, and bypass sections that would be more pushed than pedalled anyway.

The main detours are:

• A compulsory bypass around Lost Creek Wilderness, using a series of Forest Service roads over Stoney Pass via Wellington Lake and then up the Tarryall River (Pike National Forest).

Turkshead Peak

• A highly recommended, optional bypass of the high-altitude route over the Tenmile Range, using the Tenmile Bike Path (Arapaho National Forest).

• A compulsory detour around Holy Cross and Mt. Massive wildernesses, using Forest Service roads and a section of US 24 (San Isabel National Forest).

• A compulsory detour around Collegiate Peaks Wilderness, using county roads and a section of US 24 (San Isabel National Forest).

• An optional detour around Raspberry Gulch, using county roads (San Isabel National Forest).

• A compulsory detour around La Garita Wilderness, using a section of Colorado 149 and Forest Service roads over Los Pinos Pass (Gunnison National Forest).

• An optional detour around Coney Summit, using sections of Colorado 149, US 550, county roads and a 4WD road over Cinnamon Pass (Gunnison and San Juan national forests).

• A compulsory bypass around the Weminuche Wilderness, using US 550 and a 4WD road over Stony Pass (Rio Grande and San Juan national forests).

• An optional detour around the Junction Creek gorge, using a Forest Service road (San Juan National Forest).

Mountain cyclists would do well to carry a Colorado state highway map and the appropriate Forest Service maps to help with navigation, identifying campgrounds, etc.

Lost Creek Wilderness Detour
Segments 3, 4 and 5 (Pike National Forest)

Introduction

This long detour follows Forest Service and county roads around the southern perimeter of Lost Creek Wilderness. It passes several campgrounds and provides vistas of the Tarryall Mountains and the Rampart Range south to Pikes Peak. You will pass through the old mining town of Tarryall, which started life in 1896 as Puma City. The story goes that an unsociable miner, known only as Rocky Mountain Jim, grew tired of the non-stop activity in Cripple Creek and removed himself to the picturesque valley, where he discovered the first lode in the area. Unfortunately for Jim, many others quickly followed, until the town had a population of a thousand.

A more direct, but also more dangerous detour (not described here), follows FS-550 and FS-543 to Bailey and busy, winding US 285 to Kenosha Pass.

Detour Description

Begin this detour about midway through Segment 3, where the CT first crosses FS-543 at mile 8.9 (7400). Continue west and south up FS-543 for 2.7 miles to Wellington Lake. Go left here, onto FS-560, and top out 2.4 miles later at Stony Pass (8560). Then proceed along the Forest Service road another seven miles, passing a side road that leads to Flying G Ranch. Go right onto FS-211 at mile 13.6 (7470); go right again in another 5.4 miles, following the signs to Goose Creek Campground. Continue to mile 35.8 (8220) and go

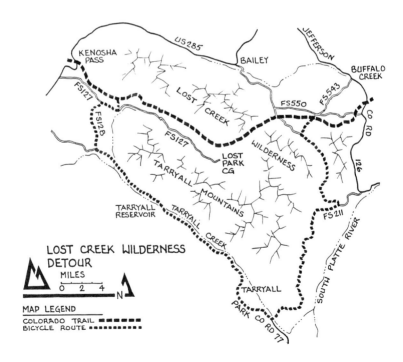

right on paved Park County Road 77. The paving gives way to gravel in about one mile. Continue through Tarryall and pass the entrance to Spruce Grove Campground a few miles beyond. Pass beyond Tarryall Reservoir to mile 63.0 (9220) and go right onto Park County Road 39 (FS-128), marked also as Rock Creek Hills Road. Continue north and go right (east) onto Lost Park Road (FS-127) at mile 68.6 (9560). Pedal to mile 70.7 (9410) and go left onto FS-133 at the sign pointing out Ben Tyler Trail. Regain the official CT at mile 72.0 (9720) where it crosses the road. In the description of Segment 5, this point is mile 7.7 (9720).

Tenmile Range Detour
Segment 7 (Arapaho National Forest)

Introduction

This optional detour sidesteps the challenging high-altitude route over the Tenmile Range by using the very convenient Tenmile Bike Path. This bypass is highly recommended, partly because it avoids what would be a very difficult route, but also because it would be a shame not to take advantage of this well planned, paved path designed especially for bicycles.

Detour Description

This optional detour begins at the Goldhill Trailhead, at the start of Segment 7.

Pedal north and then west on the bike path, which parallels Colorado 9 to Frisco. Head south as you enter Tenmile Canyon and pedal up the bike path, following the approximate route of the DSP&PRR. After approximately 12 miles of pleasant pedaling you will arrive at Wheeler Flats Trailhead near Copper Mountain. This is the starting point of Segment 8.

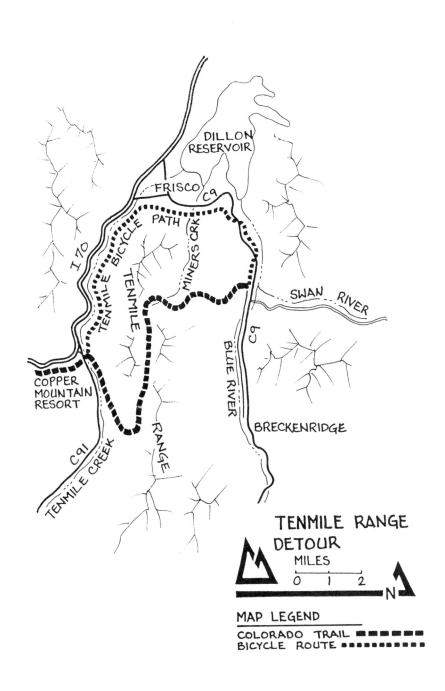

DILLON
RESERVOIR

FRISCO
C9

I 70

TENMILE BICYCLE PATH

MINERS CRK

TENMILE

SWAN RIVER

COPPER
MOUNTAIN
RESORT

BLUE RIVER

C9

RANGE

BRECKENRIDGE

C91

TENMILE CREEK

TENMILE RANGE
DETOUR

MILES
0   1   2

N

MAP LEGEND

COLORADO TRAIL ▪▪▪▪▪▪
BICYCLE ROUTE ▪▪▪▪▪▪▪▪▪

Holy Cross Wilderness/ Mt. Massive Wilderness Detour
Segments 9 and 10 (San Isabel National Forest)

Introduction

In order to detour around the Holy Cross and Mt. Massive wilderness areas, it is necessary to use US 24 and a county road. US 24 is a busy highway, without shoulders, and care should be taken when riding this portion.

Detour Description

Pedal to mile 2.7 (10,480) on Segment 9, where this detour begins on Wurtz Ditch Road.

Leave the CT and descend 0.3 mile on the road, then go left on FS-100. Continue to US 24 at mile 1.3 (10,120), and go right (south) on the highway. Carefully follow US 24 for 7.5 miles, through Leadville, and continue south beyond the town to mile 14.0 (9540), where you will turn right (west) onto Colorado 300. Proceed 0.8 mile on the latter and then turn left (south) onto dusty Halfmoon Creek Road. Take a right (west) 1.2 miles beyond and follow the signs to Halfmoon Creek Campground. Continue beyond Halfmoon Creek and Elbert Creek campgrounds to mile 21.5 (10,080), where you pick up the CT again, heading south from the Halfmoon Creek trailhead.

This is the starting point of Segment 11.

Collegiate Peaks Detour
Segments 12 and 13 (San Isabel National Forest)

Introduction

It is necessary to use a section of US 24 for this detour, but the distance spent on the highway can be reduced by using Chaffee County Road 371 for the last ten miles into Buena Vista. This detour affords unobstructed views of the Collegiate Range, especially so if

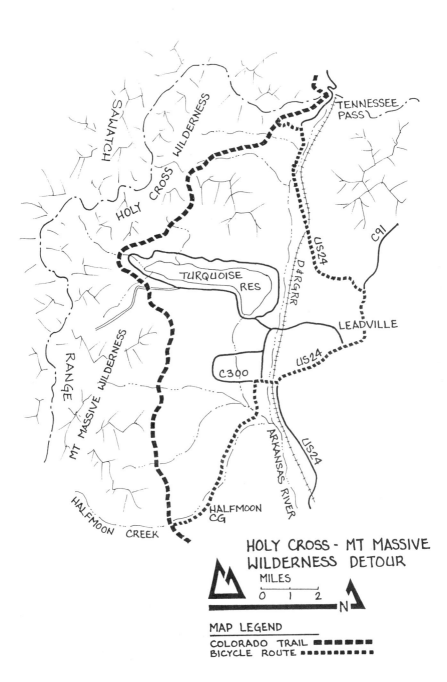

HOLY CROSS - MT MASSIVE
WILDERNESS DETOUR

MILES

0 1 2

N

MAP LEGEND

COLORADO TRAIL ■■■■■■
BICYCLE ROUTE ●●●●●●●●●

you choose to follow Road 371, which parallels the east bank of the Arkansas River through sagebrush and piñon meadows. Road 371 follows the abandoned route of the Colorado Midland Railway south to Buena Vista, using a series of tunnels hewn out of the granite basement of the Mosquito Range. The railroad was built through here in 1886 and had a whistle stop known as Wild Horse near the tunnels. Can you identify the rock formation known as Elephant Rock, which was so popular with passengers that they often compelled the train to stop so they could take photographs?

Detour Description

Begin this detour at the start of Segment 12 on Chaffee County Road 390.

Pedal east 3.0 miles on the road and turn right (south) onto US 24. Carefully continue south on US 24 for 5.9 miles, then turn left onto Chaffee County Road 371. You can continue on US 24 to Buena Vista if you wish, or you can cross the Arkansas River on Road 371 and then resume a southerly course on the abandoned Midland grade to Buena Vista at mile 18.8 (7690). Once in town, turn right (west) onto Main Street and continue a few blocks to the stoplight at US 24. Proceed west across US 24 on Main Street, which becomes Chaffee County Road 306 (Cottonwood Pass Road) beyond the city limits. Continue to the Avalanche Trailhead parking area at mile 28.4 (9360), where you will rejoin the CT. This point is mile 6.6 (9360) of Segment 13.

Raspberry Gulch Detour
Segments 13 and 14 (San Isabel National Forest)

Introduction

This optional detour avoids an extremely steep and poorly maintained section of the CT by following county roads around an unnamed summit between Chalk Creek and Raspberry Gulch. This short section of trail will eventually be rerouted around the base of the summit. Inquire at the Salida District for more information on this future rerouting.

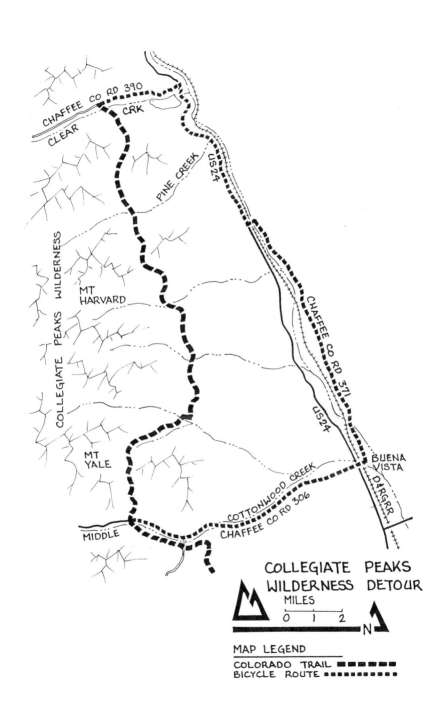

CHAFFEE CO RD 390
CLEAR CRK
PINE CREEK
US 24
COLLEGIATE PEAKS WILDERNESS
MT HARVARD
MT YALE
CHAFFEE CO RD 371
US 24
COTTONWOOD CREEK
CHAFFEE CO RD 306
BUENA VISTA
D&RGRR
MIDDLE

COLLEGIATE PEAKS
WILDERNESS DETOUR

MILES
0   1   2

N

MAP LEGEND

COLORADO TRAIL ▪ ▪ ▪ ▪ ▪ ▪ ▪
BICYCLE ROUTE ▪▪▪▪▪▪▪▪▪▪

Detour Description

Follow the official CT to mile 19.4 (8160) in Segment 13. Turn left (east) onto Chaffee County Road 162 and pedal 0.7 miles to Chaffee County Road 270. Proceed southeast, then east, on Road 270, which soon takes on a southerly heading. Continue to mile 4.6 (8200) and go right (west) on Road 272. Turn left (south) at an intersection two miles beyond and continue on Road 272 to mile 8.2 (8920), which is the Browns Creek Trailhead. Continue up the Browns Creek Trail to mile 9.6 (9600), where you will join the CT again. This point is mile 5.1 (9600) of Segment 14.

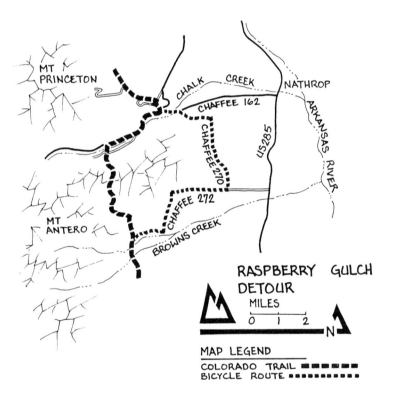

La Garita Wilderness Detour
Segments 18, 19, 20 and 21
(Gunnison National Forest)

Introduction

This mandatory detour is necessary to avoid the La Garita Wilderness and an extended high-altitude route across Snow Mesa and the Continental Divide. The La Garita detour and the following optional detour around Coney Summit are designed to be used together by cyclists wishing to continue the alternate route around the difficult, trailless CT route. Bicyclists will be pedaling along backcountry Forest Service roads that follow parts of the historic Saguache-San Juan toll road built by Otto Mears in 1874. They will also pass by the site of the original Ute Agency on Los Pinos Creek. The detour passes several National Forest campgrounds on Cebolla Creek.

The final miles are spent ascending Colorado 149 to Spring Creek Pass, where you can join the high-altitude route of Segment 22. Or you can descend Colorado 149 to Lake San Cristobal and use the detour around Coney Summit.

Detour Description

This detour begins on the Cochetopa Pass Road (Road NN14) at mile 6.4 (9760) of Segment 18.

Descend on the dirt road past two switchbacks and continue pedaling ahead (northwest) on the road as the CT bears to the left up Archuleta Creek. Continue past Dome Reservoir to mile 10.8 (8979) and turn left onto Road KK14 (Los Pinos-Cebolla Road). Pass beyond the old Ute agency to mile 19.6 and continue ahead on Los Pinos-Cebolla Road, ignoring Big Meadows Road, which forks to the left. Continue ten miles to Los Pinos Pass. Descend from the pass to mile 33.9 and join up with FS-592. Continue ahead (northwest) on the Los Pinos-Cebolla Road for one mile and go left (west) at the intersection. Gradually ascend along Cebolla Creek to mile 50.0 (11,320), where the Forest Service road joins up with Colorado 149. If you insist on pedaling the high-altitude route over Coney Summit (not recommended), go left here and ascend 7.6 miles further to

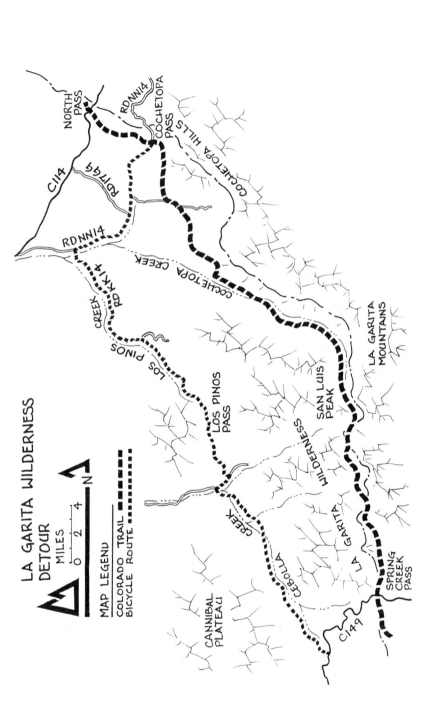

LA GARITA WILDERNESS
DETOUR

MILES
0   2   4

N

MAP LEGEND
COLORADO TRAIL ▪▪▪▪
BICYCLE ROUTE ••••

NORTH PASS
RDNN14
COCHETOPA PASS
COCHETOPA HILLS
C114
RDT744
RDNN14
CREEK RD KK14
LOS PINOS
COCHETOPA CREEK
LOS PINOS PASS
SAN LUIS PEAK
LA GARITA MOUNTAINS
WILDERNESS
LA GARITA
CEBOLLA CREEK
CANNIBAL PLATEAU
SPRING CREEK PASS
C149

Spring Creek Pass, where you will rejoin the CT at the beginning of Segment 22. If, however, you decide to continue the detour, descend to the right here on Colorado 149 to Lake San Cristobal, as described under the Coney Summit Detour.

Coney Summit Detour
Segments 22, 23 and 24 (Gunnison National Forest, San Juan National Forest)

Introduction

This optional, lengthy detour from Colorado 149 to Molas Pass avoids Segments 22, 23 and 24; it is intended to be a continuation of the La Garita Wilderness detour. Mountain bicyclists are encouraged to continue the detour here around Segment 22 because of the difficulty of the official CT route in the vicinity of 13,334-foot Coney Summit.

Starting at Carson Saddle in Segment 23, the CT is still rough but mostly uses existing trails (with the exception of short sections in the headwaters of Lost Trail and Pole creeks, where the trail disappears in thick tundra grasses). Purists who insist on rejoining the official CT at Carson Saddle (Segment 23) may do so by leaving this detour description about half way up the Lake Fork Road at Wager Gulch.

Cyclists using this route will not be deprived of stunning scenery. This detour passes Lake San Cristobal, continues up the valley of the Lake Fork, which is ringed with 14,000-foot peaks, and then ascends 12,640-foot Cinnamon Pass. The pass is a well known 4WD road that was originally constructed by Otto Mears and Enos Hotchkiss as part of the Saguache-San Juan toll road in the 1870s. The story goes that it received its name because of the glistening alpine grasses on the surrounding mountainsides.

Detour Description

Continue the La Garita Wilderness detour by turning right onto Colorado 149 from Los Pinos-Cebolla Road and descending the steep highway toward Lake City. Turn left off the **highway at mile 7.1**

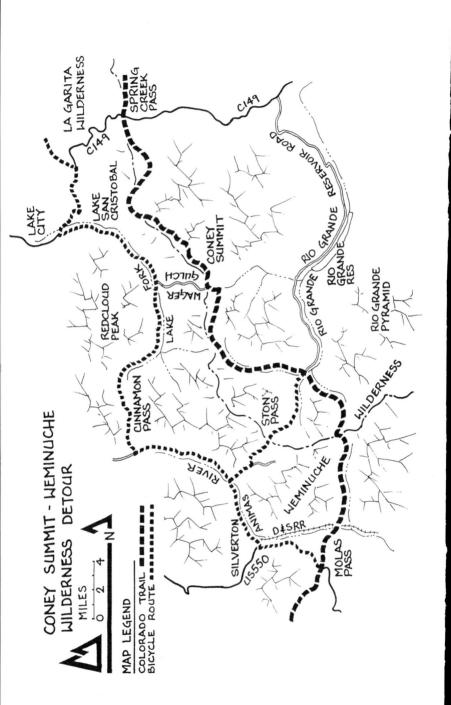

CONEY SUMMIT - WEMINUCHE
WILDERNESS DETOUR

MILES
0   2   4

N

MAP LEGEND
COLORADO TRAIL
BICYCLE ROUTE

LA GARITA WILDERNESS

SPRING CREEK PASS

C149

C149

LAKE CITY

LAKE SAN CRISTOBAL

CONEY SUMMIT

RIO GRANDE RESERVOIR ROAD

RIO GRANDE

RIO GRANDE

RIO GRANDE RES

RIO GRANDE PYRAMID

REDCLOUD PEAK

FORK

WAGER GULCH

LAKE

CINNAMON PASS

STONY PASS

WEMINUCHE

WILDERNESS

RIVER

SILVERTON

ANIMAS

D&SRR

US550

MOLAS PASS

(8880) and follow a paved road to Lake San Cristobal. Continue beyond the lake and pedal up the narrow valley, following the signs to Cinnamon Pass as the road gets progressively rougher. Top out on Cinnamon Pass at mile 28.9 (12,640). Descend 2.2 miles from the pass and make a sharp left (south) onto an intersecting jeep road just above the ruins of the old mining town of Animas Forks. Continue south, then southwest, down the upper Animas Valley until you reach Silverton. Pedal through town and join US 550 at mile 43.9 (9240). Go south on US 550 and ascend to mile 50.0 (10,880) just 600 feet north of the highway's summit on Molas Pass, where you will pick up the CT going west.

This point is the beginning of Segment 25.

Weminuche Wilderness Detour
Segment 24 (Rio Grande National Forest, San Juan National Forest)

Introduction

Cyclists who manage to make their way along the official CT route up Lost Trail Creek and down Pole Creek will have to detour over 12,600-foot Stony Pass to avoid the Weminuche Wilderness. This detour passes around Segment 24 and joins up with the official trail at Molas Pass, as does the Coney Summit detour.

The Stony Pass route, like Cinnamon Pass, is a historic and scenic bypass, originally built in 1879. Prior to that date, a burro trail over Stony Pass carried most of the traffic into Silverton, primarily because it was one of the few routes into the area that didn't cross Ute reservation lands.

Detour Description

The CT intersects the Rio Grande Reservoir Road at the end of Segment 23, where this detour leaves the official route of the CT.

Pedal ahead (northwest) on the road toward Stony Pass. The ford of Pole Creek a short distance beyond can be deep and swift until late summer. Top out on Stony Pass at mile 6.3 (12,600). Descend steeply to Cunningham Gulch Road (FS-589) at mile 10.3 (10,120) and continue 2.5 miles north to an intersection at the old site of Howardsville. Turn left (west) onto FS-586, which follows the broad Animas River valley. Descend into Silverton and pick up US 550 on the opposite end of town at mile 17.7 (9240). Ascend south on US 550 to mile 23.8 (10,880), just 600 feet north of the highway's summit on Molas Pass, where you will join the official CT going west.

This point is the beginning of Segment 25.

Junction Creek Canyon Detour
Segment 28 (San Juan National Forest)

Introduction

The portion of the official CT in Junction Creek is mostly on good trail, but it does traverse some precipitous spots in rough terrain and there are several long, deep fords, particularly in the upper end of the canyon, that are not yet bridged. By contrast, there is a very good road that begins just east of Kennebec Pass and descends at the edge of the canyon to the trailhead on Junction Creek. This bypass is intended for those cyclists who are anxious for a speedy descent to Durango, or for those interested in making a long loop trip up Junction Creek and then down the road to their starting point.

Detour Description

This detour begins at mile 2.0 (10,340) on Segment 28, just east of Kennebec Pass.

Descend 0.7 mile on the road and turn right at the intersection. Continue downhill, dropping quickly through several life zones. Don't be so distracted by the scenery that you fail to notice the many hazardous cattle guards on the road. Pass the entrance to Junction Creek Campground and continue 1.4 miles to the National Forest boundary and Junction Creek Trailhead, the western terminus of the Colorado Trail.

This is the end of Segment 28; Durango is 3.4 miles down the road.

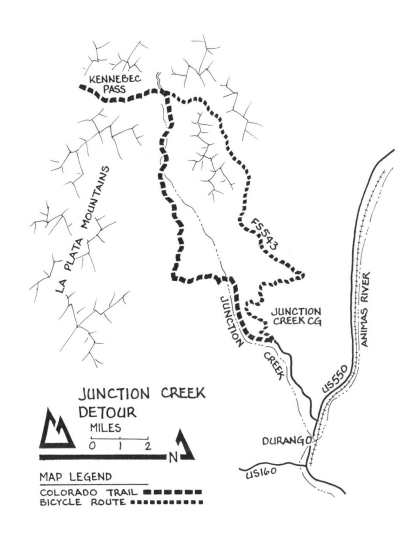

KENNEBEC
PASS

LA PLATA MOUNTAINS

FS543

JUNCTION

CREEK

JUNCTION
CREEK CG

US550

ANIMAS RIVER

DURANGO

US160

JUNCTION CREEK
DETOUR

MILES

0   1   2

N

MAP LEGEND

COLORADO TRAIL ▰▰▰▰▰
BICYCLE ROUTE ▪▪▪▪▪▪▪▪▪

Recommended Reading

Bartlett, Richard A. *Great Surveys of the American West.* Norman, Okla.: University of Oklahoma Press, 1962.

Brown, Robert L. *An Empire of Silver.* Sundance Pubs., 1984.

Bueler, William. *Roof of the Rockies.* Boulder: Pruett Publishing Company, 1974.

Chronic, John and Halka Chronic. "Prairie, Peak and Plateau." *Colorado Geological Survey Bulletin* 32, 1972.

Colorado Trail Management Direction Route Selection Environmental Assessment Report. Washington, D.C.: United States Forest Service, 1984.

Digerness, David S. *The Mineral Belt.* Sundance Publications, 1977.

Gantt, Paul H. *The Case of Alferd Packer.* Denver: University of Denver Press, 1952.

Gilliland, Mary Ellen. *Summit: A Gold Rush History of Summit County, Colorado.* Silverthorne: Alpenrose Press, 1980.

Hall, Frank. *History of the State of Colorado.* Chicago: Blakely Printing, 1895.

Harbour, Midge. *Tarryall Mountains and the Puma Hills.* Colorado Springs: Century One Press, 1982.

Hart, John L. Jerome. *Fourteen Thousand Feet.* Denver: Colorado Mountain Club, 1925.

Lavender, David. *The Big Divide.* New York: Doubleday, 1948.

Mutel, Cornella Fleischer and John C. Emerick. *From Grassland to Glacier.* Boulder: Johnson Books, 1984.

Ormes, Robert. *Guide to the Colorado Mountains, Sixth Edition.* Sage Books, 1970.

----------. *Tracking Ghost Railroads in Colorado.* Colorado Springs: Century One Press, 1980.

Pettit, Jan. *Utes, the Mountain People.* Colorado Springs: Century One Press, 1982.

Quillen, Ed. "Trail to Nowhere." *Denver Empire,* December 9, 1984.

Sprague, Marshall. *Great Gates.* New York: Little, Brown, 1964.

Sumner, David. "The Colorado Trail Takes Shape." *Colorado Magazine,* July-August 1974.

Wolle, Muriel Sibell. *Stampede to Timberline.* Sage Books, 1949.

San Luis Pass

Acknowledgements

It is appropriate that, like the Colorado Trail itself, this guide is the product of the volunteer efforts of many people. There would be no guide at all without the trail, but it would be impractical to recognize the thousands of citizens responsible for making the CT a reality. However, you know who you are.

Over the years, many corporations, foundations and other organizations have contributed money or supplies to help make the volunteer effort possible. These include Brand-It Company, Cristopher and Company, the Colorado Lottery, the Colorado Mountain Club, the CMC Foundation, Adolph Coors and Coors Foundation, the Eric Veal Memorial Fund, the Fort Collins Group of the CMC, the Gates Foundation, VOC, Jolly Rancher, Kaufman Company, King Soopers, Martin Marietta, Quick Foundation, REI, Walter Drake Company and Werpy's Bakery.

The seed which eventually blossomed into this guide was planted in 1985 by Gudy Gaskill, who continuously provided ideas and inspiration along the way, as well as unlimited use of her personal computer for compiling the text. Peter D. Rowland assisted immensely by surveying the trail from Molas Pass to Junction Creek Trailhead and writing the trail descriptions for that section. David Gaskill and Jack Dyni wrote the geology section and provided interesting geological interjections elsewhere in the guide. Dr. Hugo Ferchau contributed the natural history section and shuttled the sometimes beleaguered trail surveyor to and from access points. The pages of the guide are graced by the artwork of Jerry Albright, and the cover was designed by Robert Peltz of Christopherson and Company. Thanks also go to proofreaders Anna Thurston, Roger Gerard, Alex Carson, and Middy and Walt Langebartel.